T0278487

THE LAST CONSOLATION VANISHED

The Last Consolation Vanished

THE TESTIMONY OF A SONDERKOMMANDO IN AUSCHWITZ

Zalmen Gradowski

Edited and with a foreword and afterword by
Arnold I. Davidson & Philippe Mesnard

Translated by Rubye Monet

The University of Chicago Press CHICAGO AND LONDON

This publication was generously supported by a gift from
Randy L. and the late Melvin R. Berlin.

The University of Chicago Press, Chicago 60637
The University of Chicago Press, Ltd., London
© 2022 by The University of Chicago

31 30 29 28 27 26 25 24 23 22   1 2 3 4 5

ISBN-13: 978-0-226-63678-8 (cloth)
ISBN-13: 978-0-226-66032-5 (e-book)
DOI: https://doi.org/10.7208/chicago/9780226660325.001.0001

Library of Congress Cataloging-in-Publication Data

Names: Gradowski, Zalmen, 1910–1944, author. | Davidson, Arnold I. (Arnold
  Ira), 1955– editor, writer of afterword. | Mesnard, Philippe, 1956– editor,
  writer of preface. | Monet, Rubye, translator.
Title: The last consolation vanished : the testimony of a Sonderkommando in
  Auschwitz / Zalmen Gradowski ; edited with a foreword and afterword by
  Arnold I. Davidson & Philippe Mesnard ; translated by Rubye Monet.
Other titles: In Harz fub Gehenem. English (Monet) | Testimony of a
  Sonderkommando in Auschwitz
Description: Chicago : The University of Chicago Press, 2022. | Includes
  bibliographical references.
Identifiers: LCCN 2022003413 | ISBN 9780226636788 (cloth) |
  ISBN 9780226660325 (ebook)
Subjects: LCSH: Gradowski, Zalmen, 1910–1944. | Auschwitz (Concentration
  camp) | Birkenau (Concentration camp) | Sonderkommandos—Poland—
  Oświęcim—Biography. | Nazi concentration camp inmates—Poland—
  Oświęcim—Biography. | Holocaust, Jewish (1939–1945)—Personal
  narratives. | Jews, Polish—Biography. | LCGFT: Autobiographies. |
  Personal narratives.
Classification: LCC DS134.72.G72 A3 2022 | DDC 940.53/1853862092 [B] —dc23/
  eng/20220218
LC record available at https://lccn.loc.gov/2022003413

♾ This paper meets the requirements of ANSI/NISO Z39.48-1992
(Permanence of Paper).

Contents

FIGURE 1 Zalmen Gradowski and his wife, Sonja (Sarah) Gradowski, 1940.
Sonja was gassed and burned on December 8, 1942;
Zalmen was killed in the Sonderkommando uprising on October 7, 1944.

Beyond the Ashes

Philippe Mesnard

The members of the Sonderkommando belong to a community of witnesses who, erased from history, drift between different memorial communities without ever being fully welcomed, even today, and have for a long time been actively rejected. They cannot be considered entirely as victims because they also collaborated in the atrocities, albeit forced to do so by the Nazis. Nor have they been recognized as heroes, despite being the architects of one of the most hopeless revolts in human history, the October 7, 1944, uprising against the SS.

This foreword covers the troubled reception of the testimonies written and buried by members of the Auschwitz Sonderkommando before focusing specifically on Zalmen Gradowski's manuscripts. But first, it presents in broad brushstrokes the history of the Sonderkommando and how they were vilified as something less than human and relegated to our cultural imagery of Hell, before becoming part of the historical record.

A Short History of the Auschwitz Sonderkommando

Between 1943 and 1945, a group of Jewish deportees—together with a few Poles and some Soviet prisoners of war who had recently arrived at Auschwitz concentration camp—were conscripted to form the Sonderkommando. The first experiments with Zyklon B gas were carried out on a few hundred Russian prisoners of war and some sick inmates, initially in the underground Block 11 in the main camp,[1] and then later in waves of sporadic elimination in Crematorium I.[2] After this, it became clear that the mass murders would be perpetrated in the neighboring camp of Birkenau in its perfected gas chambers and ovens. The four buildings were up and running by spring 1943 at the north end of the camp, after two farms on the outskirts of Birkenwald had initially served as temporary gas chambers. The extermination operations reached their peak in spring–summer 1944, when convoys of Hungarian Jews arrived in Auschwitz. In about two months, including the last convoy on July 9, 1944, Hungarian military officials, under the guidance of German SS officials, deported around 430,000 Jews from Hungary. Most of them were taken to Auschwitz-Birkenau, where upon arrival and after the so-called "selection," between 300,000 and 350,000 were killed in the gas chambers.[3]

At that time, with a team of up to 900 detainees separated into two shifts, the Sonderkommando kept the wheels of this death machine turning without interruption. Even though the precise number cannot be known, it is estimated that about 2,200 prisoners were in the Sonderkommando at Auschwitz. Day after day, they participated in the destruction of their own people, the "Final Solution," while unable to reveal the truth to them, on pain of brutal death in front of the whole group of Sonderkommandos. They also facilitated the murder of prisoners deemed no longer capable of work during selections in the blocks, mainly those having reached the limits of their physical and mental capacities who were designated as "*Muselmänner*" (sing. *Muselmann*, literally "Muslim") in the camp jargon.

In exchange for performing these unbearable tasks, the men in the Sonderkommando benefited from better treatment than other deportees: they were fed, clothed, and given a bed, unlike many of the other prisoners. Some became used to the horrific work; others, few in number, committed suicide or were murdered. They mostly lived in extreme distress, but it would be a mistake to consider them as inhuman, unable to feel disgust at what they were forced to do or to feel empathy for those who were exterminated. Trapped in this untenable situation, some of the Sonderkommando planned an uprising at Auschwitz. There were similar revolts in two other death camps: in Treblinka on August 2, 1943, and in Sobibor on October 14, 1943, but none in any concentration camps. Actually, in the concentration camps, the Resistance networks, which were mainly communist, knew that it would be better to wait for the arrival of the Red Army rather than risk the strong probability of a massacre during a general uprising. This reticence is why the Jewish leaders of the Sonderkommando insurgence reproached these political prisoners in the camp's clandestine network for not having supported the preparations for an uprising.

One of the most important figures of the Sonderkommando, Zalmen Lewental, described with great lucidity the anxiety created by the constant postponement of the insurrection while more Hungarian Jews were selected to be gassed upon arrival. He wrote that the political leaders of the Resistance network always took their time in responding to the demands of help from the Sonderkommando. Since these prisoners were not directly involved with the massacre of the Jews, the more the revolt could be delayed, the better it was for their strategy of waiting for the arrival of the Red Army. It is important to consider this situation in order to grasp the extent to which the Jews were abandoned. Not only did the Allies and European Resistance fighters outside the camps fail to save the Jews — showing even less interest in the Gypsies — but even inside the camps the communist Resistance, in a very pragmatic and non-empathetic assessment, did not want to consider the daily slaughter, of which they were fully aware.

As the idea of a general uprising showed itself to be little more than a pipe dream, the most determined members of the Sonderkommando decided to attempt it on their own. The revolt broke out on Saturday, October 7, 1944, just after midday. The SS reaction was immediate. Over the next few hours, more than four hundred members of the Sonderkommando were killed. The extermination of the Jewish convoys continued at least until the first few days of November, when the surviving members of the Sonderkommando were tasked with dismantling the machinery of extermination and erasing all traces of the crimes committed there.

From mid-January 1945, a hundred surviving members of the Sonderkommando managed to sneak in among the thousands of deportees being forcibly evacuated from the camp in the so-called *Todesmärsche* (death marches). Between January 20 and 26, the SS blew up what remained of the ovens and gas chambers so that all that was left of the machinery of destruction was rubble and ruin. As Gideon Greif has pointed out, there was no systematic effort to document the testimonies of members of the Sonderkommando.

The Clandestine Manuscripts

In discussing the trauma of the Holocaust, Shoshana Felman and Doris Laub describe the Shoah as the "unprecedented historical occurrence of . . . an event eliminating its own witness."[4] Giorgio Agamben draws a comparable perspective when designating the so-called *Muselmann* as the "integral witness" who must bear witness to the unimaginable.[5]

Between 1939 and 1945, numerous texts were buried, written by individuals testifying to the events of the Holocaust as they occurred, and by groups such as Oyneg Shabbos, brought together by Emanuel Ringelblum in the Warsaw ghetto. Among these individuals was Simha Guterman, who hid his testimony[6] underneath the steps of a building in Radom, Poland, and Itzhak Katzenelson, who buried three bottles containing the manuscript for his *Song of the Murdered Jewish People*[7] in the camp at Vittel, France, before being deported with his last surviving son to Auschwitz, where they would both be murdered. In January 1945, not long before their evacuation to Auschwitz, Jewish deportees began to compose a veritable anthology testifying to life in the camp, but only the foreword has survived.[8] The literary motif of a message in a bottle thrown desperately into the sea reveals the anthropological dimension of these gestures.

In and around the crematoria at Birkenau, a similar phenomenon arose with the Sonderkommando. Between 1945 and 1980, the manuscripts of five of its members were discovered buried at Birkenau. First on February 20, 1945, Hersz Herman Strasfogel's letter,[9] written

FIGURE 2 Haïm Wollnerman and his wife, Yokhid, 1948.

in French, was found—initially it was mistakenly attributed to someone called Haïm Herman. In March 1945, Zalmen Gradowski's first manuscript in Yiddish was unearthed, and Lejb Langfus's was discovered in April. Actually, what we call Gradowski's first manuscript is, in fact, a notebook, accompanied by a letter written on September 6, 1944, which will be discussed below. They were collected and published by the Auschwitz Museum in 1971. Around the same time, Haïm Wollnerman acquired Gradowski's second manuscript, which includes three chapters. Seven years later, in April 1952, an unsigned text in Yiddish was found, which historian Ber Mark, then director of the Jewish Historical Institute in Warsaw, attributed to Lejb Langfus.[10] Zalmen Lewental's first text, written in Yiddish, was discovered on July 28, 1961. On October 17, 1962, a collection was discovered in a glass jar, also in Yiddish, bringing together Lewental's notebook, another of Lejb Langfus's texts, and a list of deaths in October 1944. Apart from Gradowski's second manuscript, these were all published first in the *Bulletin of the Jewish Historical Institute* (*Biuletyn Żydowskiego Instytutu Historycznego*) in Warsaw between 1954 and 1969,[11] and then published together in 1971 by the Auschwitz Museum in a special issue of *Auschwitz Studies* (*Die Hefte von Auschwitz / Zeszyty*

Oswiecimski) under the title "In the Presence of Crime: Notes from the Sonderkommando."

The Auschwitz Museum followed this first Polish-language issue with a German translation in 1972 and then an English translation in 1973. Langfus's manuscript was published in *Auschwitz Studies* in 1973 and could therefore be included in the second Polish general issue, which appeared two years later. Finally, in October 1980, a manuscript written in Greek was found near Crematorium III, by a fifth member of the Sonderkommando, Marcel Nadjari.[12] Partially unreadable because of its long stay in a flask in the earth, it was first published in 1996;[13] the use of new digital technologies with multispectral analysis was used to reconstitute 90 percent of the text between 2013 and 2017, which was done by Aleksandr Nikitjaev, who was working with Pavel Markovich Polian, editor of Gradowski's and other Sonderkommando manuscripts in Russia and in Germany. It was only in 1996, the year of the second German book edition of the texts,[14] that all the manuscripts found thus far were published in one volume. While the five authors and their manuscripts are now clearly identified, there is a consensus that more written testimonies were buried in the crematoria perimeter by unknown Sonderkommandos that did not survive.

Nonetheless, Gradowski's text, the longest of those mentioned above, remains exemplary of the capacity of Sonderkommando members to remain strong in the face of the alienation and terror of the crematoria. Gradowski's second manuscript, published by Wollnerman in 1977, was completely new, even if it was not widely read. In the earlier edition of Gradowski's first manuscript published by Ber Mark, Mark contended that other parts of Gradowski's manuscript likely existed and were buried elsewhere, in different locations, "under a mass of ashes."[15] It is those missing texts that form the second manuscript that was found later.

In March 1945, after four years spent in concentration camps, Wollnerman returned to his hometown of Oświęcim (Auschwitz). Sometime later, Wollnerman and a small group of friends decided to emigrate to Israel. Shortly before his departure, a young man came to visit him and offered to sell him a box that he had unearthed near one of the ovens in Birkenau. "We took out some papers and a notebook written in a beautiful Yiddish script. I flicked through some of the pages and I immediately understood that I was in possession of an important document," Wollnerman explained in the foreword to his edition. Wollnerman handed over the asking price and set about transcribing the manuscript's contents, which was a difficult task given that the pages were stuck together and certain passages had so deteriorated as to be rendered illegible. These missing sections were indicated by bracketed ellipses, [...], and are reproduced as such here.

Several institutions in Prague made offers to acquire the manuscript, but Wollnerman refused, wanting to remain faithful to Gradowski's wishes that whoever found the manuscript should seek out his relatives in the United States, in order to learn about who he and his family were and to obtain a photo to be included in the text when published. Wollnerman was able to find a photo of Gradowski and his wife, Sonja (Sarah), in 1946, but the manuscript would not be published until thirty-one years later. Upon arriving in Israel in 1947, Wollnerman contacted a number of publishing houses and journal editors to try to convince them to print the work, and by 1953 he had almost succeeded. However, despite the efforts of the Yad Vashem archive director Dr. Joseph Kermish, the manuscript was not published until 1977, when Wollnerman decided to publish it himself in Jerusalem under the title *In Harts fun Gehenem* (From the heart of Hell), printed in golden letters on a red canvas cover. This edition is accompanied by Wollnerman's foreword and two other texts: "Some Memories of Zalmen Gradowski," by David Sfard, Gradowski's brother-in-law, who was by then a researcher at Yad Vashem; and "A Word from a Former Auschwitz Prisoner," Yehoshua Wygodski, member of the board at Yad Vashem. Before discussing the text itself further, I will focus on the erratic history of this edition.

After the founding of the State of Israel, culture and state ideology promoted the heroic figures in the Zionist movement and did not give any place to the Sonderkommando, who belonged in a zone that, before being categorized by Primo Levi as "grey,"[16] had no place in the construction of the new identity of the Israeli people, nor in the historical inheritance that they wanted to call upon. Compared with the trials of the Kapos during the 1950s, which were events that Israeli

society had found hard to process, the participation of the Sonderkommandos in the destruction of their own people was not easily
comprehensible—most of the time, it was drastically reduced to a
flawed, shameful, and unbearable experience. Even after the 1960s
and Adolf Eichmann's trial, when Menachem Begin encouraged the
integration of all non-combatant victims of the Holocaust into the national culture in order to rally all different Jewish communities around
the idea of the Holocaust, the members of the Sonderkommando
were no more welcome than before. Pariahs of collective memory,
they did not belong to the community of Resistance fighters or to the
community of victims, inhabiting an amorphous space in between.

Wollnerman's edition, although relatively unknown, did receive
some public attention. David Roskies mentioned it in 1988—eleven
years after its publication—in *The Literature of Destruction: Jewish Responses to Catastrophe*, quoting from Gradowski's "The Czech Transport: A Chronicle of the Auschwitz *Sonderkommando*."[17] Roskies
inscribes Gradowski's testimony into the long Jewish tradition of
the literature of the Catastrophe, along with Simkhe Bunem Shay-
evitsh and Itzhak Katzenelson in the chapter "The Great Lament."
It can, of course, be seen as belonging to this literary tradition, but
it is clear that other factors at play here have put it in a category of
its own. The existence of the Sonderkommando has evidently per-
turbed people for a very long time. While we might have supposed
that the strength of the American Jewish community and of Holocaust studies research would not have allowed such testimony to
wither away and be forgotten, that has not historically been the case.

In fact, there has been little research undertaken in the United
States on the Sonderkommando. In 1990, Nathan Cohen mentioned
Gradowski's second manuscript in "Diaries of the *Sonderkommandos*," first published in volume 20 of *Yad Vashem Studies*; in 1994, Cohen's essay appeared in *Anatomy of the Auschwitz Death Camp*, edited
by Yisrael Gutman and Michael Berenbaum. In 1999, Gradowski's
second manuscript was partially published in a German translation
in a publication by Miroslav Kárný, Raimund Kemper, and Margita
Kárná, in *Theresienstädter Studien und Dokumente*. In 1993, Rebecca
Camhi Fromer traced the experience of Sonderkommando member

Daniel Bennahmias in her book *The Holocaust Odyssey of Daniel Ben-nahmias, Sonderkommando*. In 1999, Carlo Saletti edited the Italian collection of these texts for the Auschwitz Museum, under the title *La voce dei sommersi: Manoscritti ritrovati di membri del Sonderkommando di Auschwitz*. This book is the equivalent of Ber Mark's work, with the later addition of unearthed testimonial documents by Marcel Nadjari.

There had been little critical attention paid to the writings of the Sonderkommando until 2001, with the new publication of Ber Mark's edition of the Sonderkommando texts by the *Revue d'histoire de la Shoah: Le Monde juif*.[18] This edition republished the texts from Mark's out-of-print publication and also included some extracts from Gra-dowski's second manuscript, which was also going to be published, at the same time, in a separate edition. For reasons that remain a mys-tery, the editors at Plon refused to give the rights to Mark's edition, and so the Mémorial de la Shoah in Paris provided the necessary funds to commission a new translation. When it was released, the book did not sell very well. However, the publication of these docu-ments was a symbolic great success, and publication under the aus-pices of the Mémorial de la Shoah became a way of returning the Sonderkommando to their rightful place in the Holocaust memorial community. Also in 2001, Gradowski's entire second manuscript, ed-ited by Philippe Mesnard and Carlo Saletti, was published by Éditions Kimé in Paris as *Au coeur de l'enfer: témoignage d'un sonderkomando d'Auschwitz, 1944*, which came out in a paperback edition by Tallan-dier in 2009. In 2002 in Italy, the important publishing house Marsilio, which had already published *La voce dei sommersi*, published Gradow-ski's *From the Heart of Hell* under the title *Sonderkommando: Diario da un crematorio di Auschwitz, 1944*; then, in Spain and the Nether-lands, two publishing houses (Anthropos in Barcelona and Verbum in Laren) published both manuscripts together in 2008. Finally, in Ger-many, the following two editions came out in 2019: Pavel Markovich Polian's *Briefe aus der Hölle: Die Aufzeichnungen des jüdischen Sonder-kommandos Auschwitz* (Wbg Theiss) and Aurélia Kalisky and Andreas Kilian's edition of Gradowski's manuscript in *Die Zertrennung: Auf-zeichnungen eines Mitglieds des Sonderkommandos* (Suhrkamp Verlag).

Despite those recent publications, the historian community has not shown much interest in Sonderkommando testimonies. Instead, those who are interested in them, either academic or independent researchers, tend to be from the disciplines of literature or Jewish studies. All this being said, we must not forget that until recently there was almost no discussion of the Sonderkommando from *any* community, whether that of the Holocaust memorial or from academic circles. Until recently, the history of the Sonderkommando was not considered as adding anything of value to existing knowledge on the subject of the Holocaust, despite the Sonderkommando's key role in the Nazis' Final Solution, the extermination by gas of Jews, Gypsies, Soviet soldiers, and other deportees. Hostility, suspicion, indifference: how did these prejudices and attitudes emerge?

Historical and Testimonial Knowledge

The information needed to understand the functioning of the gas chambers and the organization of the Sonderkommando, but above all the conditions in which the Sonderkommando lived, was very quickly made available after the war. In 1946, Ota Kraus and Erich Shön (also known as Erich Kulka) had already gathered together the results of their documentary inquiry about the Auschwitz camp in *Továrna na smrt*, which was translated into German in 1957 as *Die Todesfabrik*.[19] The October 7th uprising was well known and had as far as possible at that point been documented; moreover, the surviving members of the Sonderkommando had been willing to talk about their experiences. In the first months after the liberation of the Auschwitz camp, Shlomo Dragon, Alter Feinsilber (also known as Stanislaw Jankowski), and Henryk Tauber presented their evidence on the Nazi crimes in Poland to the Soviet-Polish Investigating Commission during the hearings held on May 10, 11, 15, 17, and 24.[20] During the Auschwitz trials in October 1964 in Frankfurt am Main in West Germany, three other survivors of the Sonderkommando—Milton Buki, Filip Müller, and Dov Paisikovic—sat among the witnesses. Paisikovic's deposition is described by Léon Poliakov, in an addendum to his 1964 book *Auschwitz*.[21] There had been no witness statements from Sonderkommandos during the Eichmann trial in Jerusalem in 1961.

Although he was not a member of the Sonderkommando, Miklós Nyiszli, a famous Hungarian Jewish doctor deported during the summer of 1944, mentioned the treatment of the Sonderkommando on several occasions in his testimony. Newly arrived with his family, Nyiszli was quickly identified by Josef Mengele, who took him under his protection and authority; he became the duty doctor for the gas chambers. A section of his testimony written in Hungarian after the war was published in 1951 in *Les Temps modernes*, the French journal founded and directed by Jean-Paul Sartre, and in 1961 it was published in full under the title *Auschwitz: A Doctor's Eyewitness Account*.[22] Around this time, the influential research undertaken by Raul Hilberg was published in the United States but rejected in Israel, because examining the complicity of the *Judenräte* (Jewish Councils) was not yet tolerated. In *The Destruction of the European Jews* (1961), Hilberg describes in concise yet distanced language different Sonderkommando groups. In 1972, Hermann Langbein dedicated an entire chapter to the Sonderkommando in *People in Auschwitz*.[23]

Knowledge of the Sonderkommando belonged until this point to the history of Auschwitz and the extermination camps. In this regard, a book such as *Into That Darkness* by Gitta Sereny about Franz Stangl, the commandant of Treblinka, certainly helped to raise awareness of them. Sereny includes several pieces of evidence submitted to the court during Stangl's trial, as well as the testimony of Filip Müller, published in English in 1980 under the title *Eyewitness Auschwitz: Three Years in the Gas Chambers*[24] and published the year before in Germany. Müller was a member of the Sonderkommando who survived Auschwitz and who later featured in Claude Lanzmann's documentary *Shoah* (1985). *Shoah* provided a substantial shock to the Sonderkommando narrative: we hear many compelling voices from witnesses such as Abraham Bomba and Simon Srebnik, who were enrolled into the Treblinka and Chełmno "special squads," respectively. Outside of Auschwitz, this kind of squad was called *"Arbeitsjuden"* (Working Jews).

From the middle of the 1980s onward, awareness of the subject increased substantially, particularly through cinema, and not only as a result of *Shoah*. Released in 1986, *Ein einfacher Mensch* by Karl Fruchtmann was actually made in 1984, a year before the release of *Shoah*. Through reconstructions and fictionalized sequences, it narrates the experience of another escapee from the crematoria, Ya'akov Silberberg, who became a baker in Tel Aviv; each night, as detailed in the opening images of the film, he places hundreds of rolls in an oven. This is an especially important film because Silberberg's experiences in the Sonderkommando are retold only through fictionalized sequences, thanks to the participation of his wife, who escaped from a death march, and his children. In the 1998 documentary *The Last Days*, James Moll interviews Marcel Nadjari. Much later, Émil Weiss's *Sonderkommando Auschwitz-Birkenau* (2007), released on the French/German channel Arte, narrates extracts of buried Sonderkommando texts describing the gas chambers in Birkenau. Henryk Mandelbaum is interviewed in the 2009 documentary *Mémoire demain: Témoignages de déportés* (Tomorrow's memory: testimonies of deportees). In France, the exhibition *Mémoire des camps* (2001), which Clément Chéroux co-commissioned, as well as the media debate it triggered between Claude Lanzmann and Georges Didi-Huberman, was crucial in raising awareness about the Sonderkommando through photos that David Szmulewski and three other prisoners managed to take before and after a gassing.

After examining the different publications and films that led to a greater understanding of the plight of the Sonderkommando, we might ask if there have been more recently any important historical studies on the topic. Obviously, the work of Andreas Kilian and Gideon Greif has been decisive. In 1995 the Israeli historian Greif succeeded in publishing seven long interviews of eight surviving members of the Sonderkommando (the Sonderkommando members interviewed are Josef Sackar, Abraham and Shlomo Dragon, Ya'akov Gabai, Eliezer Eisenschmidt, Shaul Chazan, Leon Cohen, and Ya'akov Silberberg). His book came out first in Germany in 1995, translated from the Hebrew, *Bakhinu beli dema'ot*, with an English translation from the Hebrew published ten years later, *We Wept without Tears*.[25] Greif continues to work on the topic, mainly focused on oral history and the October 7th uprising. In Europe, Andreas Kilian is the most active researcher on the subject of the Sonderkommando. In 2002 he edited, with Eric Friedler and Barbara Siebert, *Zeugen aus der Todeszone,* which presents the biographies of several members of the Sonderkommando and an exhaustive list of the events of this period.[26] Despite the recent release of Shlomo Venezia's testimony, *Inside the Gas Chambers: Eight Months in the Sonderkommando of Auschwitz,* first in France in 2007, with an English translation in 2009,[27] no French historian has ever chosen the specific question of the Sonderkommando or the gas chambers as a subject of study. Not directly related to Auschwitz is Turkish historian Sila Cehreli's *Témoignage du Khurbn: La résistance juive dans les centres de mise à mort—Chełmno, Bełżec, Sobibór, Treblinka* (Khurbn testimony: Jewish resistance in the death camps—Chełmno, Belzec, Sobibor, Treblinka), published in France in 2013.[28] The most recent study of the Sonderkommando is *Matters of Testimony: Interpreting the Scrolls of Auschwitz* (2016), by Nicholas Chare and Dominic Williams.[29]

A number of documents are available on numerous websites, most notably from the depositions for certain trials, such as that of Dov Paisikovic. There is also the University of Southern California Shoah Foundation, which has posted montages of testimony by Dario Gabbai on YouTube under the title "Auschwitz II Birkenau Sonderkommando Testimony Clips."[30] A number of websites feature interviews with former members of the Sonderkommando. However, long before the Internet, the Sonderkommando was part of the collective imaginary. They are even an important touchpoint—on a level with the crime they were forced to perpetrate—for the deportees themselves.

The Sonderkommando as They Were Imagined

The paradox of the Sonderkommando is that, historically, they are unique and yet at the same time they call up numerous cultural references to Hell, especially from Greek and Roman mythology, Dante, and Hieronymus Bosch, all of which provide names and images by which we can recognize the Sonderkommando without ever getting to *know* their situation. However, the first people to attribute to them an exceptional status or to reduce them to particular aspects of their existence were the very prisoners at Birkenau or Auschwitz I who found themselves interned in the areas closest to the Sonder-kommando's quarters. Olga Lengyel writes that "in the camp, they had their own quarters and all contact with other prisoners was strictly forbidden." According to the doctor André Lettich, "Having come from far away, forced into silence and well-guarded, they disappeared without a trace, leaving a complete mystery."[31] Despite this kind of allegation, we know that the Sonderkommando did have contacts with those outside of their quarters, if only to communicate with the main Resistance leaders in the camp. Tadeusz Borowski, who was himself imprisoned at Auschwitz, recounts a macabre encounter in the final page of his short story "Auschwitz, Our Home (A Letter)": the narrator bumps into a "Sonder" who tells him about "a new trick for lighting the ovens" with dead children.[32] David Olère, who was a Sonderkommando and survived Auschwitz, drew pictures that made it possible to reconstruct, with a documentary-like sobriety as well as a kind of expressionist touch, the different phases in the process of gassing.[33]

The repulsion that the Sonderkommando provoke is illustrated, this time in terms of their external appearance, by one of the first testimonies from the death camps collected by Rudolf Vrba and Alfred Wetzler: "We already had little contact with them because of the terrible stench that they threw off. They were always soiled, unkempt, savage, indescribable and ruthless."[34] In *Aucun de nous ne reviendra* (None of us will return), Charlotte Delbo's description of a "heaven commando" (so-called because they sent their charges to "heaven") is no less frightening: "A prisoner stood in a lorry, a jacketed giant with an upturned fur collar," and, using his belt, he pulls up the deportees chosen for gassing and "throws them into the back of the lorry," grunting as he works, "like someone who knew his job well, and sought always to improve."[35] The Sonderkommandos were seen as mythological colossi who come to collect their ration of victims to feed the furnaces.

This view has hardly changed, and the general outlook on the Sonderkommando remains overwhelmed by these phantasmatic descriptions, which do not seem to have diminished with the passing of time. In 1972 Wiesław Kielar, a Pole and one of the first political deportees to Auschwitz, wrote: "The members of this special commando were no longer really men in their own right, within them, all human feeling had vanished, burned up with those who were most dear to them. They were entirely hardened, insensible to suffering and to the deaths of those around them. [...] The only feeling they knew was the fear of their own deaths, a fear that was all the more intense given their intimate knowledge of the barbaric machinery of death."[36] In his study of Auschwitz, Hermann Langbein reports in unnuanced fashion the words used to describe them: "They were the ravaged faces, the madmen."[37] Both Andreas Kilian and Gideon Greif are very critical of the depictions by historians such as Langbein that demonize the Sonderkommando. Jacques Stroumsa, who was first employed as a cellist in the camp orchestra and then as a technician in the Union-Werke offices, comes across as more moderate but unwilling to delve deeper: "While I was at Auschwitz, the word *Sonderkommando* provoked in us a sort of terror. We knew they existed, what jobs they were forced to do, but we found it difficult to believe."[38]

Is the depiction of the Sonderkommando by people who had not been deported any more rigorous? Stephan Hermlin was one of the first German writers to visit Auschwitz and wrote an essay entitled "Auschwitz Is Unforgotten." A man named Henryk Porembski appears in his text, described as "the commandant of the crematoria";[39] cross-referencing suggests that this was Henryk Mandelbaum,[40] whose family name has been polonized. Hermlin does not paint a ruthless portrait of Mandelbaum like others before him, but he attaches an overtly ideological position to the Sonderkommando's story, which conformed to Polish-Soviet propaganda about the concentration camp and inscribed the genocide within a sort of historic march toward a socialist utopia; this version recalls the clandestine photos of naked women in the convoy to Birkenau, on their way to be gassed, that were retouched after the war by the Soviets to give the impression that they had gone valiantly to their deaths.[41]

Between an impossible place in the Western imaginary and an abusive ideological reappropriation such as this, the Sonderkommando has been used to fabricate other visions too. In Otto Preminger's movie *Exodus* (1960), the sequence in which the young

Dov Landau, just after disembarking from the now-legendary ship *Exodus*, must submit to an interrogation in order to enter the ranks of the Irgun is a perfect example of how the Sonderkommando have become a kind of material, serving to feed the imagination of the depraved, genocidal world of Auschwitz. Young Dov Landau tries to hide his experience at Auschwitz, but under pressure from the leader of the group, he admits he had learned to work with explosives not during the Warsaw ghetto revolt, as he had suggested, but when he was a member of the Sonderkommando in Auschwitz. It was how they dug the pits in which Jews, after being gassed, were piled up to be burned. Such information, for those who know a little bit about the process of extermination, is completely absurd. Moreover, Dov Landau finally breaks down, confessing that the SS used him as though he "were a woman." The film thus compiles all the clichés of the "weakness" of women who, once deported, were unable to be heroic and could only provide sexual services to the SS, with the shame of those who collaborated in the gassing of their people.

However, there are other fictional films that focus entirely on Sonderkommando, their history or their condition.[42] In 2001, Tim Blake Nelson created a Hollywood masterpiece by playing the card of pathetic realism in *The Grey Zone*. Harvey Keitel plays Eric Muhsfeldt, an avowedly sadistic SS officer in charge of the gas chambers at Auschwitz. The storyline is based on Miklós Nyiszli's testimony and Primo Levi's essay about the grey zone, in which he describes this Nazi's "demonic crime" as "an attempt to shift on to others—specifically the victims—the burden of guilt, so that they were deprived of even the solace of innocence."[43]

The 2015 film *Son of Saul*, directed by László Nemes, represents a new stage in the telling of the Sonderkommandos' story. In October 1944, near the gas chambers at Auschwitz-Birkenau, Saul Ausländer, a Sonderkommando, witnesses a young boy who has survived a gassing being revived and then murdered by the SS. The boy's body is going to be taken to the medical block to be autopsied, but Ausländer wants the body to be left untouched at all costs and insists that the boy is his son. He will not let the boy's body be burned like the others, protecting the corpse up until the October 7th uprising when he is killed. In this depiction, the central character defies all the negative traits that had been assigned to the Sonderkommando. However, the fictional Ausländer is not a depiction of any Sonderkommando member we know of, although a number of other characters in the film are based on actual individuals, such as Zalmen Gradowski and one of the squad members who took a photograph looking out from the gas chamber of Crematorium V. *Son of Saul*, through its interpretation, reverses the heroic image of resistance. In fact, the plot does not conform to the canons of a genre in which courage and resistance would "naturally" be the cornerstone; such is its subtlety, the film does not give in to an alternative (or additional) generic expression of victimhood. This was in fact one of the major concerns of the director Nemes from the project's outset: no voyeuristic aesthetics, no Hollywood realism; a film that was neither lament nor Western (the end of *The Grey Zone* very much resembles the latter).

To end this journey through the different ways in which the Sonderkommandos have been *imagined*, let us consider someone from whom we might have expected a little more restraint: Primo Levi. Contrary to the idea that one generally has of Levi and his presentation of the concentration camps, in the following case he is far from impartial. In a report written in 1946 with Leonardo Debenedetti for the Red Army while they were still in a camp in Katowice, both authors focus in on the Sonderkommando. Lacking nuance, they repeat false information that they had heard: "A nauseating odor emanated from their clothing; they were always dirty and looked completely savage, truly ferocious beasts. *They were chosen from among the most hardened criminals for the gravest of blood crimes.*"[44]

Nonetheless, Levi set aside a particular place for the Sonderkommando in the central chapter of his collection *The Drowned and the Saved* (1985), "The Grey Zone." In these pages, there is a further hint as to how the Sonderkommando constituted an obstacle to wider comprehension, and Levi demonstrates ambivalence toward them. For him, it seems "difficult, almost impossible to form an image for ourselves of how these men lived day by day, saw themselves, accepted their condition."[45] As such, he suggests a suspension of judgment, an exercise that entails a systematic questioning of the stereotypes used unsuccessfully to understand them. However, a little later, Levi returns to his deprecatory tone: "From men who have known such extreme destitution one cannot expect a deposition in the juridical sense of the term, but something that is at once a lament, a curse, an expiation, and an attempt to justify and rehabilitate themselves. One should expect a liberating outburst instead of a Medusa-faced truth."[46]

We know that for Levi, the evocation of the face of the Medusa is associated with the *Muselmänner*, those deportees who had arrived, for the most part, at an irreversible state of physical and mental deterioration. The meaning of the *Muselmänner*'s image remains stable, in comparison to that of the Sonderkommando. This point creates difficulties for Levi in his efforts to understand this particular grey zone. And it is this difficulty that is exaggerated in Giorgio Agamben's *Remnants of Auschwitz* in order to devalue the humanity of the Sonderkommando. Agamben does not use the "grey zone" as a heuristic notion to question the Sonderkommando behavior—as Levi tried to do—but rather, responding to the explicative demands that led Levi to require the suspension of judgment, he utterly rejects the Sonderkommando from all communities, confining them to a radically violent Purgatory.

The Destiny of a Writer of Darkness

More than any other written testimony from this period, Gradowski's manuscripts remain out of step with general expectations about this sort of text. Essentially, the literary qualities of his manuscripts make them more than a collection of facts and Gradowski more than just a witness who chronicled what he experienced. Here, we are in the presence of a true work of literature, by a man who always aspired to be a writer. His tragic destiny is that he became a writer in such extreme conditions and did not survive to see his work published.

Where did a member of the Sonderkommando find the necessary distance to write a true literary text? It is not that there was never any free time for writing; indeed, the teams would in fact find themselves without any work to do when there were no new convoy arrivals—

but these were the moments when they were most in danger of being killed themselves. They did not lack the means as such, but they were deprived of the conditions that would allow them to exist safely, even if the basic requirements for their physical existence were fulfilled. How then did Lejb Langfus, Zalmen Lewental, Zalmen Gradowski, and those other anonymous writers, who no doubt wrote but whose texts have been lost, manage to find a space that allowed them to step back from the horror that they were forced to live with? From which perspective did they write these manuscripts? Under such circumstances, how were they able to link the act of writing to what they witnessed? The Seen to the Said? These questions perhaps carry with them the proof that there would have forever remained a trace of the Sonderkommando even if all of them had been killed, because there is always another person to read and decipher that trace, for as long as humans continue to populate the world. Indeed, it was an unlikely encounter that led to Zalmen Gradowski's second manuscript becoming entwined with the fate of Haïm Wollnerman.

If the fate of Gradowski's first manuscript is similar to that of the others that were edited by Ber Mark, the history of the second manuscript is entirely atypical. In order to fully grasp its particularity, some biographical details are helpful to provide the necessary framework for understanding his writing.

1. BIOGRAPHICAL DATA

Haïm Zalmen Gradowski was born between 1908 and 1910 in Suwałki, a Polish village near the Lithuanian border, to a relatively prominent family of very religious shopkeepers. He worked with his father, Shemuel Gradowski, a shopkeeper and businessman. While it is difficult to verify his upbringing, we are quite sure that Zalmen Gradowski was very committed to both religious and political matters, as is evident by consulting the *Yisker Bukh Suvalk* (Memorial book of Suvalk).[47] A fervent Zionist, he was an active member of the Betar Movement in his hometown and frequented Revisionist circles—a movement launched by Vladimir Jabotinsky in 1923, close to the political Zionism of Theodor Herzl and Max Nordau.[48] He became one of the leaders of a Zionist group in Suwałki, as indicated in the *Yisker Bukh Suvalk*.[49]

When Suwałki was occupied by the German forces in 1941, he and his wife, Sonja (Sarah) Zlotoyabko, settled in Soviet-controlled Lunna, a shtetl near Grodno, in the province of Białystok, where his wife's family lived. There, he worked as a clerk in a state-run company. After the Germans invaded the region in the summer of 1941, and once a ghetto was established, Gradowski was responsible for the management of sanitary issues, a role that increased when the ghetto inhabitants were deported to the transit camp in Kołbasin.

On December 8, 1942, Gradowski was deported to Birkenau with his family, all of whom were killed that same day, while Gradowski himself was quickly transferred to the Sonderkommando in Crematorium III.[50] In testimony cited by Ber Mark, Yaakov Freimark explains how Gradowski belonged to one of the teams responsible for burning the bodies in Crematorium IV. Freimark, who was from the same town as Gradowski, easily maintained contact with him because he was in the Kanada Kommando, which was in charge of the personal belongings left by the deportees. Freimark's testimony reported that, at the end of each day, because the Jewish faith prohibits burning bodies, Gradowski would put on his prayer shawl and phylacteries and recite the Kaddish.

Shlomo Dragon, one of the few survivors of the Sonderkommando, recounted that Gradowski drew up a list of gassed people on the basis of reports from other Sonderkommandos working in each crematorium, and he buried the list next to Crematorium II. Shlomo Dragon—whose brother Abraham Dragon was also in the Sonderkommando—cleaned up the barracks where Gradowski stayed, and he tried to help him to write safely. Shlomo "arranged a bed for him next to a window so that he would have enough light too. Only the barrack room duty made these conditions possible." He said that Gradowski told the small number of Sonderkommandos who were informed of his clandestine activities that the "events in the camp had to be documented so that the whole world would know about it."[51] He probably obtained the paper on which he wrote from Yaakov Freimark. At the same time, Gradowski took an active

part in the clandestine movement that formed within the Sonderkommando, and later became one of its leaders.

Gradowski's methods of resistance during his detention until his
death were informed by three factors: his religious conviction, his
political commitment, and his desire to be a writer. This latter aspect
was confirmed by David Sfard, his brother-in-law who fled Poland
in 1939 and was a researcher at Yad Vashem after the war. Sfard provided the details about Gradowski in the text that accompanies the
original version edited by Haïm Wollnerman. Sfard said that Gradowski gave him several of his short stories to read before the war;
he felt that Gradowski's style had too many poetic flourishes and not
enough concrete descriptions, and the stories lacked a literary qual-
ity. But was Sfard a reliable expert in the literary field? Nonetheless,
Sfard remarked on the extent to which Gradowski demonstrated
writerly aspirations. This fact is crucial in understanding the literary
questions that his manuscripts pose.

2. THE FIRST MANUSCRIPT

On March 5, 1945, Gradowski's first manuscript was found near Birkenau's Crematorium III by the Soviet-Polish Investigating Commission during a search carried out based on information from Shlomo
Dragon. This manuscript is currently in the collection of the Museum of Military Medicine in St. Petersburg. Inside a German water
bottle made of aluminum and with a metal cork, they discovered a
notebook measuring 14.5 by 10 centimeters, with 81 numbered pages
(there were about 10 missing pages), each page containing between
20 and 38 lines, the first few lines of which are illegible. The bottle
also contained a second manuscript, a letter, of just two pages, dated
September 6, 1944, and bearing Zalmen Gradowski's signature. Thus,
this discovery brings together the supposedly first of Gradowski's
manuscripts and the letter.

The manuscript, written over the course of autumn 1943, is dedicated to the memory of his family, murdered on their arrival at
Auschwitz, and begins with a phrase, written in four languages (Polish, Russian, French, and German), inviting the reader to pay atten-

tion to this document, which carries a very important trace for the historian—in the second manuscript this notification is only in Yiddish. Then, about twenty pages of the original text has information relative to the mass murders being committed by the German occupation troops in November 1942 in the Grodno region, over the course of what was called the *Aktion Judenrein*. After those pages, Gradowski continues with an account of his journey to Auschwitz, his entry into the camp, and the first few days he spent there. The text stops at the moment the author was recruited into the Sonderkommando.

A first level of interpretation allows us therefore to follow the chronology of the persecutions and the ultimately fatal deportation of Gradowski and his family. On several occasions, he mentions the Polish attitude toward the Jews as frequently negative. These are the most documentary elements of the text. A second level of interpretation points to the psychological dimension of his story: the anxiety, the uncertainty without any real hope, the fear. Numerous questions punctuate the text; these have disappeared by the second manuscript.

But the most striking aspect of this manuscript remains the author's sophisticated writing style. Directly addressing a fictional reader, he never ceases to call on the reader and invite them to imagine his journey. Gradowski not only gives information about the extermination process and the living condition of the squads; his writing is also very much addressed to a reader, and he tries to maintain a connection to this future reader. Gradowski guides us on this descent into Hell, using a literary style full of emotion and emphasis, resorting to numerous instances of the rhetorical repetition of anaphora (e.g., "you see, my friend"; "come, my friend," repeated frequently at the beginning of paragraphs); the text is structured by the alternation of these anaphora with questions and appeals to the reader. Different kinds of repetition are used as imaginary landmarks that delimit the outside, invaded by such extreme violence as to be devoid of the benchmarks of normal life; these landmarks help to build a distant and bearable space on which the unbearable reality can be represented. We can also interpret them as equivalent to a ritual way of holding out against the invasive reality. This occurs as though part of an effort to strengthen the text so that it can support the declarations that the author, on a psychological level, was not able to withstand otherwise. Gradowski pushes this unusual aspect even further in the second manuscript.

Gradowski's manuscripts are also filled with intertextual references from Yiddish literature such as the Yiddish tradition of the fantastic, including Hayim Nahman Bialik's poem "In the City of Slaughter," referring to the Kishinev pogrom of 1903. The influence of Mendele Moykher-Sforim's *The Nag* (*Di Klatshe*, 1873) is also apparent; just as Gradowski takes us (his reader) to see the camp, the demon Ashmedai (Asmodeus) flies the young hero into the air to show all the evil in the world, where the smoke of civilization rising to the heavens is likened to incense burning on the altar of "their god the devil." This leads us to the second manuscript.

3. THE SECOND MANUSCRIPT

"The notebook ends abruptly," writes Ber Mark about Gradowski's other texts. "The subsequent sections were possibly buried elsewhere [...] in different locations, under a mass of ashes, where the ovens were."[52] These "subsequent sections," which form three chapters of the second manuscript, came to light at about the same time as Mark's edited collection of manuscripts, finished by Mark's widow after his death in 1966. As such, Ber Mark and Haïm Wollnerman, the publisher of the second manuscript, were not aware of each other's texts at the time of publication. As mentioned above, Wollnerman needed thirty years to publish the manuscript at his own expense, with his foreword and two texts from David Sfard and Yehoshua Wygodski, members of the board at Yad Vashem. However, when editing Gradowski's manuscript, Wollnerman did not want to publish the last section, "The Reuniting," of the last chapter, "The Czech Transport." Thus, these two pages were not published until Wollnerman's grandson Avishai Zur included them in the Hebrew edition he recently edited. But Zur is not able to give any convincing explanation about his grandfather's choice. It might be because, beyond its very lyrical style, these pages end on a call for revenge.

4. THE POSSIBILITY OF BEING OUTSIDE ONESELF

As well as being longer than Gradowski's first manuscript, the second manuscript is the longest of all the buried texts unearthed thus far. It is divided into three chapters, preceded by a preface in which he emphasizes, as in the first manuscript, the importance of actual future readers. Wollnerman published the chapters in an order that we have not followed, in favor of the order proposed by Krystyna Oleksy.[53] Wollnerman's version starts with "A Moonlit Night," which is a long lyrical invocation of the moon loaded with multiple references from both religion and literature (see Arnold Davidson's "Afterword" below). The second chapter is "The Czech Transport," which deals more precisely with the extermination of the Czech Jews. Third is "Separation," the longest chapter, which describes the selection process within the Sonderkommando.

If we take into account the chronological order of their writing, these last two must have been swapped around, which is why we have altered this order from Wollnerman's edition. Indeed, as Oleksy has observed, Wollnerman's third chapter, "Separation," in fact describes events that preceded "The Czech Transport." Gradowski writes of having spent fifteen months in the Sonderkommando, while in "The Czech Transport," he indicates that sixteen months have passed. Moreover, the reduction in the size of the Sonderkommando, which he details, ostensibly makes references to the selection that took place in the last two weeks of February 1944, probably on February 24, prior therefore to the gassing of the Czechs, which was undertaken the following month. The recent German edition by Aurélia Kalisky and Andreas Kilian follows the same order as Wollnerman, and how the order of the text matters is a debatable issue. In their very documented commentary, Nicholas Chare and Dominic Williams argue that "A Moonlit Night" and "The Czech Transport" are linked because of semantic reasons related to the connection of the moon and the night.[54] But is this a satisfactory criterion to base the order of the chapters? More precisely, should semantic links take precedence over chronological order? Putting "Separation" between "A Moonlit Night" and "The Czech Transport" highlights how writing in such conditions should not be interpreted only with the categories of sense of meaning and coherence.

Regarding Gradowski's writing style, his manuscripts cannot be reduced to a collection of facts, and he does not present himself as preparing the ground for future historians. In this respect, Zalmen Lewental's intention is different in his recovered texts. This is not because Gradowski lacked information about the massacres: as Shlomo Dragon explained in 1945, "The *Schreiber* of our *Kommando*," meaning Gradowski, wrote down the number of victims and "noted down the impressions of the prisoners themselves."[55] The facts, which are certainly of decisive documentary value, function as precise anchoring elements for a text based on historical fact, but they are enhanced by the literary flow of Gradowski's writing. Even if these manuscripts were his very first pieces of writing, they are quite sophisticated. Reflecting the author's attempts to translate his experience in terms of the literary rather than the literal, they possess poetic and stylistic qualities that radically separate his manuscripts from those of the other Sonderkommandos.

Such literary gestures bring together the pain of lost or disappearing worlds with a future that is not made up solely of suffering; a space pierced only by the hope of being read. Gradowski tells us that his life's posthumous meaning depends on his readers—*which means us*—and that his future exists elsewhere away from the massacre. In order to realize his writing's endeavor and because he is without hope ("Can the dead weep for the dead?" he writes), Gradowski must extract himself from a present where every moment is suffused with the presence of the dead. That is why his writing can be understood as representing both a possibility of being outside oneself and a true act of resistance very much linked with the uprising he was planning with his Sonderkommando comrades.

Beyond the address to the reader, the stylistic attention with which he expresses his literary meaning is often charged with astonishing emphasis and pathos, which can at first be disconcerting. Gradowski's literary style is a form of distanciation that repels his horrific quotidian existence. He does not present us with a chronicle, which would have trapped him in the reality of his direct contact with the experience of those who were murdered. Literary style is for him a means of turning away from this gruesome reality in order to be able to portray it with greater clarity. This conformity to stylistic forms functions as a way of detaching himself from his surroundings, in order not to forget, but to see them more clearly. It is almost paradoxical that such a writing style manages to produce the longest testimony and was written in the closest proximity to the gas chambers.

This is why it was essential that the translator of these manuscripts respond faithfully to the lexical demands—for example, retaining the numerous repetitions and the abundant use of adjectives—as much as carefully following the rhythm and tone of Gradowski's phrasing. For the same reason, the frequency of dashes has been respected; typographical witnesses to the author's poetry, they generally mark a pause between the first half of a phrase, referring to the joyous world of "before," and the second half when that world is destroyed.

The reader encounters euphemisms, litotes, poetic, emphatic or even ironic phrases, but the most specific are anaphora, a repetition located at the beginning of multiple phrases. In "A Moonlit Night," the anaphora of "why" and "see" are addressed to the moon in the opening pages; "down there" and "there above" in those last two hitherto unpublished pages of "The Reuniting"; and "the bunk" repeated twenty-two times in the section "The Bunks" from the chapter "Separation." Constructions that appear surprising such as questions and exclamations also arise, inspired by the rhetoric of biblical lamentations. Gradowski mixes into his narrative colloquial but also more elegant expressions. He makes use of precise lexical fields that he reuses liberally to present his vision of the unworldly, or to invoke the brotherhood that links him to his people, before and after their deaths. Most of these terms are grounded in Jewish traditions and cultures. He patterns a specific style fed by his own culture. Yiddish lends itself to this rich blend of languages, allowing Gradowski to move around among them all. Such playfulness is very unexpected in a testimony on this subject. The shifting tone and style, allowing the author great flexibility in choosing his perspective, is what makes possible the transformation of the Seen into the Said.

From a literary point of view, he regularly employs free indirect speech, but is also able to hold back and imagine what he is feeling as if from the outside. He accompanies the victims, recording various acts of resistance and how the victims face the despicable spectre of their imminent deaths. He recounts each SS subterfuge to deceive the victims until the doors were closed on the "shower rooms," which were in reality the gas chambers. His writing translates a continual flow of thoughts, moving from perspective to perspective, never staying still. It weaves through the thoughts of women, of men, of two supposed lovers, of SS guards. He calls on the moon and thinks or answers for it—the symbolic use of a grand poetic gesture that is part of the ritual Jewish blessing of the new moon. Through this, he suspends the normalization and numbness experienced in the face of horror repeating again and again. If we look beyond the dark context of the setting, we can recognize an elaborate use of narrative techniques that go far beyond what Chare and Williams characterize as "ghostly."[56]

Gradowski collects each spark of life, each vibration of the bodies around him. From this comes his almost fascinated insistence, which some readers will find uncomfortable, on noting down the physicality of the women around him, who embody all that a body can offer, receive, or take, and all that a body does not cease to do or give, over the course of its life. Here he uses a whole lexicon that refers to life, as opposed to that which refers to horror, which he evokes through motifs of petrification and frozen tears.

The Sonderkommandos are precisely placed where they can aid in pushing the bodies of the victims, described as so fully alive, into destruction. In this text, the body is alive to an extreme degree, condensed whole into just a few lines—before being delivered to death. The notion of "world" is also very important and is a term he uses frequently. Beings are worlds, destroyed worlds, from a world which is itself lost and that the author magnifies; but other free worlds exist, most notably the reader's. If the writing style is a means of accompanying the dead by maintaining the glow of their lives, it also allows for a temporary suspension of the infinite debt he is subjected to every time his people are gassed, and to recover, if only while he writes, some sense of dignity.

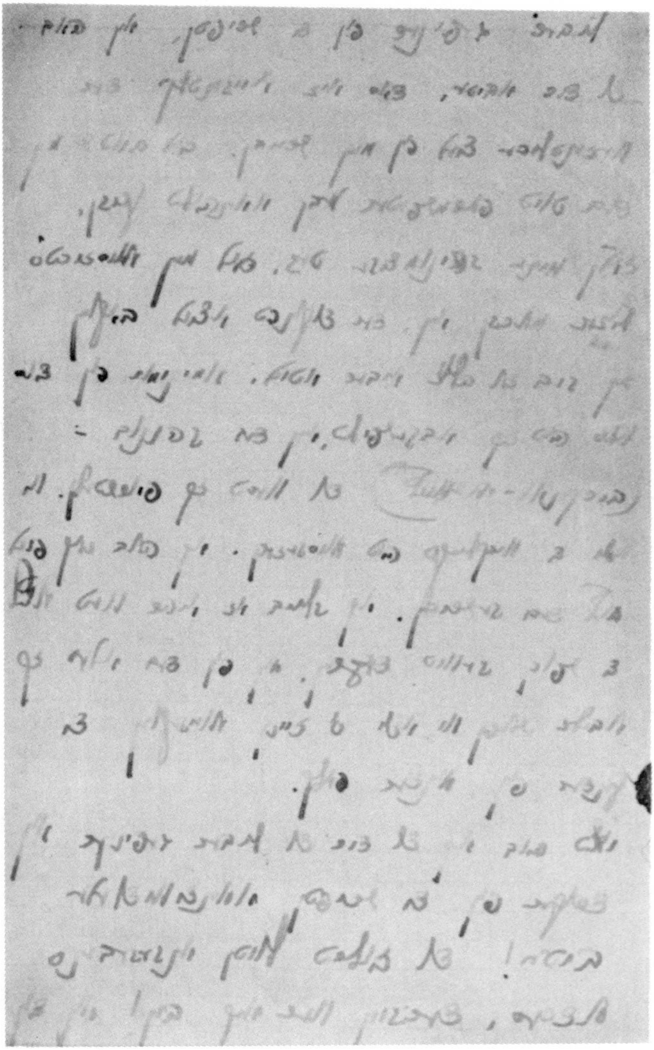

FIGURES 3 & 4 Handwritten pages from
Zalmen Gradowski's second manuscript.

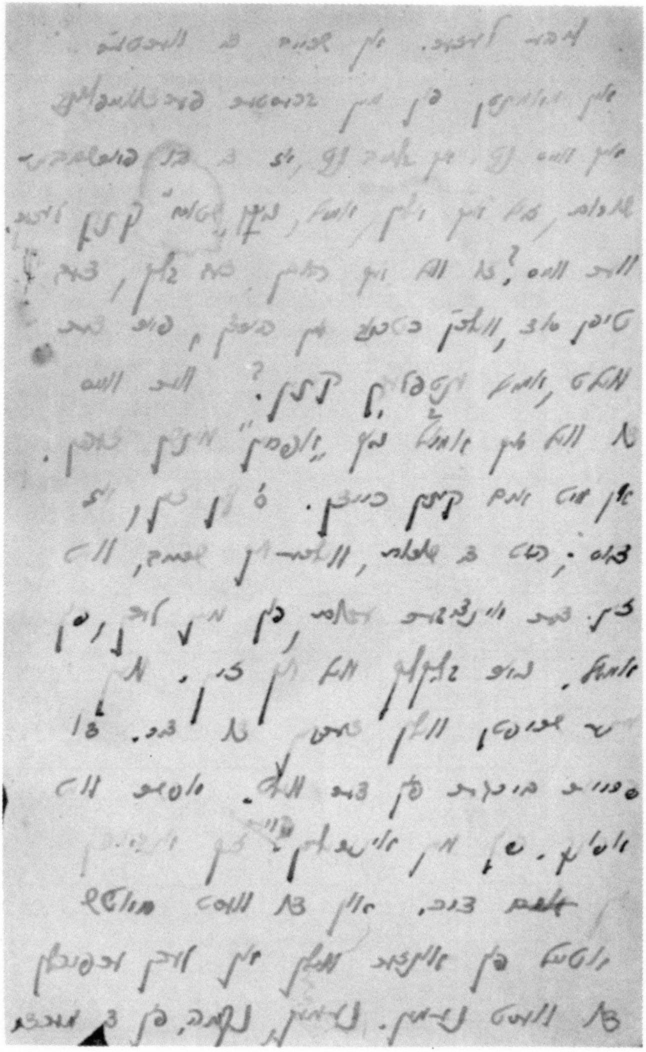

FIGURE 5 Photo taken at the Auschwitz Museum archives of an image of the aluminum bottle in which Zalmen Gradowski put his first manuscript and the September 6th letter. © Philippe Mesnard.

THE LAST CONSOLATION VANISHED

Report

After examination of a wide-mouthed aluminum water bottle

MARCH 5, 1945

Captain Popov, military investigator attached to the Ministry of Justice, in the presence of witnesses O. N. Mitenko and S. Steinberg, proceeded to examine the aluminum bottle which had been given to me [*sic*] discovered during the removal of the ashes in the area of Crematorium III.

DURING THE EXAMINATION IT WAS ESTABLISHED

The German-model wide-mouthed aluminum water bottle measures 18 cm in length, 10 cm in width. It is closed with an aluminum screw-on cap, inside of which there is a rubber seal. The bottle has a recess on one side and a small opening through which we could see a piece of paper.

When opening the bottle, it appeared impossible to extract its contents through the neck.

In order to extract the contents the bottle was cut open lengthwise, and the contents extracted.

Upon examination of the contents, we discovered: A notebook measuring 14.5 by 10 cm and containing 81 pages of notes written in Yiddish. It appeared that part of the notebook had been wet. A 2-page letter, also in Yiddish, was slipped inside the notebook. The notebook and the letter were wrapped in two sheets of blank paper.

THE ABOVE IS ESTABLISHED BY THIS REPORT

Military investigator: Captain of Justice POPOV

Witnesses: (1) MITENKO (2) STEINBERG

First Manuscript

Notebook

Dedicated to my family, burned in Birkenau-Auschwitz
My wife—Sonja
My mother—Sarah
My sister—Esther-Rokhl
My sister—Luba
My father-in-law—Raphael
My brother-in-law—Wolf

[Come] here to me, you fortunate citizen of the world who lives in a land where happiness, joy and pleasure still exist, and I will tell you of the abject criminals of today who took an entire people and turned their happiness to sadness, their joy into eternal sorrow—their pleasure forever destroyed.

Come here to me, you free citizen of the world, where your life is made safe by human morality and your existence is guaranteed

Translator's note: This translation has been kept as close to the original as possible, with the intent of rendering the characteristic style of Gradowski's prose. His repetitions and unusual punctuation, particularly his use of quotation marks (for irony or simply for emphasis) have been left exactly as he wrote them. Hebrew words have been transliterated in their standard, most widely used English spelling. Hebrew words that have become part of the Yiddish language have a markedly different pronunciation and are transliterated as pronounced by Yiddish speakers (e.g., *Shabes* rather than *Shabbat*, *Sholem* rather than *Shalom*).

by law, and I will tell you how these modern criminals, these vile bandits, expunged all morality from life, wiped out the very laws of existence.

Come here to me, you free citizen of the world, whose land is bounded by a modern-day Great Wall of China, where the claws of the loathsome devils could not reach, and I will tell you how they trapped a people in their devilish arms, and with sadistic cruelty clamped their devilish claws around their necks until they were smothered and annihilated.

Come here to me, you free citizen of the world, who was fortunate enough never to know face-to-face the rule of the cruel new pirates, and I will tell you, and show you too, how and with what means they murdered millions of a people long known as a people of martyrs.

Come here to me, you free citizen of the world, who had the good fortune not to know the rule of the cruel [...] two-legged beasts, and I will tell you with what refined sadistic methods they murdered millions of the people of Israel, helpless, alone, protected by no one. Come and see how a highly cultured people was transformed by a savage, diabolical law [born in] the mind of the greatest bandit and lowest criminal that the sadistic world had yet spawned.

Come now, while the destruction[1] is still in full progress [...]

Come even now, as the annihilation still zealously goes on.

Come even now, when the Angel of Death still has all his power.

Come now, while in the ovens the funeral pyre still blazes with its great flames.

Come, arise, do not wait until the Deluge[2] is over, when the sky will brighten and the sun will shine again, for then you will stand in amazement and not believe what your eyes tell you. And who knows if with the passing of the Deluge, all those will disappear who might have been living witnesses, able to tell you the truth.

Who knows if before the rising of the sun, witnesses will come forth from the horrible dark night, and you will certainly think that the vast and horrible destruction that you discover was the work of cannons. You will certainly think that the vast destruction that befell our people was the result of war. You will certainly think that the total liquidation of the Jews of Europe was the result of a natural catastrophe. The earth opened its mouth and through some Godlike force they were gathered together from everywhere to be swallowed up in the abyss.

You will not believe that such horrendous destruction could be the work of people, even if those people had been turned into animals.

Come with me, a solitary child of the people of Israel, alone and miserable but still alive, who was driven from his home and, along with his family, friends and near ones, found a brief respite in wet [earthen] graves and from there were brought to the so-called concentration [labor] camps and ended up at this great cemetery of the Jewish people. And there the devils chose me to be a guard at the gates of Hell, through whose doors passed and still pass millions of Jews from all of Europe. With each of them I [...] when they stood [...] I was with them to the last [...] and they confided in me the last secret of their lives. [I] accompanied them on the last steps of their lives. Until they were locked into the [...] of the Angel of Death to vanish from the world forever. They talked to me of everything, how they were torn from their homes and lived through a chain of terrible suffering until they reached their final goal, to serve as sacrificial victims to the devil.

Come, my friend, stand up, come out of your warm, safe palaces, arm yourself with courage and daring, and walk with me over the continent of Europe, where the devil has imposed his rule, and I will tell you and with facts show you the ways in which this highly civilized race liquidated the people of Israel, weak, helpless, and guilty of no crime.

Do not fear the long and tragic journey, do not fear the cruel and savage images that you will be called upon to see. Do not fear, I will not show you the end before we begin, and gradually your eye will grow blank, your heart numb and your ears deaf. Take with you, man, an assorted baggage, that will serve you in cold and damp, in hunger and thirst, for in the middle of a freezing night we may well have to stand on deserted fields and accompany my unfortunate brothers on their last road, their march to death. We may well march for days and nights in hunger and in thirst over the different wander routes of Europe that have carried millions of the Jewish masses whom the modern barbarians have driven toward their vile and diabolical goal, to offer up their lives as a sacrifice on the altar of their people.

Are you ready, dear friend, to begin the journey? Just one more condition I will set for you: bid farewell to your wife and child, for you have [...] the cruel images you will no longer want to live in [a world] where such diabolical acts can be committed.

Bid farewell to your friends and acquaintances, for you will certainly [after] looking at the horrible sadistic deeds from the supposedly cultured devil's spawn, you will want to erase your name from the family of man and will regret the day that you were born.

Tell them, your wife and child, that if you never return from the journey, it is because your human heart was too weak to withstand the weight of the horrific, bestial acts your eyes observed.

Tell them, your friends and acquaintances, that if you do not return, it is because your blood froze and could no longer flow, at the sight of the horrific, barbaric images, of how they died, the innocent, helpless children of a poor and forlorn people.

Tell them that if your heart turns to [stone], if your brain becomes a cold mechanism for thinking and your eye merely a camera, then too you will not come back to them. Let them look for you in the primeval forests, for you will flee from the world where the human species lives. You will look for solace there among the savage beasts rather than be among the cultured devils, for wild animals too have been tamed by culture, their claws blunted and much of their savagery lost. But it is just the opposite when a man turns into a beast. The more culture the more cruelty: the more civilization the greater barbarity, the higher the development the more horrific the deeds.

Come with me, let us rise on the wings of an eagle of steel and soar above the vast and tragic horizon of Europe. From there, through microscope-glasses we will observe everything, penetrate everywhere. Hold on tight to my hand. Do not shudder [...] for you will yet have worse to see.

[...] hold on with manly strength, blunt in you all [...], forget your wife and child, friends and acquaintances; forget the world you came from. Imagine that the images you see are not people but loathsome animals whose existence must be extinguished, for otherwise it will be unbearable to look.

Do not fear, when in the wet earthen graves you see living, vibrant children, for you will see them later on in worse conditions yet.

Do not fear, when in the middle of a freezing night you find a large mass of Jews, driven out of their graves and pursued in its journey, on its unknown, unfamiliar way. Let not your heart tremble at the sound of the children's cries, the women's screams, the groans of old and sick, for you have yet to see crueler and more horrible.

Do not fear, when after such a march, when the day begins to break, you will find old couples lying on the road amid red and purple stains—these are the sick and weak, shot to death when they could not endure the march.

Do not worry about those already dead, save a groan for those who for the time being are still alive.

Do not tremble as you watch this mass driven into the wagons like lifeless cargo, in such numbers that there is no more air to breathe, for they are being taken to a fate more horrible yet.

And now, my friend, having given you all the instructions concerning our trip, I will walk with you through one of the countless Polish camps, in which were concentrated the Jews of Poland and of many other nations, who [...] great suffering were sent there from whence there is no coming back, for eternity has drawn its border there.

Come, my friend, now we will descend into the camp where my family and I, and tens of thousands of Jews, lived for a short time. I will tell you what they lived through in those horrible times until they reached their final destination.

Listen, my friend, and learn what takes place here.

Here in the camp the atmosphere is oppressive; they have announced a transport from several towns together. All are frightened, those whose time it is to leave and those whose turn might come tomorrow, for they see the masters working at a quicker tempo to liquidate the camp. And now comes news that transports are being sent from the city too, and in a most bestial way. The police surround a group of streets and go from house to house, dragging out young and old, sick and weak, as if they were dangerous criminals, and tak-ing them all to the large synagogue of the city and from there under close guard to the train, where the freight wagons, made up like cattle cars, are already waiting for them. Like repulsive creatures, they are driven in, pressed together, stuffed in until there is no more air to breathe. When they see that the wagons are so packed that people are already hanging off the side, then the doors are shut, sealed with heavy iron bars, and then sent, under heavy escort, in that unknown direction, to that unfamiliar place which is said to be a work camp for the deported Jews. Any Jews who try to hide or look as if they will not go or seem to seek a way to disappear are shot on the spot.

On the threshold of the great synagogue of Grodno, blood was spilled, the blood of dozens of young lives, those who suspected where they were being taken and wanted to avoid being the first vic-tims. The authorities, refined bandits and common criminals, saw that the system of sending transports from the city direct to the train could in the future cause problems, creating groups of young men, desperate and with no family responsibilities, who would react with violence or run away to the woods to hide, better to live with animals than to remain among such men. Or they would make their way into the deep secret woods in which are hidden the few small scattered groups of heroic fighters who sacrifice their lives for the freedom and happiness of all, who hinder the oppressors in their fight for power and grandeur. To avoid all this, to be certain to fully carry out their plunder, they began to turn to other refined means that would con-fuse their thinking and cloud their understanding. They let out a rumor that the final concentration point of Grodno would be this camp, just now being emptied of the Jews from the villages. And with this opium of illusion, they lulled even those who had a real in-tuition about their future and would have been ready for battle and resistance. Thus began the deportation from Grodno to the camps.[3]

Come, my friend, today a transport is expected. Let us take the road that leads to the camp. Come, let us stand by the side to better observe the dreadful, the horrible scene.

You see, my friend, there far away, a black mass lying on a shining white road. Barely moving, it is encircled by tall black shadows that continually bend toward the creeping mass and repeatedly rain down blows on the deeply bowed heads. We do not know what it all represents. Is it a herd of cattle being driven or a group of people who have lost half of their height? See, now they are coming closer. It is a mass of Jews, thousands upon thousands of them, young and old, now on the road leading to their new home. They do not walk but crawl on all fours. So has ordered the young bandit who holds in his hands their fate, their life and being. This awful scene he wanted to see with his own eyes, how a huge mass of people can be turned into animals. He wanted to sate his sadistic, cruel heart with emotions of human pain and suffering. You see how, after the long distance they have marched, they stagger to their feet, broken and exhausted, and must now sing and dance to amuse their guards.

He, the ignoble pirate and his henchmen, from the first step stamped out their egos, sacrificed their souls to his Aryan god and turned them into tragic living automatons, with no will of their own, no aspirations, who obey in every way the orders of their oppressors. All that is left is their wish to remain automatons, with the deep heartfelt hope that in the nearest future they will reclaim their ego and breathe in a new soul.

See, my friend, how numbed and stiff they march in ranks. No cry nor scream of a child will you hear, do you know why? Because every cry of a child is snuffed out by a blow to mother and child. So was it ordered, such is the will of the savage beasts whose bestial tendencies grew ever stronger, who only sought after victims and wanted to drown their cruel thirsty souls in warm Jewish blood. The mass must obey the most horrible orders, for their lives are in their hands and their broken bodies will soon be found sprawled on the ground in red rivers of blood, with no one to take them to their eternal rest.

See, my friend, how mothers clasp their children to their breasts and smother their cries. They press the little heads under their shawls so as not to hear the whimpers of the children slowly freezing to death. Notice how one Jew squeezes another by the hand as a sign he must keep still. Be quiet, remember, do not give up your life before your time. This is how it looks, my friend, the march of thousands upon thousands of Jews being led, for the time being, into the concentration camp.

And now see, my friend, [...] and now found [...] for themselves the thousands of [Jews] [...] who just yesterday served as useful elements and were even privileged for their useful and productive work, and have now been reduced to wanderers, psychologically broken and physically exhausted, not knowing where the devil will lead them. Whose only wish is as quickly as possible to find a living grave in order to rest their bones.

My friend, we have just heard dreadful news. My family, friends, acquaintances, and myself, along with thousands of Jews, must be ready to take the road today. Dark thoughts fill our minds. Who knows where they will lead us, who knows what tomorrow will bring. A horrible foreboding will not let us rest. For the actions of the authorities contradict the stated aim. If they needed us as a work force in the future, then why do they so quickly deplete our strength? Why do they hasten so to drain our blood? Why turn strong Jewish muscles into weak and useless hands? Why liquidate useful sectors of work for which there are no replacements aside from us, and leave them idle, dead. And no one seems concerned. Why is the government work here so useless, so unnecessary, that it can be broken up, dismantled, and there at the concentration camp, it will be greatly needed and important, why?

Who knows if it is not all a tragic bluff, from the vile, seasoned criminals who want to chloroform us with promises of work so that they can more easily, with less difficulty, carry out their great plan of extermination. Such thoughts possess us now as we prepare ourselves for the trip.

I see, my friend, you have something to ask me. I know what it is you cannot grasp. Why, why have we come to this point? Could we not have found a better place where we could live in safety? To this I will give you a complete answer. Three factors made it easier for the devil [...] the extermination process of our people. One factor was general and two [individual]. The collective factor was the fact that we lived among Polish people in the majority of whom we saw and felt a great visceral anti-Semitism. As soon as the devil arrived, they looked on with satisfaction at the cruelty he unleashed upon us, with feigned regret on their faces and inner pleasure in their hearts. They listened to the horrible heartrending news of the hundreds of thousands of Jewish victims exterminated by the enemy in the most cruel and savage ways. Perhaps they rejoiced in their hearts at the coming of the pirate-people to do the work they were not yet capable of, for they still have a touch of human morality and conscience. The only thing that did frighten them, and rightly so, was that once they had finished their war against the Jews, at that instant when the target toward which all the cruelty and barbarity had been directed disappeared, they would then seek a new victim to sate their bestial instincts. This fear was in part well founded and its consequences were soon seen. Great masses of Jews tried to find a place in the towns or countryside where they could be swallowed up among the Polish population, but everywhere received the same refusal: No. Everywhere they found before them a closed door. At every place an iron wall stood before them and as Jews, they stood out in the open, where the enemy's hand could easily reach them.

You ask why the Jews did not mount a resistance. Do you know why? Because they had no trust in their neighbors, who would have betrayed them at the slightest setback. They could count on no elements who would seriously help, who at a given moment would have taken on the responsibility for the struggle, for the uprising. The fear of being handed over to the enemy sapped the will to struggle, destroyed all bold impulses.

I see, my friend[, . . .] why did we not run into the thick forests to grow by uniting with others or to train our own parti[san] cadres, who would fight for a better, more beautiful tomorrow?

In this case the reason resides in the two individual factors that worked like an opiate on the great Jewish masses, who let themselves be led with no resistance to the great and horrible slaughter. The first factor, which led astray even the young people, was the bond of family. The feeling of responsibility for parents, wives and children bound us all and fused us together in a great indivisible mass.

The second factor was the instinct to live, which banished all black thoughts and drove away like a storm wind all evil ideas, on the pretext that all that was feared, all that was whispered about, was no more than the product of age-old pessimism and they allowed themselves to be easily taken in by such thoughts.

For how is it possible that they, those in power, even if they represent the lowest, most dangerous bandits, could have in store for us, not just a life of chains, cold and hunger, but something even worse.

Who would believe that they could take millions of people without rhyme or reason and lead them in so many different ways to slaughter.

Who would believe that they would lead an entire people to destruction for the diabolical desires of a gang of common criminals.

Who would believe that they would sacrifice an entire people to compensate for their lost war for power and greatness.

Who would believe that a people would blindly obey a law that carries with it death and annihilation.

Who would believe that a highly civilized people [would] turn into devils whose only ideal is murder, whose only aim is extermination. This underestimation of the extent of depravity and criminality, the decadence and lowness of [...] people to a large extent combined to extinguish the will to resist even in those who would have been capable of it.

My friend, I think you understand us well now and feel for us in this sad time we are now living through. Now come, [do not tremble,] we will take a walk among the deep earthen graves where they [are] now making feverish preparations for their departure.

You hear crying and screaming. These sounds rise from deep within the barracks, barracks that hold the terrified Jews who are about to leave. Come into one of them, you can hear—there is much noise and tumult. Everyone prepares his belongings for the trip, choosing only the most essential. They put on as much as possible and the rest, all that they brought here at such great risk, they distribute with no regrets among friends and acquaintances, even strangers. Everything that yesterday, or just hours ago, was still worth something, and to which they were so attached, now in the last hours before the journey has lost all value and is of no importance. As if they already sensed that in that future nothing is needed, everything is expendable.

You see, my friend, those two Jews walking, one holds a candle to light the darkness; the other carries an open bag. They are representatives of the towns about to leave. They are carrying out the last orders of the power: to take from the travelers anything of value, under threat of death if any such object is found.

Women take off their most beloved jewelry, which is […] part of their lives. With tears in their eyes and pain in their hearts, they give up these precious things, gifts from their parents, handed down from generation to generation, which they had treasured as holy objects, which were woven into a thread of their history. And now they tear it off and throw it with a sigh into the collection bag. Some like to see a consolation in this. The power wants to strip them of the means to make their lives easier in the future. When the collection is over, the two Jews carry it with satisfaction, like a ransom, out beyond the fence and into a small building, where there sits the tall blond bandit who is supposed to insure our protection.

Yes, he understood what to do. He wanted his share of the loot. To you, eminent masters who reign from afar, I send their bodies and souls, and I get to keep their belongings.

Come, my friend, into another barrack. Again you hear the cries of women and children. These cries are of little children who have not been able to sleep. They rub their pretty little eyes and try to get to sleep. But no one lets them sleep. They dress them in warm clothing, which is very uncomfortable for them. They cry, they beg: Leave us alone. They can't understand what people want from them at this hour of night. They cry and the mothers cry too, over their bitter fate, over their misfortune, why were they born to be so unhappy in this world?

Friends and acquaintances now come to say goodbye. They fall weeping into each other's arms, and kiss with great emotion. It is terrifying, each kiss seems so meaningful. These people who so warmly press their lips seem to know something about what is in store for us. Their warmth is an expression of deep sympathy. Their tears an expression of compassion.

You see, over there stand several families completely shattered, helpless, not knowing what to do. They are those who have family members in the hospital and must now be separated from them.

[...]

They feel encouraged, the sick patients are leaving in [...] which is [...] and the family will not be split up. There are mixed feelings. They are happy that they are [...] those who have their sick relatives are delighted with the momentary happiness and cannot think beyond that.

[...] others see in this a bad sign, for surely the sick are not being taken to do any work. But whatever the case, no matter how dismal the future may be, no one will be separated from his family, for who would perform [...] a surgical operation [...] on his own heart? Who can be such an abject egoist as to leave a wife and child, father and mother, sister and brother to seek salvation for himself, even if you know that you can save your own life. Who can leave their dearest family, with whom you have already gone through the worst moments, to leave them alone now on such an uncertain, unknown, frightful journey. No, we must all remain together.

Come, my friend, the hour when we must leave has struck. See, an enormous mass of 2,500 people have come out of their dark earthen graves and line up in straight rows. Each family together, hand in hand, shoulder to shoulder, a unified, tightly bound mass of hundreds and hundreds of families that have grown together, fused together in one great inseparable organism and have set out on a road that will lead them in the direction chosen by the power, where they are being sent to work.

A cold, frosty night with stormy winds. Thousands of people stand and stamp their feet to warm their toes, already frozen from the cold. The women clutch the children tightly to their bodies and take their frozen little hands in their mouths to warm them. Each fixes his pack so it will be easier to carry. The weak father and mother, who have been relieved of carrying even their own light bundles, to make it easier for them to merely drag their bodies to the train, sigh for their poor children who from the outset have to bear the weight of their baggage too. All is ready to march out.

In the nearby barracks stand men and women and look at us with [...] eyes and send us their last greetings, their wish for our [...] We exchange looks, expressing our wish that we may in the future see each other as free men.

The gates open and we leave the barbed-wire-enclosed camp. A dark thought flashes through my mind. This is the second time the gates to the free world have opened for us, and how cruelly freedom has deceived us. We left behind the barbed wire of the ghetto and passed through the free world to be brought here into these dark graves. And who knows what fate these second opened gates will lead us to. Who knows where and in what direction the open eyes of the camp are looking.

The first time our stopping place was close to our home. We breathed in the air of our familiar surroundings and that gave us a little assurance. But now who knows where the road will lead. For we are going there, getting ever closer, deeper, into the land of our worst enemy. Who knows if the arms he stretches out to us will turn into a devil's hands to ensnare and smother us. Who knows?!

We went out into a large free world that dazzled us with its whiteness and frightened with its endless breadth and we trembled at the contrasting blackness of the great boundless heavens. How symbolic it all looks. A white earth with a black lid covering the great mass that moves over the whiteness. An extraordinary stillness hangs over the world. It seems to us that apart from us, black shadows, no one else exists. As for us, they have led us out into the world to do with us some sort of important work that the day must not see.

We give each other searching looks in the [...] we want to see a sign of life and existence. But we search in vain, only dead, frozen stillness.

We hear echoes of the thousands and thousands of footsteps that through the [world] reverberate anew, the footsteps of a new march of exile of the ancient, oppressed, persecuted people. But what the exile represents now is more horrible, more terrifying. Then, in ancient Spain, we left a land because of our national pride and religious consciousness [...] spit [...] in the faces of those who with open arms wanted [...] and even wanted to lead us into their reigning temples for the price, in order to remain, of denying our specific cultural and national identity. We answered their pleading looks with mockery and contempt. And those who were willing to give us all our civic freedoms just for religious conversion, at them we looked with disdain and disgust. Then, we left as a proud, unbending people as from afar shone for us the open doors of the world, welcoming us with open arms. But today [...] we are not leaving a land, they are driving us out, not as a people but as loathsome creatures. We are driven out not because of our national pride but because of an ignoble, sadistic diabolical decree. We are driven out not toward the borders of another land but, on the contrary, nearer to itself, deeper into the heart of the land that wants to rid itself of us.

We are going, and the road seems endless. So will we go into eternity.

An instinctive shudder now went through us all. We see in the distance, on the whiteness of the earth, great tall shadows, between them shine small, barely noticeable, fires. All our hearts were beating quickly with fear. A dark thought [...] who knows, perhaps they are taking us now [...] into the domain of [evil] shadows in the [...] of the night's devils who await our coming and are making the final preparations to receive us. Who knows? Perhaps the fate that awaits us is the same as that of the hundreds of thousands of Jews before us who were taken, in such dark nights in such shadowy places and found there a cruel death. Who knows? But until we pass the forest, get through safely, free [...]

We go on. It grows harder to walk. We go through a hilly area and remarkably it seems, for [...] a familiar place, but now it is unknown to us all. Perhaps down below, the earthen mouths are already there, open and ready to swallow us alive, as had already happened to tens of thousands of us, who knows? We stand firm hand in hand until, with beating hearts and great anxiety, we get to the top of the hill. A sudden joy came over us all. In the distance we saw twinkling fires of electric lamps, proof of a nearby railway station. We all feel our strength and faith renewed, we have reached the railway. Twenty small wagons are waiting for us, calculated to take 120 people to a wagon, so as to have a standing place for each. This is a great comfort for us. Each family tries as hard as possible to stay together in this grueling, stifling journey. Some of the sick people stand and look out the train windows in fear, to see if their sisters, brothers, children or old father and mother are coming. But there is no trace of them. As we learned later, they […] were broken in […] and were swallowed up in the wagons […] closed and locked the last […]

[…] to flee […] we will be shot […] with a cynical smile on his face and an inner determination stood the blond beast — our protector […] wagons. Yes, he has an important mission to carry out […] he has [led?] [two thousand] five hundred who disturb and sends them [now] to the highly cultured […] who must carry out their sentence.

A muted whistle cut through the air. It was the signal of the starting train. Like an animal running off with its prey, so the train pulled out from its spot and gradually disappeared. From all their hearts came a painful groan. Now they all felt the horrible pain of really being torn from their homes.

The entire mass rocked as if about to fall. Already at the outset they felt the harshness of the discomfort. All try to make themselves as comfortable as they can, at least enough to endure the trip. The children are held on laps and it is quickly agreed that if you sit now, later you will give your place to another. They create an atmosphere of peace and unity within this net that is taking them into the hands of the devil, who he is they do not yet know. Religious Jews say the prayer for a journey and wish each other: As prisoners we are led away and as free men may we return.

Come, my friend, let us walk along the speeding floorboards. You see: here sits or stands a despondent, desperate mother, sunk in deep nightmarish thoughts. The monotonous chugging of the wheels weighs on the mass and its ceaseless pounding adds its own harmony to the sad, discouraged mood. It feels as though the trip has already

lasted an eternity. We have boarded the train of eternal Jewish wandering, which stands forever at the disposal of the nations, and we
must get on and off according to their will, their judgment.

You see, my friend, by every window people stand as if fused together and look out at the free world. Everyone wants to look his fill,
his eyes wander in all directions as if they already had a foreboding
that he is seeing it for the last time.

You have the impression that they are sitting in a moving fortress,
before which the world unfolds like a film with its varied colors as it
bids farewell to those imprisoned in the train.

It seems as if the world is telling them [...] at me, look long and
hard, as long as you can still see me because in [...] myself to you for
the last time.

Notice, my friend, there stand two young people—a man and a
woman gazing fixedly in one direction. They do not speak but their
thoughts commune and soft sighs escape from their hearts, as a flash
of an interesting memory has enthralled them and torn them away
from reality. They think of the past, the not-so-distant past. Here at
this place, at this familiar station of Lososna,[4] they would so often
meet to spend their free time together, and their longing turned into
a passionate love.

[...]

[...] flowed by like this. Every day they [...] offered so much joy
and pleasure [...] enchanted by its many colors. Each [object] winked
at you with a smile, everything expressed the [...] of life. Now a dark
thought crosses their minds [...] Who knows? Who knows? Will [...]
the magical memories still survive this place? They stare now at that
point from which [...] now vanishes from [...] they look in the direction from which they were so brutally torn. A piece of li[fe] has
vanished into eternity.

Come a bit further, do you see the two young people standing
there as if transfixed, looking around at the world. Do you hear the
few words the woman has just uttered to the young man: Do you
remember, dearest, do you remember that sym[bolic?] trip, that
gloomy winter's day when we were complete strangers and met in
the compartment, became acquainted and through that trip were

united forever. That path led us to a happy life. It opened for us a flower-strewn road through life. It seemed we were going the same way, in the same direction. Then we boarded the train of life. Who knows where this train will take us, who knows what track our train is on now.

Go further, you see, here stands a woman with a small child in her arms, nearby stands her husband. They look out on the world they have just passed through and instinctively they keep looking over at their pretty little child. They are weighed down by heavy cares though still young and full of life. And it is so enticing, this world they glimpse through the window. Everything calls them to life and existence. Now they have someone to live for, to work for, to strive for. They just recently had their first child and with its coming they wove themselves a place in eternity, became partners in developing and building the world. And soon, with their very first steps into this world, they were stopped, told to go away, move out of the place where they had begun to build their nest.

Now they are not thinking of themselves. Only one thought occupies them, what will become of their dear little child, so essential, so promising.

For them this child is their greatest joy, their chief consolation, their common ideal in life—but for those terrible bandits—a useless plaything that has no worth nor any right to live.

See how they look at their pretty little girl with eyes like black cherries and from their troubled faces you can read what they are thinking[:] You, dear child, it is you who give meaning to our lives. How much pleasure you have given us, child, when your first word fell from your lips: Mama.

Oh, how jealous the father was at that moment. And how happy he was when the child recognized him as her father and pronounced for the first time: Papa. Oh, dearest child, who knows if that thread of eternity that you have just begun to weave will be brutally cut off. Dear child, who knows if you will continue to be ours and we yours. The mother presses the child to her heart and tears fall on her little head and the father gives her a warm and tender kiss.

Come, let us walk a little further. Do you see that mother with her two grown daughters beside her? What painful thoughts now overcome the mother and daughters both! The mother thinks: My entire life I sacrificed, my dears, for you, my entire life I devoted to you, for you I gave up everything just so I could live what I so long yearned for, to enjoy a mother's happiness and pleasure. And it was all an empty dream. Your dear devoted father was dragged away somewhere by the bandits and who knows if he is still here among the living. Who knows if you are already orphans. Your dear brothers were taken from me and who knows where they are now. And I remain alone and broken. You, dear children, were my only comfort and who knows what's in store for you.

Who knows, my dears, if you will be able to bear the harsh new living conditions that you will face and who knows if you will be capable of carrying a double load of despair, mine and your own. Who knows. But now she isn't thinking of herself. About her own life the mother does not think at all, for how can a mother think about herself when she is still uncertain about the life and existence of her children. The daughters look at their mother and heave a sigh. A deep sorrow comes over their faces—who knows if our dear mother, who with worry has grown old and gray and from sleepless aching nights become weak and worn out, won't her pained appearance make her look older than her years and won't she be counted as one of the unneeded, unnecessary ones, who have no right to exist. Dearest mother, who knows if we will be fortunate enough to be of help to you. Who knows if they will tear you from our arms and we will remain alone, broken, with no mother, no brother, alone and lonely in a vast desert world that terrifies us with its cruelty. Who knows?

Thus you will find in every compartment of every car numb people sitting or standing with deeply bowed heads, weighed down by painful torment.

The train pursues its long monotonous journey. We are now nearing the city of Białystok. Everyone tears himself away from his thoughts for a moment and rushes to a window to look at the approaching station. What will they actually see and who can be waiting for them here? But instinctively everyone wants a glimpse of this city, for which all the travelers feel such a strong attachment. Everyone has family, friends or acquaintances here. They want to look even if just from a distance at the city where there still lives a friend, a child, a relative. They want to send greetings through the windows and give them a last look of farewell. Perhaps they will see a Jew from the still-quiet city of Białystok,[5] who will by a look be able to explain to us the meaning of our journey.

We have arrived at the station and stopped on a siding, an unused line, a dead line. Already cut off from the road of life. How dismal the station now looks, once so lively that it used to make heads spin with its clamor, and now it stands wrapped in fog, no trace of life to be seen . . . The only sign of life, a newly created life, is the soldiers marching with bayonets and helmets. A siren sounds from a factory chimney. A reminder of life, a greeting from sisters and brothers [who are in there contributing their work and effort] now within the arms of the large factory buildings, giving their energy, industry and strength for the bandits who now rule over us. They work for the price of hope, the hope that the factory walls will serve them as a protective rampart.

A whistle cuts through the air, the train moves once again. Stay in good health, you Jews of Białystok.[6] May the factories be for you [...] so the enemies lying in wait will not be able to find you. Go on living calm and safe and may we in the future be able to come back to you as free men. The train moves faster. Now all have sunk once more into a deep despair. Their despair grows deeper with every kilometer. What is happening here? We are getting closer to the station of Treblinka, now a well-known name to Jews, for according to various rumors that have reached us, it has swallowed up and exterminated the greater part of Polish and also foreign Jewry. Everyone looks out the window, eyes searching in silence. Perhaps they will see something. Maybe find a sign that will tell them the truth, maybe someone along the way will shout out something to them, where they are being taken and what awaits them. Oh, how terrible! Two young Christian girls stand looking up at the train windows and run a finger across their throats. A shiver runs through all those who see this, who notice the gesture. They move away as silently as a ghost. But they keep still, say nothing about what they've seen. They don't want to make greater yet the anxiety that is growing by the minute. It feels as if something is imminent, who knows what the coming minutes will bring, who knows if they will be taken down that siding, leading to the place that has become a vast Jewish cemetery. Everyone presses to the windows. Each wants to be the first to see where the wheels will carry them. Thousands of hearts beat in unison, thousands of souls tremble. One thought gnaws at them, gives them no rest. Who knows if the last minutes of life are drawing near. Could it be that they have reached the border of eternity. Each examines his conscience. Religious Jews say their prayers and think about making their final confession.

Every family presses together to form its [own] group. They want to pour themselves, weld themselves together into one large inseparable organism. They hope thereby to find protection, to seek consolation.

The mothers clutch the children in their [arms?] [...] their little heads. Even grown children press close to their parents, as if they want in the last minutes of life to feel the sweet taste of a mother's or father's tenderness. They feel their father or mother [will] as always, take them under their wings and protect them so no evil will come to them. The tension mounts with the movement of the wheels. Now they seem to be slowing down. A sign that they are nearing their destination, coming to the culmination point. Tension is at its height. The train has stopped, for a moment 2,500 people stop breathing. Teeth chatter in fear and hearts beat quicker. The great mass waits the next minutes in fear of death. Each second—an eternity, each second a step closer to death. All stand frozen and wait for the outstretched arms of the devil who will soon take them in his claws and fling them into the abyss.

A whistle wakes them from their stupor. The train has torn itself away from death and continues on its way. Mothers kiss children, women kiss their husbands, tears of joy are shed. Everything wakes them to a new life, they breathe more freely. New thoughts are woven, full of hope for life. [...] So the panic was over, the fear dissipated. A new wave of comforting thoughts swept over everyone. The idea began to grow that all the rumors were false. All the dire predictions were groundless and had come to them through the misunderstanding of some atrocity that was surely horrible but was not mass murder. So you see them now, infused with courage and the certainty that they are being taken to life, a hard life, but still to life. Now you hear happier sounds, sweet tender notes [...] enchanting women's voices rising in an ecstatic melody that spreads to an ever-growing circle. Through melodies like this one Jews voice their deepest questions. It expresses the great suffering of those bound here in chains, being taken to an unknown, unfamiliar life that frightens them terribly and robs them of their calm. The melody prays to their Creator[:] Liberate us from the deep abyss and take us to a bright, shining tomorrow. The melody begs: Lead us further on the line of life as you have until now, and may the final destination end with nothing worse than a fright.

We are now nearing Warsaw. Each would now give up a portion of his life to see just one Jew from Warsaw. How happy we would be if we could meet one of those whose brothers and sisters were supposed to meet the same horrible fate.[7] And maybe one of them would be able to tell us the truth [...] the destination of our long journey. But unfortunately there is no sign of a Jew to be seen at the Warsaw station once so full of Jews. You see people roaming about with serious, hostile faces, waiting for a train leaving in their direction. But they are all strangers to us and the sight of them awakes in us a horrible hatred and jealousy. Why are they free to go where they [will] why can they buy a ticket for a train that takes them to a warmer, safer home [?] why can they travel to a place, to a destination, where a wife or child awaits them, who will stretch out loving arms to greet them. And we, we are being led against our will, not to some warm home but to a desert. There, no woman's smile will await us, no mother's open arms, no carefree laughter of a child, only hostile, angry looks from our dreaded bitter enemies, whose outstretched arms hold, as we so well know, a whip, a knife, or firearms if necessary. Into such nightmarish thoughts sink the mass of people as the journey goes on.

The silence is broken by a man who comes in from another car and calls out happily: Friends! I bring news from those who left our camp on an earlier transport. He had found on the wall of his car a written greeting showing the entire route from departure until the time they arrived in *Yekke* land.[8]

Everyone was delighted to have even a distant greeting from those who seemed to have vanished into the abyss. Reading the words, we feel as if we are talking to them. They seem to tell you everything. There they are before you, living, vibrant Jews who were taken weeks ago, leaving no trace, which deeply disturbed us all. And now, we get a living greeting from those whose fate we imagined so terrible! And how clever they were, those earlier travelers, to understand how frightened we would be about their existence, how it would rob us of our calm. So they left a living sign from themselves to bring us comfort and a sense of security. And now we will follow their example and write a greeting for those who will board the same train in the coming days. Let those who come after us also be grateful to us for thinking and worrying about them.

But all at once the joy vanished. Happiness turned into sadness — anxiety once more caught us in its net. One sentence as if with [...] plunged us into sorrow again. "We are arriving in *Yekke* land!" And with that the greeting ended. Here the thread was broken. Until then we were together and now they have disappeared from us. They had written the story of their lives until they came to *Yekke* land. Until they fell into the heart of enemy territory. They let us hear of their lives, until they were clasped in the arms of the murderous barbarians.

[...] a still, dark night came over the world. The train stood still. How dangerous to ride with abject criminals when there is no light. In the middle of a station [unused] stands a train twenty wagons long and in its arms 2,500 children of the oppressed, persecuted people. The wagons are dark and gloomy. From the train windows look out the frightened, tormented, exhausted children of a people under sentence of death. In the dark of night they look for a ray of light to light their darkness and bring a bit of life into their lifelessness, but their searching is in vain. The terrifying night speaks only with darkness. The sorrowful black wagons do light up from time to time, but it is a foreign, cold, dead light. The light is from our escorts inspecting the prison cars to make sure there isn't someone from our dangerous gang trying to escape in the blackness of the invisible night.

The first of the dreadful, nightmarish travel nights has begun.

Now two horrible factors began to torment the great inert mass: hunger and thirst. See, my friend, how they have lost all human senses. Each thinks only of one thing: where to find a piece of bread to still the hunger, where to get a drink of water to still the thirst? See how the fortunate ones standing near the windows stick out their tongues and lick windows covered with mist. They try, through the mere [idea] of dampness to refresh their faint and weakened hearts. You hear the children crying: Mama, give me some water, just a drop. Mama, listen, give me a crust of bread. I'm weak. I'm fainting. I have no strength left. The mothers comfort the children: Soon, child, I'll get you some soon. And sometimes, there are a few fortunate ones who still have something in reserve. They give what they can to those already faint. But the great majority are totally worn out from hunger.

The children are impatient and cannot wait and continue to beg for the promised bread and water. The mothers grow despondent seeing the suffering of the children and have no other choice than to shout at them. Fear makes the children keep still and they snuggle weeping into their mothers' anguished bosom. The grown-ups, who suffer no less than the children, console themselves that at the nearest station the power will surely provide us with food and water. Why would they deport a people intended to form a mass of workers and then let them die of hunger and thirst?

In another car we hear the frantic cries of older children, bustling around their mother, who could bear it no longer and has fainted. They try all they can to bring her to, [until] she opens her eyes. A joy for them amid the sadness: their exhausted mother has come back to life. They had been so frightened, what if they lost her and remained motherless in the world.

A few people with cool nerves tap on the windows to our guards, to beg them to do something, at least throw in a little of the snow ly-ing on the ground. We hear the cynical laughter of the cruel beasts, whose only answer is to show us their loaded rifles, ready for anyone who would dare to open a window. How appalling! You look out the window. The ground is covered with a white, wet mass of snow, which could revive the faint hearts, freshen the weakened bodies! Which could bring them some life. The whiteness glistens before us—it has in it so much life, so much comfort, so much happiness, that white mass. It could inject a new wave of life into those dead wagons. That white mass could liberate 2,500 people from the claws of a horrible death by thirst. It could bring into the despairing hearts a new wave of hope and courage: and how close it is to us. Just there in front of us. It shines so with its whiteness and beckons with its magic. So horrible—just open the window and—reach out your hand to touch it. That white mass, it seems to us, has been imbued with life, it rises from its bed and wants to approach us. It sees how we draw it to us with our looks. It feels how we yearn and long for it and it wants to console us, it wants to breathe life into us, but the cruel bandit is there with his frozen bayonet on his shoulder and answers repeatedly with the dreadful word—No. He cannot permit it. Nothing can budge him, not the pleading of the women, not the crying of the children. He is deaf and unmoving. Everyone moves back from the windows, resigned to turn away their eyes from the taunting whiteness and sink back into deep and troubled thoughts that break through the dead stillness with heartrending groans.

[…] separated from the living, moving line, so as to disturb no one on the way.

The train is as black as night and the misfortune of those who repose inside is deeper and blacker even than the night. From time to time we are awakened by the whistle of a train passing quickly through. All rush to the windows to have a glimpse of those others who also […] travel through the night. You see well-lighted wagons, moving with clamorous joy, as if they were hurrying to some happy destination. We catch sight of people from the free, civilian world. Those looking out our windows are overcome by a deep aching. The others seem to be people like us, innocent, having committed no crime. They travel and we travel. But how different our journey is! They are following the line of life and we, who knows! From over there the light shines out and from us all that is visible is the terrible, frightful darkness. Over there now sits a mother, calmly and in safety, riding to a destination she has chosen of her own free will. But these here have been taken by force, against their will. And who knows where and to what purpose?

They back away from the windows. Another drop of despair has found a place in their hearts. Each one has absorbed another bit of sorrow and despair. And resigned, each one looks for a corner where he can lean his deeply bowed head.

When the night began to recede, our train moved out again, dragging itself monotonously. Always giving way for the better, the superior race, which will not let it stand long in its way. We are nearing a city. Everything there is awake to life. You see women running to buy their household needs. And now we see in the distance a large group of people advancing toward us from another [...]: surely they are going to work. All are curious to see who they can be, those marching toward us now. Could there still be in this region too [...] useful Jews. From afar it is impossible to be sure of their nationality, but as they come nearer we are filled with joy. We can see the large yellow stars. A sign that there are still living, working Jewish masses. Hope and consolation fill us all. But it is striking that at every station where we stop we notice people standing around who wink at us in the train and make meaningful gestures with their hands. They run the edge of their hands over their throats, or else they point a finger toward the ground. It seems some sort of dark fate accompanies them on their journey and at every stop these apparitions seem to spring up from the earth to make their diabolical gestures. What do they mean by it[?] Why do they so worry these travelers who are already frightened to death. Each tries to drive away the evil thoughts that grow out of those gestures. We want to cloud our own brains, to stop thinking of that picture that is always before our eyes—of that woman earlier who ran her hand across her throat.

The train pulls out and we continue the monotonous neverending journey. We approach another station. Here too people stand looking at our train with curiosity and this soon plunges us into deep sadness. Between two trees we see two women who stand and look at us and with handkerchiefs they wipe the tears running from their eyes. Aside from them we see no one nearby. You cannot understand. Why are they crying? Why has our arrival had such a terrible effect on them as to make them cry? Why are those [saddened women] crying? Are they the tears of a personal tragedy or do they cry out of sympathy with those looking back at them from the train? What do we mean to them, that we should make them all cry—and now again we feel man's two great enemies, the torments that will not let us rest and demand their due[:] hunger and thirst again began to torture the exhausted mass. We tried again to find a way to move our cruel escorts, that they might allow us to get at least a little water. There facing us stand some women, perhaps Jewish by the look of them, who want to give us, to throw to us the balls they have made out of snow. How happy we would have been if we could open the window for just a minute and reach that white, wet substance. Hands reach up to us, frightened but brave, certainly Jewish, who could certainly expect to suffer some unpleasant consequences—but our pleading eyes had such a strong effect on them that they forgot the reality of the situation and came to stand at our windows, so close that they could reach us by throwing. They hold ready in their hands the large, cold, wet balls of snow, waiting to throw them to us. Just one thing stops them from doing this good deed, which would have given us new life, infused new strength into our faltering hands. These closed windows—but the firm and diabolical order stands and will not let them budge. One sign of good will, one wink to say yes, would have been sufficient, would have relieved us of our terrible torture. But—unbending and hard as stone—in their hearts there is no feeling, no will and no understanding. The tension grows stronger by the minute. People go wild. And now [...] fainted from weakness. And the desperate mass, forgetting all proportion, tearing itself away from reality, began to bang at the doors and push against them. They banged so hard at the windows that several guards jumped up together, suddenly terrified that something may have happened here that could cause unpleasant consequences for themselves. What does she want, that woman crying and screaming, they ask with a sneer.

Those who have not yet lost the power to speak explain that her child
has fainted from thirst and the mother is begging for a little water.
The guards laugh, relieved to know that it's no more than that, and
they are ready to step back and continue on their way. But the mother
pounds harder and the windows are about to shatter. People try to
pull her back, to calm her for fear she will bring some misfortune to
them all. But she will listen to nothing. If she loses her little girl, her
only child, then her life is worth nothing in any case. She begs: Let
me out, let me run just to bring back a drink of water for my child.
Several brave people come to her defense and let her return to the
window. She screams in rage. The bandits return and, seeing that
this woman's outrageous actions could embolden the whole desperate mass, which might be fatal for them as well, they decided on a
diplomatic gesture, and with a nod of the head gave permission to
open a window. All were overjoyed. A gust of fresh air with brazen
joy burst into the wagon, driving out the musty stinking air. Everyone
felt infused with new life. They grew agitated, the tension reached its
height. Now, soon, in a minute, a second, a ball of white snow will
come flying in and he will take it in his hands—then right into his
mouth, and slake his thirst and revive the strength of his weary heart.
Some of the snowballs found their target, but many fell on the floor,
which has no want nor need of it. The ones who are lucky enough to
catch the white treasure throw themselves on it like madmen, sharing
it with the closest family members. All swallow it right down, paying no mind to its icy cold. They fight, they scramble for the smallest shred, they pick up any pieces that were carelessly dropped. But
very few were fortunate enough to still their thirst and the rest of
the great mass still sat in despair and torment of hunger and thirst.

The train moved from its spot. All wave to the few brave women and
wish them the greatest happiness for their noble heroic deed. The
train picked up speed, we passed various towns and hamlets, most
of them unfamiliar.

  [...] now by soldiers [...] it is driven. The train stops [...] we are
[...]

[...] all stand [...] station. They [...] who are traveling [...] battle with their second enemy [...] great people of the East.

They look with spiteful disdain at their enemies who are already caught in their net. They would now love to throw themselves [...] wild animals, on us, "the guilty ones," with all their zeal, because of whose [insanity?] they were forced to leave their homes, say good-bye to their parents, sisters and little brothers. They had to leave a wife, crying hysterically, and a child who wouldn't take his hands from around his neck and begged: Papa, don't go away.

They see us, weak, helpless, broken, and for them it is we who brought this great misfortune on them, we who brought the peoples into the arena of war. And if we let them near us, they would have devoured us with sadistic cruelty, broken our bones with murderous fury. Why are they being sent over there to that distant enemy, when they have here under their noses [...] a greater, more dangerous enemy than the one they are now being taken to. Let them make this their battleground and they will demonstrate their [Aryan] strength. Let them remain here, here in their horrible ghost-world—here—and they will show what they are capable of.

But no, you vile bandits, gullible [...] pirates, go off there to enemy number two, the enemy with all its strength and power. Go show your valor there, show your [...] you go there where you will be met by the huge steel birds and the massive moving fortresses, driven by the great patriots, the courageous heroes fighting for freedom and happiness for all humanity. Go, you vile [...] creatures, you abject criminals, there, on that battlefield, where light fights against darkness, freedom against slavery—there you will lose your barbarity, your strength will vanish, your existence will be expunged. Your lives will sink there into the bottomless pit.

The trains pull out. We are headed west and they east. We both face the same fate, we for no reason and they by their own fault.

We are approaching a town. From afar we see the huge factory chimneys. You begin to notice the presence of extensive human endeavor. And when we got really close, there before us was one of the great cities of Upper Silesia. There over a vast territory stood many buildings, large and small. Everywhere, the great chimneys reaching toward the sky bear witness to much hard labor. This was once the center of Polish heavy industry. They are all seized by a single thought[:] Surely, they are being sent here to these huge factory buildings which have need of human hands and there they will be swallowed up, like their predecessors, who surely found their place here.

We continue our monotonous journey, deeper into Silesia—the surroundings are sheathed in fog. It is as fearful and gray as life itself. On the railroad lines run huge, long trains loaded with coal. We feel that this is the heart of the Polish black gold country. Each one is oppressed by the thought, what if they throw him into one of the deep underground coal mines—who knows if his physical strength will hold out and if he will be able to survive the conditions his well-known bosses will impose.

Or will he, after the exhausting weeks of hunger and privation, will his weakened muscles be able to shoulder the responsibility he carries for his wife and child, father, mother, who knows. We travel as far as we can until the night imposes her reign and then we stop again. From time to time the train moves forward, goes a few kilometers, then stops. A heavy nightmarish night has wrapped its arms around the pained and frightened mass of Jews. They know they are now close to their destination. According to the travel plan they are nearly at the culmination. And who knows where it will be, what will await them when they get there, when they reach that point up to which their predecessors wrote their story.

[...] who very soon now [...] will have to follow the same road [who] knows [...] doubt held them all [in] its grip—just one ray of hope gave [...] faith and confidence [...]

This underestimation of the enemy intoxicated them all like opium, gave them courage and poured a drop of consolation in their hearts. The mass sleeps exhausted, in anguish for the coming morning. A long night passed, sunk in melancholy. A gray morning rises over the world, struggling to pierce the thick black fog that will not part with the world and vanish with all its power.

[...] and not [...] he has the [...] wrapped in more grayness and has [...] shown no more [...] sorrow and melancholy—speaks of [...] death—the world is in mourning—this is an accursed day.

On this day of sorrow and [...] 2,500 innocent [...] children were taken to a bestial death.

We arrived at the station Katowice. You see before you not a city, yet what appear to be outlines of buildings. We are overcome by the oppressive atmosphere. We see that we have nearly reached the final goal. Another hour and we will have to leave the train. And who knows what awaits us—some fear this final point and have already become so accustomed to their monotonous life of travel, despite the unbearable conditions, that they would [...] for all eternity go on traveling to be carried off to a desert somewhere among wild [...] or animals, only not get off here [...] They dread the cruel murderous faces of [...] will come to get them. They fear the reality to which they have been brought. They fear the enemy country, they fear the unfamiliarity of the place [because] if, back there, close to their homes, they were treated with such murderous brutality, what can they expect here. Some, who are already physically and morally exhausted, have resigned themselves to whatever fate has in store. Let it be whatever it is, as long as we leave this cramped, locked fortress, which will soon have robbed them of their lives. And perhaps once we're freed from this, things will be better, safer. There still throbs a ray of hope.

[...] and to the last station [...] all utterly broken [...] and themselves, all are [...] frightful thoughts. Each [...] was in a state of tension. Gnawing thoughts rise up from the deep, the same tormenting questions[:] where are those who [...] got off before us—why is every trace of their lives—lost—why have they vanished as if into eternity and left behind for us no sign of existence? Why? Here we are practically at the final point and soon we will have to write the final words: "We have come to that land and now what?" All cut short, all vanished, why? Perhaps it is really true the horrible news of the Jews of Warsaw [...] met their death in Treblinka.

[...] bandits—have a another [...] famous [...] who knows [...] do they no longer hear the final sounds of the wheels.

Who knows, if they will ever again be able to board the train of life?

Who knows, if today could be their last morning[?]

Who knows, if they will once more see a sunrise?

Who knows, if their eyes will once more see the world?

Who knows, if they will once more enjoy life?

Who knows, if they will again be able to bring up their children?

Who knows, if you, children will have a mother, and the mother a child?

Who knows, if you will [...] for me, my [...]

The train slowed down and turned off to a side track. It is a fact, we have come to the final destination. The train stopped, the mass swayed and shook itself back to life while still in the wagon. All push and struggle to the exit, all want to breathe in some fresh air and also some freedom . . .

We got out of the train. So see, my friend, what is happening here? See who has come to welcome us. Soldiers with helmets on their heads, rifles in their arms, accompanied by big fierce dogs. Are these the open arms that have come to greet us [...]? No one understands why there is such a guard. Why such a terrifying welcome? For what? Who are we that they need to meet us with the force of arms and the savagery of dogs. Haven't we come to work as calm and peaceful people. Then why all the security measures?

But wait, you will understand.

Right at the exit, the knapsacks, the small bags with minimal belongings, are violently torn from them and thrown into one big pile. No one can take anything, can have anything with them. This order throws everyone into deep pessimism, for if you are told to give them even your barest necessities, it is a sign that the necessary is unnecessary, the most needed, not needed. Here in this place you need nothing for any human use. But you have no time to think longer about this, for at once a new order cuts through the air[:] Men apart, women apart. This cruel and horrible regulation struck everyone like a thunderbolt. Now that we are at our final destination, when we are already at the border, they ask us to separate the inseparable, to sever what is so tightly bound that it has become one great indivisible organism.

No one moves from his spot, for they don't believe the unbelievable, that this unreal scene should be a reality, should become a fact. Only when a hailstorm of blows fell on the first rows did the following rows begin to move apart.

Even as they were being divided, no one [...] believed, no one grasped that this was the moment of separation.

They thought it was merely a formal procedure, to confirm the actual number of arrivals of each sex separately. Pain came over them [...] together now in these grave moments, to give each other courage and comfort. They still felt the strength of the unbreakable family ties. Here they both stand, on one side the man, on the other—the woman and child. Over there stand elderly men, an old father and facing him a weak mother. There stand brothers on one side looking at their sisters opposite. No one knows what is about to happen. But they feel somehow they will soon be separated [...] phase. They seem to be asking people's age and profession. They are divided and [...] stand here. But something is not clear. Those asking the questions seem to pay no attention to the age or profession, simply if they happen to like the look of someone—this one here, that one there.

And the mass is now divided into three groups: women with children, men—young and old, and a small number, amounting to about 10 percent of the transport, are placed in a third group. No one knows where it's better to be, where it's safer to be. Everyone thinks they are being chosen for various kinds of work. Women and children—to the easiest jobs, the younger men, as well as the elderly—to other bearable work. And the smallest group, which seems to include the most capable, has been chosen for the hardest jobs of all [...] It makes your heart bleed to look from the side at the women, weary and exhausted from the trip, who must still carry the children in their arms and [...] at least to help with something, relieve them in some small measure, but a hard, dull instrument comes down with such a bang on your head that you instantly forget what it was that made you move toward the other side. The women, seeing what awaits their husbands if they try to help them, gesture over to them to stay calm and not move from their spot. Too bad, to be alone now in these difficult minutes [...] but no, you are disturbing their [...] They console themselves that they will soon be reunited and go on their way together again.

All sorts of thoughts are jumbled in your brain and you stand helpless and unprotected. The only thing one feels now is the pain of this sudden separation. For if they plan to send the women and children to work and they, the men, will not be there to help them, then the whole idyll they had lived with until arriving here has been a bluff. The whole familiar opiate so long used has suddenly evaporated and left us standing with the deep aching pain of the surgical operation carried out just as they left the train.

Trucks arrive to take the women and children, who have to be [...] and when will he see his wife and child again, when will he meet his father and mother again? How can he [help] his dear sister? The men stand on the side and look on as they are loaded onto the trucks driven away. Each has his eyes riveted to one spot, one point, where his dear wife with the child in her arms is moving off. There a mother with her two daughters is carried away, under the gaze of their brothers and fathers. Oh, how awful, how horrendous is the image before you: one of the soldiers who was loading the trucks has now mounted one of them and with all his strength pushed and shoved the women and children as if they were dead cargo [...] now formed in their minds—what if his wife and child [were crushed] in his brutal hand and if [...]

In these hard moments, so heavy with responsibility, they so wanted to be with them, to protect them. Take them under their wings, hide them—wife and child, mother and sister, with their shoulders. Oh, how happy he would be if he could serve them as a protective wall, that no harm might befall them. Each one sent his wishes to accompany them, that they might find them again in the coming hours in good health and good spirits. The women look down to the rows of men. She cannot tear her eyes away from her husband, her father or brother. How happy they would be if they could only be together now in these fearful moments. They would feel safer and be able to face more bravely the minutes to come. Now they stand alone, helpless and frightened. There below stand their faithful, devoted husbands and brothers. There below are the [...] and want to help them and comfort them. But the fierce, sadistic dogs won't let them near and [...] brutal sadistic murderers, why? Why won't you let these men, who are ready to give up their lives for us, stay with us together, to make things easier for us in these painful moments. Why?

But each woman consoles herself that it won't be long. As soon as the reception procedures have been completed, she will be reunited with her husband and under his protection. She will have the help of her brother. All will be reunited, all will come together as before and in common they will weave the threads of their lives. No matter how bitter the future is, it will be sweetened by [...]

The area empties out. There begin to arrive [...] and full trucks hurry away in one direction. Our eyes follow them until they disappear and new ones come and take new living passengers and carry them off in the same direction.

The stronger ones, the small group, who were presumably chosen as those most apt for hard labor, try to find comfort in this, that taking the women and children and the older and weaker men is an expression of a [humanitarian] sentiment. Perhaps the power wants to spare them the ordeal of going on foot after such an exhausting journey.

They put us in rows five by five and order us to march in the direction that leads to the camp.

Look, my friend. Walking over there is a small group of over 200 men, just a part of the larger mass that had arrived. They walk with heads bowed down with cares, with hands hanging at their sides, resigned, sunk in despair. They were thousands when they arrived together and now so few remain. They had come with wives and children, father and mother, sister and brother, and now left so alone, so lonely. No wife, no child, no father, mother, sister, brother. Everywhere they were together. As one they had left the ghetto, together taken out of the camp, locked together in the train. And now at the final destination, when they have reached the culmination point, so fearful, so terrifying, now they have been separated [...] who knows how [...] the exhausted wife, who has [...] little children [to care for] who knows, who knows how she will manage at such a time and without his help. Will she in her helplessness receive a blow from the cruel, frightening bandits. One man thinks, what will his old father and mother do now that they're all alone. Won't they be treated with spite and contempt, receiving blows as well, from their new hosts. Who knows how his sister and brother are doing. Who knows if they are even together. Did they put them together again in that place to which they were taken, so that they can help and console one another.

[...] go in the direction [...] only with their families [...] such — nightmarish thoughts [...] oppress the [...] now small group of people.

It was as if they had all wakened from a sleep. They saw a group of men marching in, all dressed alike, who look well and give an impression of brave and carefree people. When we get closer to them, we see that they are Jews. We were overjoyed. This is the first time we have seen people from the camp, a sign of life, a sign of good relations and humane treatment. This strengthens their belief that nothing worse is in store for them too. And the only worry they now have left [...]

[...]

[...] small buildings. We can hear [...] counting the rows. We go past. Several soldiers standing there make fun of the way we walk. Once the rows have been counted we enter the newly fenced-in [area?]. We look around on all sides. We are hoping to find, through the barbed wire, those who only minutes ago were torn away from us. We hear voices of women, adults or elderly by the look of them. Through the barbed wire we can see women, some in civilian dress, others in camp clothing. There is such a clamor, such a din over there — this must be where our wives and children were sent. It is surely — my mother and sisters over there and now they are carrying out all the necessary hygienic preparations.

[...]

[...] could happen. But one thing is now clear for us, that something has been set up here [...] and we have been separated [...] the women's camp, well fenced in with barbed-wire fences. We have experienced the first rupture, felt the first pain. We are not yet able to fully grasp it. But a deep abyss seems to have grown before us. We take some measure of consolation from the fact that they are not taking us far away. We will remain nearby. Through the barbed wire we will be able to exchange glances and maybe sometimes even come into contact. We pass through another gate and enter the men's camp, also well fenced in. We step onto the muddy ground [...] but not yet [occupied]. Some men standing near two brick buildings look us over from head to foot. We cannot tell if they are Jews or Christians. We don't understand why they peer at us so insistently. Surely out of curiosity to get to know the new arrivals. We see people who frighten us by their appearance. They walk on the muddy ground pushing wheelbarrows filled with mud. Some carry burdens on their shoulders — one carries bricks, another mud. We tremble at the sight of these figures, once human, now shadows. Could this be the work? Is this the concentration camp that is supposed to provide occupations for the millions of deported Jews — can this be the important work, so essential for the nation, for which we had to sacrifice everything — the most useful, the most necessary jobs of all?

[...] what you see because you are too worried about the fate of your near and dear ones. They are led into a wooden building. They had hoped that they would find their brothers and fathers, who were taken here in the trucks. But there is no trace of anyone. Who knows, perhaps they have already gone through all the procedures and been assigned their places. A couple of Jews come in, little Jewish bandits, accompanied by several soldiers, and give an order[:] Everything you have you must now give to us. No one understands what they want. They have already given everything away. Why do they want the smallest object, the tiniest things that might be hidden in a pocket? Why!!

[...] clubs that [fall?] upon the heads of the newcomers, just for asking you get a blow from the [...] They ask us to give up even our identity cards, the most basic, the most important document there is, especially in wartime. You may have nothing at all here, not even the proof of who you are and where you're from. We don't under-stand why we must give everything up. And when they have been stripped of everything they are taken to the baths.

The Jewish escorts make fun of us. No one understands their mysterious questions. Who told us to come here[?] Could not you have chosen a better place? No one answers, because they don't un-derstand the question. They are taken into the famous disinfection bath, but they don't get washed, just have their hair cut off and are given [...] with some kind of wet rag. They are led into another room where they are given new clothing. They go in looking like human beings in normal civilian clothing and come out in clothes that make them look like horrible criminals or the worst madmen. No one has a hat, some in shoes, some in boots, ill fitting and too big. The clothes are too big for some, too small for others. The new prisoners are al-ready coming back, beginning to fit in with the old established camp-family. They are set onto the rails of camp life, the rails they will have to follow in their new lives.

One thought occupies everyone now. One question gives them no rest: How can we find out where our families have vanished, how can we even get word of them, how do we find a trace of them?

A rumor had spread that every S[unday] we would be able to meet at [...] Where this news [came] from [...] not yet. We are happy to get [...] We come back to the same barrack. We are told to stand in one row. They have to take down our identity information. We all try to talk to the old-timers to learn something from them. But how low, how criminal they seem, those we talk to. How can they be so sadistic as to make fun of forlorn and broken people. And when we question them, where are our families, how can they so easily answer, with no expression on their faces, They are already in heaven. Has the camp so affected them that they have lost all human feelings and can find no better entertainment—to get enjoyment from another's pain and torment. That is the impression we have.

[...] conceive such horrible [words][:] Your families are already gone in the flames. We are gripped by fear. Our hearts tremble at the mere sound of the words: Your family is no longer alive! No, it's impossible. How can it be that these people now talking to us came, like us, with their families and now remain alone because all those who were taken on the trucks went straight to the gas chambers that swallow living, vibrant beings and spew out cold, dead bodies. No, it's not possible! How could they possibly speak so lightly of it. How could they open their mouths. How could they find words to express it [...] because they themselves would not be part of the world any more [...]

[...] that [...] this devilish game which [brings?] to this horrendous camp life but nevertheless—their words leave deep traces which burrow into my heart and mind and evoke and weave dark and awful thoughts. The enemy of our spirit has now come to life. Hunger begins to gnaw. And human beings grow weak in the face of the greatest inner enemy. It never lets you rest, never lets you think, until you have paid him his due. Then the hungry men are fed. There is a moment of consolation—their bodies have at least in part been satisfied. The tattooing begins. Each receives his number. From that moment you have lost your very self. Your human being has turned into a number. You are no longer what you once were. You are now a walking number, saying nothing, worth nothing [...] a hundred such numbers are then assembled [...] all led into their new homes.

It is already dark outside, one can hardly see the path. Here and there we see electric bulbs, which emit a faint light. The only bright light is one large searchlight that hangs over the gate, seen from a great distance. We slog over the muddy ground, nearly falling. With fear and torment we arrive at our new graves. No sooner did we arrive at our new home, before we could even take a breath of air, when already some of us were clubbed over the head. Already blood gushes from a split head or a bashed-in face. This is the first welcome for the newcomers. Confused and stunned, we look around us, what is this place we have fallen into [...]

One who moves off to one side [...] the other's [...]

Each thinks only how best to protect his broken body from more blows. We quickly get a brief explanation that this is the [bouquet of flowers?] of camp life. Here reigns an iron discipline. Here is a death camp. Here is an island of the dead. People have come here not to live but to find death, some sooner, some later. Life has not elected residence here. This is the home of death. Our minds are dulled, our comprehension numb. We do not grasp the new language. All we think about is where is our family, where have they been put, how will they ever get used to such conditions. Each of us thinks, who knows if any now […]

[…]

Criminals and sadists like these and […] now of the terrified child watching as they beat his mother.

Who knows what the ignoble bandits, of whichever sex they may be, are doing now to his poor sick mother or his dear beloved sister. Who knows where, in what possible grave, his father and brother have found their rest. How are they being treated. All stand helpless, tormented, despairing, lonely, alone and broken. They assign bunks — these are bed frames made for 5 or 6 numbers together. And they order us to lay our bodies in them. Only the head must be visible, crawl in deeper, you cursed people.

Let yourself be seen as little as possible. The old-timers, those who have been guests here for a long time, approach the bunks and ask how many we were to begin on arrival and how many were brought into the camp. These questions are incomprehensible to us.

We cannot grasp what is the difference. Where are the others, those who left on the trucks. They look at us with cynical smiles. And we hear from them a deep sigh, a sign of human sympathy. Among the old-timers we find someone who came from our camp with one of the earlier transports, from whom we had heard nothing, of whom we had found no trace, and here is our greeting, here is a sign of life. Will we be able to have a greeting from *Yekke* land, too. But what is he saying, this man, what is he telling us? Our hearts tremble, our hair stands on end. Hear what he says[:] My dear friends, we too, like you, arrived here by the thousands and only a small percentage of us is left. Those who were driven away in the trucks were immediately taken to their death. And those who were led away on foot, they will follow a painful road, some a longer one, some a shorter, to death from exhaustion. Horrible, unbelievable words. How is it possible that people can talk about the death of their wives and children, mother, fathers, sisters, brothers and can still be here, can still exist[!] An uncertain thought creeps into our minds. Perhaps the camp atmosphere has made these people so insane, so cruel, that they take special pleasure in seeing others in the most painful suffering. They find comfort in this, they want to increase the number of sufferers, the number who share their pain. But one thing is incomprehensible, that all of them, irrespective of age and character, tell the same thing.

[...] who is not here, has long vanished from among the living and this has such a [deadly] effect on each of them until he is utterly broken and doubts begin to invade his mind. Perhaps these people are really telling the truth!

Come, my friend, and see how men lie pressed together here, from 3 to 6 to a bed, in a tangled ball of pain and suffering. Each weeps and wants to pour his heart out to another. They don't want to think about the great misfortune but already the tears of pain have begun to fall.

Listen my friend, as one man speaks to another[:] Dear friend, can it be true? Have we already lost everything, have we really no one left, no wife, no child, no mother, no father, no more sisters and brothers. Our whole family gone? How frightful,—how horrible— can it possibly be? Can such brutality gain power over life? Can such sadism [...] thousands and thousands of innocent people to their death and still have a place on this earth.

Oh, how happy we would be if we could only be there together. How happy we would be now if they hadn't separated us and we could go together to our fate, no matter how horrible and terrifying it is. Why did you divide us, you vile bandits, [...] are your hearts divided in two, one for death and the [other] [...] for each yet remains. Why [...] is [soul?] for the second [...] allowed us to find ourselves together in the arms of death [...] not to find a place of suffering [...]

[...] clear thinking, who had from the outset a horrible foreboding [...]

[...] then why had he held on to the death pills till the last moment and he does not know that he is lost.

Oh, how good it would be, how happy we would all feel if we had such fine, wonderful death pills. We would have taken them now with such pleasure and how happy we would be if we could find our final rest in a sweet eternal sleep [...]

[...] and on the waves of splendid dreams reach the beloved family and be united with them forever.

A blow of a club on one of the heads that was too far out of the bunk cut short the thoughts, cut short the painful talk. The pain of my newfound brother had such an effect that we began to think a little of ourselves. To protect one's inner self, to protect all that is now left from additional pain and suffering. The new camp "father" comes over to our bunks, the tall, blond, heavyset man, and with a pleasant smile, he addresses us, the newcomers[:] Children, be informed, that I, whom you see before you, is your [...]

[...] [I] [...] am left [...]

[...] children in [...] can still keep your bodies alive [...] several days from now deep in the camp your bodies will [...] and die in horrible torment.

Remember, this place where you are now—is a death camp. People don't live long here. Conditions are very harsh here and an iron discipline is imposed. Forget everything. Remember only yourself. That way you can stay alive. You must think first of your shoes and boots. That is the first commandment of camp life. Go barefoot—and you're quickly liquidated. Keep yourselves spotlessly clean though who knows if after a hard day's work you will still have enough strength to go and eat. Just don't lose your will. The speech is over. Good night, my dear ones.

His words barely entered our heads. Why should death frighten us? For us it is no calamity. Only one thing took root in our minds. That was his instructions for how to protect ourselves, protect our bodies from useless pain and suffering. That frightened us all. We all wanted to avoid physical pain. Suffering until death was something we wanted to spare ourselves.

The talk both consoled and frightened us. Consoled by its tone and frightened by its content.

How does it look, this work place to which we are being led? Who knows how much [pain and] suffering we will have to endure [until] we come to the final solution. Who knows?

Already done with everything and coming back into our own world—into the [...] abyss of suffering which claimed us again. We hear the sound of a man's voice singing. We are losing our minds. What can be happening here in this graveyard, a song of life, here on this dead island a song of life. Here in the death camp can people still sing and others listen to them with interest? How is it possible. Have we come to some sort of devilish world where everything is upside down, where everything that is done is contrary to human reason.

It grew noisy in the block. Everyone is hurrying to crawl back into their beds as quickly as possible.—What has happened. The well-fed *Stubendienst* had arrived, those in charge of the service, those who will serve in place of our mothers, wives, and sisters. They let fly with their big fat sticks at the frightened human shadows, exhausted from the day's work. What do they want from them[?] Why do they torture them so[?] Why do they beat them left and right for no reason[?] One had a broken head, another maimed and you don't dare say a word—if you say anything against them you get thrown to the ground and like a repulsive [...] stamped on with their feet. So that's how they look [...] to my dear sisters. Woe to my brothers who must look to you for [...] comfort, woe to the children who try to find in you a mother's tenderness. Woe that you are their providers.

They come to our bunks and complete the speech of the block chief. They tell us and show us how we must behave with them and with our work. Remember you must become automatons and move according to our will. Forget one step of what we dictate, and you will have to do with our third hand, our stout and heavy club, that will bend you, force you down so low that you will never pick yourselves up again.

However bitter the poison may be—it has no power now to affect us—it does not frighten us, nor does it hurt us. We are ready for anything and go fearlessly toward the terrible tomorrow. It is oppressive to us all, makes us feel ill at ease, to have to attend to all our physical needs in the block, right here at the foot of your bed. And later others will have to carry it outside. And what is so horrible, so fearful to contemplate, our morals and ethics have also met their death here.

It grows quiet in the block. Everyone lies in the bunks, sunk in sleep.

Only in the newly occupied bunks, the new arrivals, those who have just become brothers, can find no rest, they cannot help thinking [...] graves of their families. Sleep cannot take hold of them. [...]

See, my friend, how they lie now, with pain and suffering on every face [...] one shouts, one cries in his sleep [...] others groan. They are reliving now [...] the [sorrow?] of this last day.

Asleep, when one is alone with oneself, one can better grasp the vast and boundless sorrow. Now on a face you will see a carefree smile. In his dreams he has found once more his lost family. All is asleep.

The first night is over. A loud ringing awakens everyone and we, the newcomers, are instantly [...] sent outside. There are exercises that they must do with us to prepare for the coming roll call.

The street is still quite dark. A wet snow falls. You hear a commotion in the camp. Now from the barracks numbers are coming out for roll call. We are all seized by the cold. We feel it quickly through the camp clothing and our bare feet. Shouts ring out: Stand up, straighten the rows. We are getting ready for roll call. Our block elder [gives] us the last instructions, how we must behave at each command. We quickly grasp all the commands.

[...]

[...] a yellow band on his arm, that is a kapo, the leader of the commando. That is the man who can, with [...] do what he will. Your strength, your body, are at his disposal.

[...] See to it that you can serve as good work elements. Just remember one thing. If he tries to take your boots, that you must not give him. And if you are too weak to react, at least note his number. He can do anything with you. He may take your life, but not your boots, for that is the source of your life. That is the protection of your existence.

The sky began to turn gray. Before each barrack grow great masses of people arranged in short rows. A commotion is heard. The last orders are shouted.

Attention, hats off[!] A second man, of a lower rank, walks toward us with majestic grandeur. This is the block leader, the one who calls the roll. He counts the standing rows and signs his paper. The numbers match. Hats on. At ease. The roll call is over. He walks to another frozen mass, verifying that everything is in order. Our looks follow them, the proud-looking military personnel, as they walk to each block. And what we notice, next to practically every block, near each standing mass, lie one or sometimes 3 or 4 [dead] bodies. They are the victims of the night, those who did not survive. Yesterday at roll call they were still [living] standing numbers, and now they lie motionless, the count is correct. Of no importance whether they are living, what matters is the number. The number is right.

[...]

[...] in a certain direction. How horrible they look, as if [...] they had just come out of a [night?] of war. But these are only further signs of yesterday's day of work.

We are split into groups. We are called the K.S. group! A kapo with a smiling face takes charge of us. His expression was a consolation to us. Those standing nearby are looking at us. They look at our numbers and wonder at our appearance, which is far too good for the camp. But when they see our numbers, all becomes clear, we had just arrived yesterday. Not yet tasted the life of the camp, not yet felt the taste of work, not yet breathed in the camp atmosphere.

We hear the sound of music. What is happening here? Music in a death camp? On this island of death to hear the sound of life? On the battlefield of work to have our senses roused by the magical notes of our former lives, here in this vast cemetery, where everything breathes with death and annihilation, you are once more reminded of the life of before. But here all is possible. This is the harmony of barbarity. This is the logic of sadism.

We march out to work. We go through the gates and our eyes turn toward the women's camp on the other side. We see before us young as well as older women [...] we went down into the deep, wide pits and there again raised our heads upward where there are [...] and took it and tossed it up again. Yesterday others stood here on this spot, and this morning at roll call they were found lying dead, dead numbers. Today [...] new numbers to fill the gaps. A number goes away—another comes to take its place. [...] sad, symbolic.

This was the work. We all begin at once to dig the ditches. All the newcomers hold their heads deeply bowed, we push our spades into the earth and our tears fall endlessly. We look down at the ground and think: Who knows? Who knows if here in these depths our beloved ones found their final resting place[?] But no, it's not possible. A man consoles himself. Such a tragedy cannot come to pass in life, no one wants to contribute to such a disaster.

Next to me stands a Jew from our district. His number is 7,000 lower than mine. He came a few weeks ago. We strike up a conversation and I tremble with every word he says[:] Lift up your eyes and take [a look] in that direction. You see there [...] [clouds] of black smoke, rising to the [skies]. That is the place, where your nearest and dearest [were killed].

[...]

[...] [his attention] his vigilance [...] and bent low when a large club [comes down] [...] on his weakened body, after each blow we hear a cry, until he falls and is stamped on until he is powerless. No one comes near, not even to bring some cold water. No great misfortune, if he can't walk back alone, he'll be carried. [...] No crime has been committed here. On the contrary, they will still consider him a good overseer and when he goes back past the little wooden house[9] with a dead number, they will welcome him back with a smile as an expression of recognition.

You are pensive—dejected and sunk deep in sorrowful thoughts. You keep moving, to avoid being an object for the fat blond bloodthirsty bandit.

The first day of work is over.

Hunger again takes hold of the mentally broken and exhausted man. Hunger, the hard-hearted enemy who drives and goads—who feels no pain. [...] demands his due from man, calculates only what's in his stomach, refuses to know of any other pain or anguish.

[...] if you still want to live, no matter for what reason, to enjoy some pleasure or even to live in sorrow [you must] [pay?]. You must give your master his share [...] if you want to go on thinking, no matter if your thoughts are of life—of joy and happiness, or thoughts [...] horrible, that speak of death and annihilation. [...] be aware you must not mistreat the stomach. He can wait for you, but not too long. He can [...] you the moment of payment. But remember, if you [...] and if you should treat him lightly, he will break you, grasp you in his claws, and you will have to seek a way to be either with him or against him . . . you will be his slave. Your head will think of nothing else but him, how to satisfy him. All your thought processes will do his bidding. Aside from him nothing will exist for you. He will be the ruler of your very self, he will own your soul. You will have to do anything, you will have to find a way to make your peace with him, if not, you must say goodbye to the world, break away from everything, cut yourself off from everything. And disappear into eternity.

[...] possible phenomenon. It would be abnormal for all the numbers [to come] back just as they went away. We march to the sounds of music. Our eyes [...] to the barbed wire—of the nearby women's camp.

[...] everyone searches, perhaps he will see one of his [...] there still pulses a ray of hope. You don't want to believe that they are already gone forever [...] camp and we reach the block—[...] with the midday meal which is given out in the cold and get ready for the second roll call, all is [...] stands a great stiff mass of broken, dejected shadowy people [...] once again we hear the orders[:] In line, stand still, caps off! And the roll call is over.

Near our block there also lies a dead number. We walk over, have a look. Just this morning he was at his work and now he lies motionless. No one is troubled by this. No one even breathes a sigh about it. You, man, if you were a child with your parents, what would be taking place around you. Your mother would be lying near you and crying with heartrending cries. Your father would be walking incessantly, sobbing like a child. Your sisters and brothers would be sitting around you, crying bitterly and mourning your death. Your friends and [...] would come to you and each would [...] the house would be filled with sorrow [...] together in this terrible misfortune.

[...] sisters and brothers as if a [stone?] [...] fallen into the camp and when a stone falls [...] it is no great misfortune. Their sorrow has [...]

[...] after roll call they let us into the block. Then they order the newcomers back outside. We are all frightened. Who knows what it means? Here any news is bad news. They take us to the baths, where the same high-ranking soldier[10] stands with several others beside him. They make us all walk past them and ask our age and occupation. One on this side, one on the other. Those who find favor in his eyes are sent into the baths. The others are sent back. A rumor spreads that they are choosing workers for a factory. All the others envy us that we will be able to leave this place and work in better conditions. They count us, note down our numbers and tell us to be ready to move when they come for us. They give us military jackets with numbers. We return to the block. The older ones envy us that we can leave the camp. They also give us hats, a sign that we will be taken [away]. No need here [to be properly dressed].[11]

I wrote this ten—ten months ago. I came from Lunna district, Grodno, from Kołbasin camp.

I had buried it in an ash pit. I considered it to be the safest place, where they would certainly dig, in the crematorium area. But recently [...]

The Letter

I have many relatives in America and in Eretz-Yisroel.[1]
I give you here the address of one uncle:

A. Joffe, 27 East Broadway, New York, N.Y., America

I wrote this in the period when I was in the *Sonderkommando*. I was brought here from the Kołbasin camp near Grodno. I wanted to leave these and many other notes as a memento to the future world of peace, so they may know what happened here. I had buried it in the ashes, thinking it is the safest place, where people will surely dig to find traces of the millions that were exterminated. Lately they have tried to wipe out those traces, in every place where there remained a lot of ashes, we were told to grind them finely, then take them to the Vistula and throw them into the stream. We emptied many mass graves. Now there remain two such open pits on the site of Crematoria I and II.[2] Some are still filled with ashes. It is possible that they were merely forgotten or else they were purposely hidden from the superior officers, for the orders were to destroy everything as quickly as possible. Not having carried out those orders, they kept it a secret. Because of that the two pits full of ashes still remain at Crematoria I and II.

A lot of ashes from [burnt bodies] of hundreds of thousands of

Jews, Russians and Poles were spread out and plowed over on the crematoria grounds. There are also some ashes on the grounds of Crematoria III and IV,[3] but less. There the ashes were ground to powder and dumped into the Vistula immediately, for the entire area was designated for "burning bridges"!!! This notebook and many other notes were laid in these graves, soaked with blood, partially burned bones and bits of flesh. This was quite recognizable by the odor.[4]

Dear finder, search everywhere, on every bit of land. Underneath are buried dozens of documents, mine and those written by others, which cast a light on all that happened here. Here we buried many teeth. We, the workers of the commando, deliberately spread these over the entire area as much as we possibly could, so the world could find tangible traces of the millions of murdered people. We ourselves have already lost all hope of surviving until the liberation. Despite the fact that we are now hearing good news, we see that the world is making it possible for the barbarians to annihilate to the fullest, to tear out by the roots what remains of the Jewish people. Before our eyes are now being murdered tens of thousands of Czech and Slovakian Jews. These might very well have expected to be liberated, but the barbarians, whenever they feel endangered, from every place they must flee, they drag out all that is left of Jewish survivors and send them to Auschwitz-Birkenau or to Stutthof,[5] near Gdansk. We know this thanks to the testimony of those who come here to us from there.

We, the *Sonderkommando*, have long wanted to put an end to our horrifying work, which we were forced to do on pain of death. We wanted to mount one great action. The people in the camp, some Jews, others Polish or Russian, held us back with all their might and forced us to put off the date of the uprising. But the day is near. It may be today or tomorrow. I write these words at a time of great danger and excitement. May the future judge us on the basis of my notes, may the world see in them at least a tiny segment of the tragic world in which we lived.

Zalmen Gradowski
6TH SEPTEMBER 1944

Second Manuscript

Preface

Dear Reader, You will find in these lines written here an expression of the suffering and woe that we, the most unfortunate children of the entire world, endured in the time that they "lived" in the Hell on earth known as Birkenau-Auschwitz. I believe that the world is already quite familiar with this name, yet surely no one will believe what actually transpired here. Some may consider and believe that if somewhere on the radio there were reports of this barbarity, of the atrocities and brutality inflicted on people here, that these are no more than "horror-propaganda,"[1] so I want to show you that all you have heard and all that I write here now is but a minimal part of what really took place here. This is the place that was created by the bandit-power as a special extermination site for our people and in part also for other peoples. Birkenau-Auschwitz is one of the little corners spread over various locations in which by a variety of means our people were murdered.

My aim in writing is that at least a tiny part of this reality should reach the world and that you, world, will then take revenge, revenge for everything.

That is the only purpose, the one aim of my life. I live with the thought, with the hope, that perhaps my writings will reach you and will help at least partially to achieve in life that which I and all of us who are still here long for, and which was the last will of the murdered sisters and brothers of my people.

To the finder of these documents!

I have a request for you, dear finder of these writings, it is the wish of a man who knows, who feels the approach of the last and final moment of his life. I know that I and all the Jews here have long been under sentence of death, only the date of judgment has not yet been set. And so, my friend, I ask you to carry out my wish, the last wish before the final execution! You should, my friend, make contact with my relatives at the address given here. From them you will learn who we are, my family and I. You should take from them our family portrait—also the portrait of my wife and myself—and you should add these to any of my writings that are published. Let those who see them at least shed a tear or utter a sigh. It would be for me the greatest solace to know that my mother, father, sister, wife, my family and perhaps my brother did not simply vanish from the world without a tear.

May their name and memory not be so quickly erased!

Alas! I, their child, here in this Hell, cannot even cry, for I drown each day in a sea, a sea of blood. Each wave chases the others. There is not a moment when you can huddle in your own corner and sit and cry, cry over the Destruction. The continual and systematic death, which is here the only life of one's whole life, drowns out, bewilders, numbs your feelings. You cannot feel, you cannot perceive even the greatest pain. The individual destruction has been swallowed up by the general one.

Yet sometimes the heart is stabbed, the soul is pierced—why do I sit so "calmly," why do I not cry, not mourn, over my tragedy? Is all feeling frozen, numb, atrophied? Sometimes I hoped, sometimes I consoled myself that a time would come, a day when I will have earned the right to cry—but who knows . . . the ground is shaky, already it trembles under our feet.

What I want now, and this is my only wish, since I cannot cry for them, may a stranger's eye let fall a tear for my loved ones.

My family, who were burned here on August 12, 1942, a Tuesday at 9 o'clock.

my mother Sarah
my sister Libe[2]
my sister Esther-Rokhl
my wife Sonja [Sarah]
my father-in-law Raphael
my brother-in-law Wolf

Of my father, who happened to be in Vilna[3] two days before the German-Soviet war and remained there, I had news from a woman of my town who came to the crematorium with a transport from Lithuania. I learned that on the night of Yom Kippur 1942 he was captured, along with tens of thousands of Jews, but she would not tell me more than that. I also had a sister Feigele and a sister-in-law Zisl in Otwock[4] and they were part of the Warsaw transport to Treblinka, where they were probably gassed. Two brothers, one Moyshl and the other Avrom-Eber—from the same woman from Vilna, Mrs. Keshkovski, I had word that they were, for a long time already, in a concentration camp. What happened to them later, I do not know. Who knows if they did not long ago pass through my own hands, living or dead, as "*Muselmänner*," who are brought here from everywhere.

This is the sum total of my family—of my world of the past—and as for me, I must go on living here—and here I stand, at the edge of the grave.

A Moonlit Night

I loved her and with trembling I awaited her coming. Like a faithful servant I would stand hours long and admire her splendor and her magic. Like one riveted to the spot, hypnotized, my eyes would gaze at her kingdom, the deep blue night skies, adorned with bright glittering stars and wait in solemn suspense for the moment of Her Majesty's arrival. And she, the Queen, arriving in all her splendor, in the company of her retinue, was calm, carefree, happy and joyous, as she came out for her mysterious rounds, to have a look at her realm, the world of night, and bestow on mankind a ray of her light.

The world longed for her mysterious light. A thrill of holiness came over mankind, a new source of life, of joy and love, ran softly over the world and filled the hearts of young and old.

Entranced, enraptured, captive to her magic, the people would sit in fields and woods, on hills and in valleys, from tall palaces and deep cellars, eyes looked up at her with longing and she, the moon, wove for them a new world of romance and fantasy and filled their pining hearts with love and joy and countless pleasures. She was man's closest friend. In her he confided the secrets of his life and to her he revealed all. In her kingdom he felt safe and secure. Happy and overjoyed, infused with hope and courage, he would spin new threads for an idyllic, happy and fantastic world.

From the calm, quiet, softly lit earth, sweet melodious notes would rise to the highest skies, from hearts filled to overflowing with love. It was mankind singing songs of joy and happiness, a hymn of praise for Her Majesty the Queen of Night and thanking her for the newly revealed world.[1]

That was all before, when I would see her in my still free sky, when I was still a man like other men. A child of my parents, I lived with brothers and sisters, a wife who loved me, and the moon was then for me a source of life and joy, for she intoxicated me with her generous hand and enchanted me by her magic and beauty.

But now, now that I am alone, left solitary here, my home, my family, my world, my people wiped out by the pirates cruelly and for no reason, and I, alone among millions, under sentence of death, sit enchained in my prison and suffer the pain and fear of death, today when I see her, I run from her as from a ghost.

When I walk out of my grave on this cursed diabolical earth and see that she, the moon, has shamelessly pushed aside a piece of the darkened world into which I have sunk so deep that it is part of me—I run back, back into my dark grave. I can no longer look at her light. Her dreamy carefree stillness taunts me. With her rising she tears away chunks of the skin that has with time grown around my bleeding heart. She storms and churns my soul, wakes in me a stream of memories that will not let me rest, that tear and pluck at my heart. The churning waves carry me away in a sea of pain. She reminds me of those times, of the magical yesterdays, and shows me the horror of today.

I no longer want to see her shine, for she causes me more grief, makes my pain deeper, my torment stronger. I feel better in the darkness, in the reign of the dead and mournful night. She, the night, is in harmony with the feelings in my heart and the torments of my soul. The dark of night is my friend, the weeping, the screams, they are my song, the fire burning the victims is my light, the atmosphere of death is my perfume, this Hell is my home. Why, for what purpose, cruel moon, do you come to disturb people in their unconscious misfortune? Why do you wake them from their frightful sleep and show them a world that is a stranger to them now, a world to which they can never, never in their lives again return?

Why do you show yourself with your magic and beauty and remind them of the past that they want only and forever to forget. Why do you come to them with your wonderful light and tell them of the life and joy that some people still have, people who live where the pirate's foot has not reached?

Why do you send your rays, which here turn into spears that pierce with pain the bleeding hearts and suffering souls? Why do you let your light shine on this accursed hellish world, here where the night is lit by gigantic flames—by the fire of the burning victims, innocents who are murdered here?

Why do you shine on this tragic plot of ground where every step, every tree, every blade of grass is soaked through with the blood of millions, millions of human lives?

Why do you show yourself here where the air is full of death and extermination, where to the heavens rise the heartrending cries and screams of women and children, fathers and mothers, young and old, innocents driven to a bestial death?

Here you ought not to shine!!! Here in this horrible corner of the earth, where people are tortured with savage atrocity, constantly sinking in a sea of blood and affliction and wait in fear of inescapable death, here, here you ought not to shine!!!

Why do you show yourself here with your splendid beauty, do you expect from them a longing gaze? Just look at the pale, thin shadows, wandering like madmen from one grave to another, who look trembling not at your light but at that fire that rises from the tall chimneys up to the skies. And their hearts are filled with dread: who knows whether he tomorrow, like his brother today, will burn in those flames, and his body, still moving today, still striding through this dead isle, will tomorrow simply vanish into that smoke? And that will be the final act of his life, of his world?

Why do you still walk as majestically as before, carefree, happy and content, and do not feel for them, the unfortunate victims who, somewhere in a land of Europe, lived in a warm home, whole families together. In your light they dreamed and imagined better times, thought and fantasized about a world of joy and happiness. And today the trains are moving with savage brutality, filled with the victims of my people, taking them quickly as a gift to their god, who is hungry for their flesh and thirsty for their blood. Do you know how much suffering, how much pain and torment they live through as they speed past lands and regions where people still live in peace and calmly enjoy the world, enjoy your magic and your splendor.

Why do you not feel for them, the unfortunate victims, who fled from their homes to hide in fields and woods, in ruins and dark cellars so no pirate's eye should reach them, and you with your light add to their misfortune, increase their sorrow, double their fear. Because of your light they are afraid to show themselves in the world, afraid to drink in a breath of fresh air or to go in mortal fear to find somewhere a piece of bread to still their hunger.

Why do you shine so beautifully on this cursed horizon and taunt the victims who, in these brightly lit nights, are taken by the bandits from their wooden graves, packed into trucks by the thousands and driven to their death in the crematoria? Do you know how much torment you caused them when by your light they saw again the beautiful and enticing world from which they have in all innocence been so cruelly torn away? Would they not feel better if the world were in darkness and they could not see it at all in the last moments of their death?

Why are you so selfish, moon? Why do you taunt them so sadistically when they stand at the edge of the grave and you don't give way even when you see them take their first steps toward the abyss? And then, with outstretched hands they send you their last regards and give you their final looks.—Do you know how much they suffer as they go to their graves because seeing your light reminds them of the beautiful world?

Why won't you hear that last song that reaches up to you from loving hearts, even as they sink deep into their graves and cannot part with you, so strong is their love for you? And you, you remain serene, continue your course, go on your way.

Why don't you give them one last look? Grant them one tear from your moon-eye so that their death may be easier because you share their pain.

Why do you come today as deep in love and dreams, as enchanted as before, and you do not even feel the great disaster, the great misfortune that they, the murderers and pirates, have brought with them to the world?

Why do you feel nothing? Don't you miss them, the millions of vibrant lives that once, in all of Europe, lived calm and carefree until the storm arrived and drowned the world in a sea of blood?

Why don't you look down, you dear, kind moon, on the wilderness of our world and see all the homes now emptied, the lights extinguished, the lives vanished, and wonder where the millions of throbbing lives, exuberant worlds, yearning looks, joyful hearts, singing souls have gone to?

Why don't you feel, moon, the terrible sadness that has enveloped the world? Amid the idyllic harmony don't you feel the absence of the hearty sounds of the young full-blooded lives that once sang to you with such joy and wonder?

Why do you still shine today with such magic and splendor? In clouds of mourning you should shroud yourself. And no more bestow your light to anyone on this earth. You should mourn together with the victims, flee from the world, vanish into the highest heavens and show yourself no more to accursed mankind. Let the world forever be in darkness. Let it be veiled in eternal sorrow just as my people were led into eternal sorrow.

The world in not worthy, mankind is not worthy of enjoying your light. No more should you cast your light on the earth where such atrocities, such barbarity are perpetrated against people for no fault, for no reason. They should no longer see your light, these people who have been turned into murderers and savage beasts—for them, for them you should no longer shine!

Also for those who still sit calmly because the pirate's foot has not yet been able to reach them and spin fantastic dreams in the light of your shine and dream of love and grow drunk with joy—for them too you should no longer shine! May their happiness now be destroyed forever, because they did not want to hear our laments, our cries, when we struggled in the fear of death. They sat then calm and carefree and drank from your springs of happiness and joy.

Moon, gather up all your light, come here with your splendor and enchantment. Stay here forever with your magic and your charm. Then clothe yourself in black as you go your way across the tragic unfortunate horizon, and in sorrow and mourning you should also clothe the heavens and the stars, that your kingdom should forever be in mourning. Let dark clouds be drawn forever across the heavens. Let just one ray fall on the earth, a ray for them, a moonbeam for the victims, the victims of my people, for they have loved you to their last breath and could not part with you even by the grave, and their last farewell they sent to you as they had already sunk deep into the abyss, and from those depths too, their last song, their last living sound they sent to you.

Come here, moon, stay here and I will show you the grave, the grave of my people. This is where you should cast your only beam. You see, I look out at you from the bars of my Hell. I am in the heart, in the heart of this Hell where my people are being annihilated.

Listen, moon, I will tell, I will reveal a secret. Not of love, not of happiness will I talk to you now. You see, I sit here alone on this earth, sad, lonely and broken, and you are my only friend. For you, for you I will now bare my heart and tell you everything, and you will understand my unhappiness and my boundless sorrow.

Listen, moon, a people of culture, a people of strength and power, has sold itself to their god, the devil, and in his name and by his will has sacrificed to him my people. And they, his slaves, men of culture who became savage pirates, brought my brothers and sisters from all the world, from every place, brought them here and sacrificed them here on his altar. Do you see that large building there, that is but one of the temples they have built for him, and here they bring his victims by force and with cruelty. Sacrifices offered to their god, to sate his hunger and his thirst with our flesh and our blood.

Millions of lives they have already brought him: women, children, fathers, mothers, sisters, brothers, young and old, men and women all together, all are swallowed by him without a pause, for his mouth is always ready for victims of my people. From everywhere they are brought to him, by thousands, by hundreds, sometimes even one by one. Jewish blood is dear to him, even a single individual may be brought from very far, for their god does not want one single Jew to remain on earth, wherever he may be.

Moon, dearest moon, look down with your bright eyes on this cursed world and see how they run wildly, insanely, slaves of the devil, barbarians of the world, how they search out, sniff around, in houses, in streets, perhaps they will find yet another victim. See them run through fields and woods, pay rewards to other nations, to help them find more victims for him, for their number is still too small—he swallowed up too many years ago—and now he is hungry, savage and insane, and waits trembling for more victims.

See how they run to government cabinets to try to convince the diplomats of other countries to follow their "cultural" example and bring victims of the defenseless people—a gift to him, their mighty god, who thirsts for their blood.

See how the wheels turn, the trains carry victims in abundance from all the countries of Europe to this place. See how they are taken from the trains and packed into trucks and led, not to work but to the crematoria.

Do you see, do you hear the great tumult, the great commotion? It is the sound of the victims who have been brought here, who had no choice but to let themselves be taken although they knew there might be no going back. You see the mothers with the children, little babies held pressed to their breasts, they look around at the building and their eyes grow mad and wild when they see the fire and smell the smoke. They sense that the last minute has arrived, the last minute of life is approaching, and they stand here lonely and alone, their husbands snatched away from them there by the train.

Did you see then, moon, the frozen tears visible in your light? And the last look they gave you then? Did you hear the last greeting, the last song they sang to you then?

Do you see, moon, how still it has grown in this place? The devil has already captured them. Already they stand naked, all together—just as he wants it, the devil, as he demands the victims—they march now, closely packed in rows, whole families together, into the vast grave they go together.

Do you hear, moon, the moans and screams, the horrible cries for help? The cries of the victims as they wait for death. Come here, moon, cast your radiant eyes on the dark and cursed earth and see: from four gaping holes, four eyes dug deep into the earth, thousands of victims look up at the heavens, at the twinkling stars, at the bright shining world and await in dread the coming minutes.

Do you see, moon, those two marching in, two slaves of the devil, carrying with them the death of millions? With "guiltless" steps they draw near to those open eyes that look at you and pour in the deadly gas, the last greeting from the world, the gift to them from the devil. Still and motionless they lie. That god has swallowed up their souls and now rests calmly for a while.

Do you see, moon, the flames shooting out of the tall chimneys and up to the heavens? Already they are burning, the children of my people, who just hours ago were alive and now in minutes no trace of them remains. Do you see, moon, that vast grave there? That is the grave, the grave of my people.

Do you see, moon, those other graves, the wooden ones, from which look out the wild and frightened eyes? Those are the victims who wait their turn. Perhaps today the last hour of their lives has already been decided. They look at you and look at the fire, who knows if they, like their sisters and brothers, fathers and mothers, will burn tomorrow, and their world, their lives, be lying in the pit.

Come here, moon, and remain here motionless forever. Sit down on a mourner's bench at my people's grave and shed at least a tear for them, for no one else is left here to weep, to mourn for them. You alone, sole witness to this misfortune, to the destruction of my people, of my world.

May your only ray, your mournful light, burn forever at my people's grave. May that be their *yortsayt-likht*, their mourners' candle that only you can light for them!

Separation

Dear Reader!

I dedicate this work to my comrades, my beloved brothers, who were so unexpectedly torn away from us. Who knows where their lives have been carried off. We have an evil foreboding, for we know "them" only too well.

I dedicate to them these few lines as an expression of my deep love and attachment. If you want some day to understand, dear reader, if you want to know what was our "I," then you should carefully contemplate these lines, for they will give you a clear picture of us — and you will also understand why we were as we were and not otherwise.

I also dedicate these lines to you, so that from them you may learn, at least in part, how and in what way the children of our people were murdered. And may you at least take revenge for them and for us, for who knows if we, those in whose hands lies the factual proof of all the atrocities, who knows if we will survive until that time of freedom? Therefore I want through my writing to wake some feeling in you, to sow a spark of revenge, which will burst into flame and take every heart by storm, and may they drown in seas of blood, those who made of my people a sea of blood.

I also have a personal request. My name, which is not given here, you should find out from my friends, and it should figure in these writings. Let my name once more be remembered with a sigh by a friend, by a relative.

And one more request I have for you. You should obtain the photograph of my family, of my wife and me, and have it published with the rest.

Let my dear loved ones also benefit from a sigh, a tear—from someone's eye. For I, their most unfortunate child, accursed man, I "cannot," I am unable to let out even a groan, a tear for them. In this hellish life in which I find myself, for nearly 16 months now, I have not yet had a day, a day in which I can withdraw into my own world, to know, to feel, to get a sense of my own misfortune. The constant systematic extermination process of our people, which I live through every day, drowns out the individual misfortune and numbs all feeling. And there is another factor here: that my own life already hovers under the wings of death. And who knows if I will one day be able to cry, to feel my horrendous pain, who knows?

My family, burned here on December 8, 1942:

My mother—Sarah
My sister—Libe
My sister—Esther-Rokhl
My wife—Sonja [Sarah]
My father-in-law—Raphael
My brother-in-law—Wolf

My father was captured by "them" in Vilna on Yom Kippur 1942. Two days before the outbreak of the Germano-Soviet war, he had gone to Lithuania to see my brothers. My brothers were interned in a camp there in Shavel[1]—what became of them after that I do not know. One of my sisters, Feigele, was in Otwock with my sister-in-law and was taken away with all the other Jews to Treblinka. That is the sum total of my family.

$(7)(30)(40)(50) — (3)(200)(1)(4)(6,6)(60)(100)(10)^2$

Roll Call

The sound of a whistle cut through the noise, din and clamor that had risen in the block as soon as the comrades had come in after roll call.

Often, for one reason or another, a whistle would drive us back outside the block for a second roll call. But this time the whistle drove straight into our hearts like a breaking storm. For just an instant a thought flashed through all our minds. Who knows? Is this whistle directed against us? What will they do to us? Separate us, divide us, tear us apart? Or will they take us away? Perhaps it's true, the rumor that circulated yesterday, that on Friday a transport will leave with those comrades who have not been listed for "crematorium" work. One reason to believe this was provided by the explanation we got from the *Oberscharführer*, that no transport is planned at this time. If he says no — that surely means yes.

We all stand lined up in fearful expectation. Who knows what is about to take place here? Perhaps they will liquidate us all. Or if it's only some of us, well, that too is the beginning of the end. If my brother is no longer needed — then I'm of no use either. One talks to another, trying to find out what he's thinking, how he sees the situation. A loud shout is heard from the *Blockältester*, "*Achtung!*" The camp commandant has arrived with his whole suite. Their faces are well known to us, but never before have they come to a roll call. The only time they came was 15 months[3] ago when they first assigned us to this tragic work. And now? The thought crosses our minds, and now if they plan to liquidate us. We look at each other with anxious, fearful eyes. Even the "yellow armbands"[4] look pale, a sign that something serious is taking place.

We are all united now in one thought, our minds occupied with one problem. A common mood of sadness dominates us all. We are together in the same fear and trembling, all prisoners in the tension of the coming minutes. We have realized, sensed that the 15 months spent together in this wretched, horrible, tragic work have cemented us, have made us into a united, tightly welded group of comrades, an inseparable, indivisible family of brothers. And so we will remain until the last minutes of our lives. All for one and one for all. Each of

us feels in his heart and soul the common pain, the collective suffering. We have already begun to feel the torment of the sufferings to
come, though we had not yet guessed what they will consist of. But
everyone surmised that "something" was going to happen, and any
"change," as we well know, will mean a passage from life to death.

Before long the situation became clear. The *Rapportschreiber*
starts to call the numbers of those comrades not listed for work.
And it was striking how the mood gradually changed, the general
tension began to fall. The collective fear became an individual fear.
Those who were now 100 percent sure that their numbers would not
be called began to free themselves from the common trembling. It
was then that the great rift cut through our family. Slowly, invisibly,
unnoticeably, an abyss grew between us and them. The tight skein in
which we had all been bound together began to fall apart. The brotherly thread, the family ties, slowly, imperceptibly, began to break.
And we could now see how weak, how naked is that being that is
called a man. The survival instinct that smolders deep inside us turns
into a kind of opium which, unseen and unnoticed, takes hold of the
man, the comrade, the brother and begins to dissipate his fear, his
anxiety. "Not you"—means that you can still be calm, for the time being only "others" are being called—and it makes you forget that the
other is your brother, your wife, your child, your father and mother,
your whole family, all you have left in the world. And the "former"
brother, he too, intoxicated by that opium, also forgets that once they
cut into the body, then your own life is no longer needed. The hope,
the certainty, that "for the time being" the numbers they are calling
are not yours, offers new consolation, gives you new courage, and
a feeling of estrangement grows—in place of the former love. Each
new number called is like a silent dynamite, blowing up the bridges
that had once united us all.

Now fear took hold only of those whose fate was still in doubt,
still open to question. Will his listed number ensure that he will remain "here"? We also began to notice how those whose numbers
were not called moved closer to the wall. They would have liked to
run away. Disappear to a place, somewhere, some corner where the
sharp eyes, the piercing looks of the camp commandant and his suite

could not reach them. For who knows whom his eye will fall on next? And one word from him and you are already severed from the mass, the group in which you feel better, safer than elsewhere.

Each of us wants the list to be read out faster, quicker, so that the numbers, the ranks should be complete. Everyone wants to be free of his anxiety, his uncertainty.

The ones who felt the pain most deeply were those whose numbers were taken off the list unexpectedly, to go and fill a blank left by the "privileged ones" who at the last minute didn't "feel like" going or else they believed it would not come to that, trusting in the assurances of their "protectors," "*Sturmführer*" or "*Lagerführer*." Their anguish was double. He had already been listed among "those" and now he must leave to fill the place left empty by another, to fill, it seemed to him, a grave left empty by that "other," that fortunate escapee.

Two groups were formed: listed and not listed.

The dark clouds that hung over everyone's horizon slowly moved from one group to the other and it seemed to us that a piece of our sky had become lighter. And "those" over there, the group on the list, is from one minute to the next cloaked in a black cloud of mortal fear. The fear lifted, the trembling vanished from those who were now sure their number would remain. And a terrible anguish now possessed the spirit of those who had been selected for transport. And the nagging question: Where? To what?—filled the entire space in which they stood. A question hovered before them in the air. Before their eyes hung the words: Where to? Their whole being, their heart and soul, was prisoner to that nightmarish thought, which assaulted and tore apart their very core. Why, what for? For what purpose are they being taken?

Belief

We, all of us, were certain it would not go smoothly. At the first try, the first attempt to break up our family, we, the brothers of the "*Sonderkommando*" will show them who we are. We will show them for the simple reason that we are those who cannot be fooled. They will never convince us that they are taking us to jobs for which they need us and no one else. We who have witnessed the thousands and thousands of lives that were the most useful, the most needed, taken from munitions plants and brought here to the crematoria, we cannot be convinced by those schemers, the highly educated and refined bandits, that they "need us," our hands are needed for work somewhere else. No! Their deception will not work with us! From the first minute that they try to lay their barbaric hands on our tightly welded organism and attempt to start the beginning of the end, we will, all together as one, awaken, rise up like a wounded animal and throw ourselves at them, the murderers and criminals who massacred our innocent people. That will be the decisive moment and we will say our last word. And our desire for revenge will erupt like lava that has so long been seething deep inside us, like a volcano. And put an end to the horrific nightmare of these last 15 months that held us in its grip.

We hoped, believed, were deeply convinced, that the moment we stand face-to-face with the danger of losing our own lives, we will sober up. The tragic reality will show us the naked truth, that all those hopes and dreams were nothing more than empty fantasy, based only on illusions by which we let ourselves be taken in, and did not see the tragic menacing danger that constantly hangs over us. But once we feel that there is no chance, no hope that we can remain alive, to be able one day to pay back the barbarians for the unspeakable attack they committed against our people, an attack never before seen in history—then we will wait no longer, wait no more for the inevitable end. As soon as we sense that the grave is being dug for us, that the abyss is about to open, then the great moment will come. The long gathered rage and hatred, the pain and torment left behind by the horrendous months of tragic work will all come together, all that forged in us the striving for revenge. All of that—the danger of losing one's own life, the shared desire for revenge and the instinct of self-defense—all that will stir up, enrage and ignite our very being. Then will come the explosion.

All, all with no exception, with no differences of physical strength or individual character, will be caught up in the hellish fire of revenge.

All of us at the edge of the grave, at the edge of our downfall, before the last quiver of life—will give our answer, why and for what purpose we have lived and existed in the heart of Hell, breathing an atmosphere of death and extermination of our own people.—That was what we believed.

One Man

The atmosphere was charged, feelings were turbulent, the air incandescent and the people—a powder keg, all it needed was a spark and the fire would break out. That spark was smoldering in all our hearts, and the slightest breeze would set it off—but then a wave, a wave of cold water came to extinguish the spark.

They, the seasoned criminals, whose only occupation is to think up the ways and means to capture, to catch in their trap, those whose lives they prey on, they pondered, pried, sniffed out our common thoughts. They bored into the deepest reaches of our soul and there they saw our nakedness. And to avoid any negative consequences, to remove all possible obstacles that could stand in the way of the great attack they were preparing for us, they adopted the old familiar motto of British politics: "Divide and conquer."

They tore our family apart, broke up the common danger and directed all of it at one group, that of the "unlisted." And the moment those on the list for crematorium work realized that they could stave off the danger of being removed from their temporary supposedly "safe place"—at that moment the common thinking, the common striving, was broken. Those who could go on weaving the fantastic illusion that they would live and survive were now disarmed. And the desire to fight slowly weakened in them. The deep-rooted survival instinct prevented any impulse to fight for revenge from rising to the surface. Two groups were thus formed, divided into two elements, and threatened by two different types of danger.

One group for whom the danger hung clearly over their heads and another for whom the danger was still hovering in the air.

What had been two brothers now became two worlds—one stood there helpless, as the supposed "temporary" safety atrophied and dulled the common feeling of brotherhood, of collective responsibility, of all for one and one for all.

But the thread that bound them was not completely broken—as even for the listed ones the danger had not lessened. Each of them felt that a chunk had been torn from his body, but the privilege that the listed ones had been granted gave them a reason to demand that the first to enter the arena of battle should be "the others," those who are already being torn out by the roots. Human weakness—not wanting to put oneself in danger of losing his life, even his dead life—thus found a good reason, a good excuse for his conscience.

They all looked at the ranks of "the others." If only they would make the first move the rest would follow their example. Any attempt they made would happily be taken up by all, and all wait tensely during the coming minutes.

But on the other side too, the enemy's arrows had hit their mark. The division, the separation, had troubled and confused them, too. It seemed to them that an iron wall had sprung up between us and them, and they felt alone and abandoned, with nothing to bind them together with us. And this error led us both astray. If there had been one man, just one whose mind could free itself from the intoxicating opium of "division" that the bandits used intentionally to paralyze our hearts, and that one man had risen in combat, the miracle would have happened. His will would have inspired us all, his act would have become a tempest, and the deeply smoldering spark, which had not gone out in any of us, would have blazed into a hellish fire—and the world would have heard for the first time the wild scream of a murdered pirate, and the song of joy from the child whose people he had assassinated.

There had been a chance, a moment, we felt the pangs of childbirth, of revenge, of the birth of a hero, but when the child was born, it was the child of fear.

In the Block

We, the so-called fortunate ones, were led back into the block, back into our happy grave. While "they" stood there in the courtyard, guarded by the camp bandits.

We ran into the block and stayed there, numb and confused, as if we were seeing it for the first time. No one knew where to put himself, it was as if we were struck dumb. No one had the heart even to go to his bunk to sit or lie down. No one had the heart to open his mouth, to disturb the dead silence by uttering a word aloud.

Everyone knows, feels that something tragic is happening here, a terrible act is now being played out, in which he himself is a fellow actor. But his mind cannot penetrate it yet, cannot comprehend what is actually taking place. Each confines himself to a small group so that his sorrow, his pain, can be shared with another. He feels a heavy sadness in the air, a sadness that comes from "out there," from that mass standing in the courtyard, and it fills the space of the entire block and it penetrates everywhere, and lies like a heavy weight on our heart and soul—but what it contains and what it expresses, we still could not fathom.

One thing we did feel, that there beyond the wall stand my dearest comrades, with whom we walked out together an hour ago, as one, linked, bonded together, and as one we should have come back, and suddenly, unexpectedly, this great misfortune struck. They had been detained out there, beyond the wall, and they will never, never again be here with us. They will never, never again, be permitted to set foot in this block. All at once, an iron wall has been erected between us and them. And two worlds have been created. We were one united family organism and they, the bandits, the murderers whose victorious cry we can now hear—they have split us in two.

They took up their cruel surgical scalpel and began to cut, to cut into our body, but we still felt bound to our comrades by thousands of threads. We are in the block and they stand outside the wall, in the courtyard, but already we feel the pain, the torment of the great incision that they are about to inflict on our organism. We already hear the quarreling, the dissensions among the comrades. We know that we are now hearing the sound of their voices for the last time, but to judge the significance, to think about the deeper meaning of this great misfortune—that we are still unable to do.

The Separation

The echo of a bestial voice snarling an order savagely cuts through the sorrow-filled block, startling the mass and waking them from the deep sadness into which they are sinking. The new order rings out: *"Alles raus!"* None of us can stay in the block because they, our brothers, now standing in the courtyard, must soon come in to get their belongings, eat their meal, and take leave of their home. They must say farewell to their camp life—they can no longer remain with us—their dearest friends, the only friends they had left in this world of the dead. We, the last of their brothers who are still alive, the last on whom the pirate has not yet laid his hand, we cannot stay with them, at this hour in which a brother who is everything for them, father, mother, wife or child—cannot have the pleasure to hold their hand, to kiss them goodbye. We cannot tell them the brotherly feelings we so want to express now in this moment of separation.

They push us out into the street.

No one can stand calmly in one place. Nervous and frightened, the comrades walk back and forth, some talk, some are silent, all cloaked in melancholy and living through long minutes of pain and suffering. All know, all feel, that their place is not out here, that they belong inside, in the block, where the others are "preparing" for departure and we would like to be together with them. Each of us feels bound by thousands of threads to that mass, to those men inside the block, running back and forth getting their things. Each feels that he himself, standing out here on the street, is also "in there." "He" and the "other" are one body and soul and cannot be separated, cannot be divided, will not be torn apart, but a cruel hand has taken hold of them, severed their hearts that had grown together, torn apart their souls bound in one. They feel, they sense the anguish and pain of the surgical operation about to be performed on them.

Each of us would like to comfort them, give them hope and courage to help them hold fast and not break down until the final moment. Each of us feels the pain they are now enduring. Now when he must part with the bunk he has been in these past 15 months, say farewell to the block that for 15 months was his home. Each of us feels that there beyond the wall the eyes of brothers are looking to him, tear-filled eyes that so want to see their brothers' eyes, that long for one last look. Some press their ears to the cold wall, trying at least to hear what the brothers are saying in these last moments before they leave. The wall is now the only separation, a *mechitza*[5] erected down the middle of our heart and soul.

All at once it grew still, they cast one last look at their camp-grave and then were driven out into the street.

They're coming out, says one comrade quietly to another. Our hearts are torn as we all feel that "something" will soon happen. The last act will soon play out, the last act before the separation. Each of us shudders at the thought of the minutes to come. He knows that he too has a part to play in all that is about to take place here, that what is being done here concerns him, too.

Everyone came together, all the scattered groups moving together to one spot facing "them." Each of us would have wanted to tear himself away from the so-called lucky ones and run toward them to exchange a few words, to say something, to press them to our hearts and express the brotherly feelings that grow stronger by the minute, and look for a way to get close to them. Each one who, only hours before, had become like a stranger, is now again a dear beloved brother. We want to embrace them, to hug them to our bosom, at least one of them, anyone, to kiss him, let a few hot tears fall on his neck to penetrate his aching heart and relieve his pain. There is now so much to say and a last secret to confide. They would like to offer a piece of their own so-called good fortune as consolation, to give courage and hope—but no one can budge. They stand there with their arms held out—as a row of guards forms a separation wall between them.

Only looks were we able to share. They look at us with envy in their eyes. We can see and feel, their eyes tell us, how they envy us. They know what our final destination will be but "for the moment" we are still there. Soon we will return to the well-lit block and sit in the exceptional warmth of a stove. Or lie down in our bunks and enjoy a few hours of sleep to help us forget our yesterday and the horrible today and the still more horrible tomorrow. While they, they will soon be taken to the bath, as they were 15 months ago. They will be stripped of the warm clothing and boots they now wear and given the striped prison outfits and a pair of wooden clogs that drag on their feet like chains. They will shiver in the cold and wind, just like the thousands of others they see every day. And then they will be led away—who knows where? Who knows where they will be taken? Is the fate that awaits them the same as that of the millions of sisters and brothers who were torn from their homes and led supposedly to work camps? And where did they end up? To the crematoria they were brought and there in those fires of Hell every last trace of them was expunged from the world.

[...]

We feel their pain, we would like to offer them a word of comfort, relieve them of a part of the suffering that weighs on their hearts and take it upon ourselves. But we must remain still and repress the seething emotions that will not let us rest. The final hour has struck, the last minute is here.

Already the large mass stands lined up in rows—"Attention!"—and they begin to count. The count is correct. Two hundred, 200 of our brothers have been severed from us and soon they will be led away to an unknown, frightening and mysterious destination.[6] We look toward them with compassion, we are ready to bring them help, to give them all we possess, all that could be useful, necessary to them. And yet, we stand still in our tracks and cannot move.

We hear the order: "Forward, march!"

A deep sigh issues from our hearts. We feel the pain of final separation, the tearing of the last thread. Our family is broken, pulled apart. Our house torn down, our family collapsed. They march off. Our hearts now beat in rhythm, the hearts of two brothers, the one leaving and the one who stays. All our eyes follow them. Quietly, we murmur our wishes for them. And through the air are heard the warmest blessings from the unfortunate brothers who have remained behind.

There in the distance a great moving shadow is still visible, marching on a dead and deserted road. The 200 brothers are on the road the devil has chosen to take them to him. They walk in fear, with bowed heads. We cannot take our eyes off them, it is the only thread still linking us with them.

And then it is gone. The yard is now deserted, their place remains empty. And we ourselves are here, alone, forlorn. Our eyes still fix a spot in that direction where they, our brothers, have vanished.

Back in the Block

Like mourners who have just laid their nearest and dearest to their eternal rest and are now coming back from the cemetery—that was the way we felt. Like mourners who cannot tear themselves away from the place where they've just left a piece of their own lives and look instinctively to that corner, to that place that has taken from them the best and finest that they possessed and still feel connected to it and cannot part from it—that was how we felt in the minutes when they ordered us back to the block.

Like mourners returning from the cemetery with heavy tread, heads deeply bowed, and cloaked in gloom and sorrow—that was how we felt.

Like mourners who still feel in themselves the fresh and painful wound made by the barbaric death—that was how we felt.

Like mourners whose whole being is imbued with the tragic and horrible experience of the passage from life to death—that was how at that moment we felt.

Like mourners who feel that a piece of their life and soul lies sunken there in the deep abyss and are now returning home battered and torn, feeling that a piece of their own life is missing and without it they will not be able to survive—that was how we felt when we went through the wide-open doors of our block.

Like mourners coming back to the home from which the cold dead body of their loved one had just now been taken away—that was how we felt. A wave of sadness and death filled the entire space of the now-empty block.

Like mourners, with unsteady stride we walked on the ground, now imbued with the immobility of death, and with distressed looks gazed at the belongings thrown on the ground, strewn about, lying in disorder everywhere, as if a desperate hand had wildly and thought-lessly thrown them there in a moment of panic.

Like mourners, shattered, entering the room in which the de-ceased had lain and it seems to them that death wafts from every corner—that was how we felt now as we entered the large common, indivisible barrack in which they too once lived. In the air, from the walls, from the bunks, the breath of sadness seeps out on every side. You feel that everywhere is missing a piece of life, life that had just now left its imprint at every point, in every corner, and all at once the beating pulse of life has vanished. And in its place is now a dead, cold, empty numbness, as terrifying as a ghost and inescapable as doom, that penetrates your heart and soul until you feel as if you too have been captured by him—by death.

Like mourners who look with weeping eyes at the things left be-hind by their near ones—that was how we felt when we found strewn on the ground near their bunks various possessions that a few hours earlier were loved and cherished and now they lie orphaned, like a doctor's prescription after the patient has died. Abandoned, no one needs them, no one has any use for them. All they do is arouse pain, remind us that these are witnesses to a life once bound to you by a thousand threads and now where has it vanished, that beloved life? You step on something and feel a stab in your heart. Not long ago it was held by your comrade, your brother. You can still feel the warmth of the hand that held it. The last look he gave it still rests on it, before he threw it on the ground in his despair.

Like mourners, that was how we felt then, when we lifted our eyes and saw the awful emptiness that exudes death. From that emptiness of death you could feel invisible hands reaching for those who are left to fill their emptiness.

Like mourners who see death floating before their eyes and can-not break free because they have been bonded together with it—that was how we felt then. We sensed that we were still tightly bound with the others, that other half who had so arbitrarily been eliminated. Death and life, a synthesis of both extremes, everywhere else separated, painfully indeed, but nevertheless disconnected, set apart, but here in this case we felt that they had been fused together, death and life walking arm in arm.

Like mourners who cherish the memory of that being because they were once bound by a thousand threads and even now after death their image is engraved deep in memory, in heart and soul—that was how in that moment we breathed and lived with them. We felt that they, the now-separated brothers, had worked their way into our organism. In all our limbs we feel a piece of their lives, lives that we now miss, without whom we cannot go one step further.

The Bunks

The bunk is the most cherished, the most intimate corner you have left on this, the most accursed, most unfortunate piece of ground in the world.

The bunk is your closest and most devoted friend, truest brother that still remains in your tragic life.

The bunk that now embodies your home, your family, your wife, your child, your whole joy and happiness, is all you have left in your hellish world.

The bunk, which is like a sensitive heart, all that is left to you in a world of cruelty, brutality and barbarity, a world where all human feelings are numbed.

The bunk now stands like a mother, cloaked in sorrow, mourning for the children who have been suddenly torn from her.

The bunk, each one is in itself a mother. As soon as you come close to her, you hear her tear-filled voice. She shows you photos of her beloved children who were brothers to you and who are now gone forever.

The bunk, each tells a story, each reminds you that every child it held in its bosom is someone you have known for 15 months. You would see him daily, by day and by night. You lived through so many experiences together. You still see them living, speaking, pulsing with life. You still feel their gaze. Familiar eyes look out at you from each […] as if a diabolical game is being played. You still feel their lives, still hear their sounds—and suddenly it has all vanished, as if sunk in the deepest abyss.

The bunk—each of them sheltered whole worlds, all different in character and in appearance. Down at that end, pious Jews would sit every evening and by the light of a candle read with deep devotion a chapter of Mishna,[7] or concentrate their aching minds on a thorny point of Talmud. Up above sat a penitent who devoutly recited Psalms or portions of Scripture or listened with deep religiosity to the reading of a law from *Shulkhan Orukh.*[8] A bit further away were children, seemingly carefree even in deepest sorrow—like little children who amid great misfortune can amuse themselves with nonsense. They liked to dress up, covering their inner sorrow with outer insouciance.

The bunk—from each of them shone a different sort of life, which added a multitude of colors to the monotonous black and gray of our tragic life, of our presence in this world.

The bunk—from each of them came a particular tone that added a certain sound to the harmony created in our hellish world.

The bunk—from each of them emanated a life, which invisibly, by its mere existence, by its sole being, gave meaning, created a certainty and could sometimes bring courage and hope.

The bunk—from each of them were spun invisible threads that wove us into an indivisible family of brothers and now they stand like open graves, from which looks out fearsome death.

The bunk—when you stand near it now you see its deep yearning eyes, yearning for the children who only yesterday at this time sat in its bosom, were caressed in its arms.

The bunk—it tells you now of the pain and anguish that the children lived through, who warmed themselves under its wings.

The bunk—it tells you of those days and nights, when it was the only one who heard the deep silent weeping that issued from the aching, bleeding hearts of its unfortunate children.

The bunk—it tells you of tragic days, of the horrendous suffering the children endured, when they searched for a friend in their misfortune, a heart that could feel their pain. But there was no one then who could hear their suffering, for all, all the others were drowning in the same sea of pain and torment and each was looking for a friend with whom to share his dreadful world. And so they had to repress the pain, bury the suffering, drown out the misery, and the heavy burden grew to become a long chain of affliction that confined, oppressed and shattered them.—It was then that they came to the bunk. It stretched out its great warm arms to the tragic, aching, broken children and drew them into itself. Gave them a place to lay their aching bodies. It embraced him, covered him like a child in a warm blanket, pressed him to its heart. And that warmth and tenderness it shared with them melted the frozen numbness that had imprisoned them. Their eyes opened and streams of hot tears flowed from […] Their hearts grew lighter—content that a tear, a tear had fallen.

The bunk—in its bosom, while he was wrapped in its arms, snuggled under its warm wings—then a child could remember his home, his father and mother. A man, in his memory, could recall his wife and child. Before his eyes he could see, rising from the deep abyss, the life that once was, when he was with them all together, a child with his father and mother—a man with his wife and child and they lived happy and satisfied. And now he lies here alone, lonely and forlorn, without a home, without father and mother, without wife and child. Why? He recalls the horror that he saw with his own eyes, the horrifying image of his loved ones going up in flames. He had stood there then, stunned, petrified, and could not grasp what was happening, and only today, in the moment of remembering, a spate of tears poured from his eyes. He had long dreamed of a time to come when he would be able to cry over his father and mother, wife and child, sister and brother, but he never could, for always, his every feeling remained numb and frozen. But today, with the sensation of warmth, he experienced a moment, just a moment, of feeling so deep it pierced his ice-cold heart and the tears washed his forever incurable wounds. Ah, how good, how fortunate he felt then.

The bunk—it had become as one with its unfortunate children. When they left it for their work each morning, it longed for them and waited impatiently for their return. It wanted to hear what they had lived through that day, what their eyes had seen. How many lives, how many thousands had been killed before their eyes? In what lands, what places on the map had they been captured, what kind of death had been reserved for them? Yes, how many secrets, how many tragic tales were buried deep in its cold, mute boards?

The bunk—like a mother who stands at the bedside of her beloved children, it shared with them their sleepless nights, as they tossed and turned in pain and suffering and could find no rest, tossed on the stormy waves of the terrible misfortune.

The bunk—like a frightened mother it watched over them through tragic events and physical exhaustion. They would come back broken, resigned and dejected and like mown-down stalks fell helpless into its arms and let themselves go under the wings of sleep, and then it heard the deep and painful moans that issued endlessly from their bleeding hearts. One child mutters, Oy . . . mama . . . mama . . . Another, from the depths of a terrible nightmare, utters over and over the same word—father; a third lies tossing in his sleep, screams, calls for help and breaks into hysterical crying, mumbling in a muffled voice the names of his wife and child. They all went through this in the world of night, living anew and suffering anew the horrible misfortune that had struck their families so long before. They relived how they had come to take the loved ones who were with them, whom they held in their arms, and had torn them away with savage cruelty. And those who came were so frightening in appearance, with looks like spears and faces like bandits, with revolvers and rifles in their hands. He begged and screamed, but no one heard and he ran away [...] and in minutes he saw them already naked. His mother, his father, his sisters and brothers, his wife with the baby clutched to her breast. They were chased out of a wooden barrack and driven across the ice-cold earth. Storm winds lash their naked bodies. They shiver with fear and cold, they cry and scream, casting terrified looks all around, but they won't let them stop for a minute. Madly barking dogs throw themselves at them, biting, tearing their flesh. One dog with his sharp teeth snatches a child from its mother's breast and drags it on the ground. Screams, shouts ring out to the skies. Mothers beat their heads with their fists. This is some sort of diabolical game with naked men, women and children being played on a hellish earth, the whole game led by maddened dogs, driven on by men in military uniforms, with clubs and whips in their hands. From out of the awful chaos, the horrendous screams, he hears a familiar voice. He sees his dear sweet mother lying on the ground, the dear little sisters stand by her weeping, and try to pick her up, but can't. Someone comes running with a club and strikes the sisters and the mother on the head. He is frantic, tries to move, wants to run, wants to save them, but can't.

A minute later, he shudders, again horrified to hear the dear sweet voice of his wife, there amid the broken ice, she has fallen with the child in her arms, fallen in the water and calling out for help, and standing near her are strange men, fully clothed. They pull her by the arms like a corpse and the child sinks into the ice-cold water and the men stand there and laugh, holding on to their dogs, and with cynical smiles as if a comedy were taking place. Now he springs from his spot, wants to run to his drowning wife and child and take them in his arms and run away with them somewhere and dress them in warm clothing—but he feels like a prisoner, bound hand and foot—so that he cannot move.

There in the distance now he sees them all, his father with his brothers and sisters. His mother lies on the cold cement floor and the sisters hold her head in their hands and kiss it, the father weeps, the brothers weep, and where is she, his wife with the child, he looks for them. Now he sees her, lying with the child stretched out on the ground and someone stands over them with a revolver and gets ready to shoot. He screams wildly, roars like a wounded animal. His comrade lying near him, awakened by his screams, rouses him from sleep. He lies there in confusion, tries to catch his breath, as if he were coming back from combat, from a battlefield. Though his bunkmate asks him to tell him his dream—he doesn't want to. Overcome with tears, sunk into the nightmare from the world of Hell he just lived through, he lies there mute—until it's time for morning roll call.

The bunk—it can tell you of happy nights too, nights that flowed like a spring of living water through the desert of death where everything is fixed and frozen. It can tell you of nights that were for him like the arms of a loved one, who pressed him to her heart and softly caressed him. They were nights in which sleep put her trembling hand on the most unfortunate child in the world and led him back to the life of long ago, to the happy world of yesterday from which in broad daylight he was torn away. The kindness of night gave him back his home, his parents, his sisters and brothers, his wife and child. You can see him now—he who in the morning is a sorrowful, resigned and broken shadow—lying carefree, happy and smiling, as he finds himself with his whole family. There they sit, all together. His father, his mother, his sisters and brothers, even those who had gone to live elsewhere, were there now. And he with his wife and child, the whole large family sit around holiday decked tables—eating, singing, laughing, telling jokes. And he, the young father, plays happily with his child, who dances and jumps on him. All are happy and joyous. Today is a holiday in their home. Spirits are high and all floats on the waves of a carefree life. Suddenly the sweet sounds of a woman's voice are heard, it is his wife, who bursts into song, her lyrical songs go straight into the heart and soul and flow into all the limbs. They are carried along on the sweet melody and soon we hear the harmony of choral singing. On wings of song they float high in the worlds of fantasy. And he himself is so happy, so full of joy. A fantastic new world has opened itself to him.

Suddenly, in the midst of the singing, he hears a sound and wakes with a start—it is the camp bell calling to wake up. He lies there stunned, his consciousness lost. Where is he? Was it all just a dream? Their faces still float before his eyes, he still hears their carefree laughter. His hands still feel the warmth of his child, whom he had just now held to his bosom. His wife, right here, had just been talking to him. He still remembers the content of the carefree familiar talk. Was it only a dream? And all of them, his father, mother, sisters and brothers, his wife and child—all are already long gone from this earth—burned long ago. And he is left alone here in this hellish world. Alone, lonely, miserable and devastated. Ah, why, for what reason, did the gong have to wake him? Ah, how happy he would be if he could be left—to sleep forever in his idyllic dream. What a happy death it would be.

Dejected and resigned, he raises his tired miserable head and, groaning, jumps into his prison clothes, back into irons and chains, and walks with unsteady steps to stand in the ranks of five and return once more to his hellish work.

The bunk—lost in dreams, alone and lonely, for its dear children have been taken away, and it stands now in mourning and waits and longs for a child to come and comfort it in its misfortune.

The Roll Call of Mourning

They sent us back out to the courtyard where not long ago the awful separation had taken place. Now they lined us up for the first tragic roll call. We must now establish the number of those left and confirm and accept the operation carried out on our organism.

We line up as always, ten in a row, and half the courtyard is completely empty and what exudes from the emptiness is like a slab of death. You can feel it, sense it, touch it with your hands. Earlier today at the first, the normal roll call, he stood next to you and now in his place there is a space, a grave.

You feel that half of your organism has been amputated and you stand here now with half a body. You feel the half that is missing and you cannot stand erect on the ground. The wound is still raw. The blood of the awful slash is still warm.

We all stand with heads bowed in mourning. No one speaks, no one utters a word to disturb the mood of sorrow, numbness and death. Each is a captive to the sorrow that now hangs over the entire space, creeps into every corner, penetrates every crack. You feel as if you're drowning in a sea of sorrow.

They call out the numbers—the count is correct. The amputation has taken more than half of our body. Only 191 of us remain. We stand in one row according to our numbers and wait. The *Schreiber* calls out the names and numbers from the file cards. He calls the name and number of each card.[9] Someone answers and there is still life in the card, the card of its dead prisoner, and the next card lies there without answer, orphaned, abandoned, its owner no longer with us, for he is now elsewhere, waiting, waiting in fear. One number stays here, another is laid aside.

The file cards seem like living beings, each bound and tied to all the others. They are all together like a united, cemented family. Each warms the other, it is a tightly forged chain. And now—forced against our will—we play out the last act, the last step of the separation. We feel as if we ourselves have been torn in mourning, just as we tear our clothes in mourning. You see, you feel, that the last trace of their lives, of their connection to us, has been torn out by the root. As if our family of brothers was no more than this small number when we came here.

The final separation is ended.

There stand two boxes of separated cards. It seems to you they move like living beings, they can feel, sense and think, and now they are saying their last farewell. You feel that if you were to bend your ear you would hear the last wish of the 191 who remain, speaking to the 250 that were laid aside, torn from us, and we now want to accompany those brothers on their way, wherever the devil may lead them, and who knows where that will be?

The First Night

Each of us goes to his bunk, and feels as if he is sitting on a *shive* bench [mourning stool] and mourns. We talk about the great tragic act that has just played out before our eyes.

Like mourners who have to be reminded that they have a body, which must also be given its due, so now each comrade reminds the other that perhaps he should eat something. One comes to the other's bunk. Each looks for consolation from his comrade, his brother.

Comrades who slept next to those who are now gone walk to the bunk of the missing and with trembling hands take the remaining blankets and carry them around looking for a corner where they can rest their grieving bodies. They cannot bear to stay in their former place. Only yesterday, his brother slept there next to him, he can still feel the warmth of his body, and now his bed, his place, is cold and dead and the remaining brother cannot lie down again in the half-dead bed.

The hours creep by, in sorrow, lie like a heavy slab of monotony. Even those with a resolute, unbending character now feel weighed down by the tragic atmosphere. Gradually, they all disappear into their bunks and crawl under the covers. They want to free themselves, remove the pressing load of melancholy, seek consolation under the wings of sleep.

Now come the late-night hours. The block is quiet. The dead stillness is broken only by the heavy breathing and sighing of the unfortunate children who find no rest even in sleep. Further away, from the half of the block now empty, comes a sadness that fills the entire space. It seems as if two worlds are present. Over there, a numb dead world, bound up with a tragic life lived under sentence of death.

Over there, a small lamp burns with a mournful shine. It shines on the empty graves that weep and moan for their children, who now lie somewhere in fear and trembling, tortured by sleeplessness. They have no place to lay their heads and these, their tombs, remain here empty, sad and lonely. In the still of night is heard a painful question: Why, why did you capture my children and where, where is their path leading them?

The lamp burns there and shines its light on a dead world.

You look on from a distance and it seems the light is burning for the victims, for the 200.

The Morning of Bereavement

The camp alarm rang out to tell us, with its monotonous sound: Enough, you have rested long enough, you enemies and criminals. To work, to your hellish work, put on your harness, you cursed child.

Today—unlike other days—all the comrades get up early. For hours now they have wanted to free themselves, to push away the sleepless, nightmare-filled night. They could hardly wait to get out. No one lay in his bunk like yesterday and snuggled under the blanket to drag out the minutes, just to make the night last longer. By the first gong they have all put on their clothes.

In the block they feel that something is missing. It is too quiet, the noise is missing, the bustle, the palpitation that the family of 500 made every morning when they got up. On that gray morning, we once again saw, felt and sensed death. There on the other side the empty graves stand numb, motionless, the pulse of life has vanished. No one stirs, no one moves—no noise, no sound of a word reaches you—all is dead.

Every morning the first greeting, the first call to life, would come from over there. From over there came the first news to tell the whole block that daybreak was coming. While you still lay under your blanket and only dim rays of morning sun came in, from over there one could already hear the sad, entreating sounds of prayer that carried over the entire block and quietly penetrated your heart and soul, and carried many of us into a world of remembrance. He would remember that in his old home he had heard sounds like these from his father or grandfather in the morning hours when he was still a child. Or it reminded him of his own life, that he himself, when he was religious, had said his prayers with that same melody, prayed for life and happiness—for himself, for wife and child. And now—the sound of these prayers wrenched a deep sigh from many hearts. But today that call, that sound is no longer there. That harmony is missing. Without the sigh those sounds called forth, the harmony of our tragic life is gone. Every quiver, every movement that flowed from each man separately, was like a cog in the machine and without it we cannot get the machine to move.

The whole block feels a portion of life is missing. Every morning we would hear the familiar alarm and drink our coffee, but today no one wakes you, no one calls, as if [...] had become a useless thing needed by no one.

Everything moves slowly now, we are quiet and apathetic. It seems that those who were over there had taken with them the pulse, the vigor and the impetus. When they left, all was gone. By cutting into the organism they had cut into its life, and those who remained were left without taste or feeling, the pulse of life extinguished. Wherever you went, wherever you took a step, you could feel their absence. In the washroom, the toilet, the courtyard, everywhere it was perceptible, you could touch it with your hand, the absence of those who had been the most living part of our organism.

That was how it was, that first morning of our separation.

Eintreten—To Work

"Line up!"—came the strident voice of a kapo—"Today everybody goes to work!" All, each one, will have an important role in the commando. Like a man whom death has robbed of half of his children. No one lingers in the block, we all want to escape from the emptiness, the sadness it exudes. Lined up in the street, each of us feels that something is missing. Yesterday at this time he walked in the same row with such-and-such a comrade. He still remembers what they talked about then. And today, who knows, who knows where they are taking them. Each of us would like to get to the gate as quickly as we can. Maybe, just maybe, he will see them again. See their faces one last time in light of day and one last time exchange a look of farewell. But even this pleasure was not given to us. As we were marching to work, they had already passed through on their way to the train. As we were told later, they were ordered to take off their good warm clothing and put on prison clothes and wooden shoes. So from the very first steps they were morally and physically oppressed and broken.

As we walk we feel a trembling. Here just half an hour ago, my brother walked, led by dozens of guards with machine guns, and who knows, who knows where the road will lead them? And who knows how long, how long we ourselves will be kept here. Is it not the beginning of the end for us all? Who knows?! We walk with lowered eyes. Each of us feels their cynical looks boring into us, looks that say "something," that penetrate our hearts and seem to ask, question, call out to us. The looks demand an accounting for yesterday's vanished evening. They had thought, they had believed, that something would happen, that the operation would be felt not just by our organism, but also by them, those who carried it out, and then surely "something" would happen.

Those looks force us to reflect, to make an accounting for ourselves. And at times we think perhaps they were right, it could have been the beginning of the end and we are to blame. But instinctively we raise our eyes to see, who is it that demands from me an accounting? Who is the force that would have been set alight by the fire we had lit? I saw the face of a Pole who, though he himself is behind bars and fences, murderously strikes a Jew and shouts, "Dirty Jew!" I breathed more freely. I saw the faces of those who would have worked, not only passively but also actively, to put out the fire together with those in whose hands they too are prisoners. Then I felt that we are alone not only in our individual lives but also alone in the common striving that smolders deep in our hearts.

In the Commando

The kapo calls out each group. They have all been reduced by half. Only one group has been entirely eliminated, one name completely extinguished, wiped out, the "*Reinkommando*." This had been made up of the weakest comrades, and its work was to clean the hair of thousands of shorn heads of Jewish women, young and old.

That commando is the only one that was completely liquidated.[10]

As we work we feel the absence of the others. Even those groups who are working normally feel an emptiness, feel that here in this place, on this very spot, stood a comrade, a brother — and today? Everything reminded us, everything spoke to us of the need to remember them.

I go upstairs to see what's happening there, behind the tall chimney, where dozens of older men, and also some younger men, used to sit, and whose real task was to hide from the eyes of the guards and pray, one reciting a chapter from the Book of Psalms, another a page of Talmud, or saying the daily prayers. And we, in doing our work, did only enough to show that something had been done. The work could be done very quickly or else drawn out, and it was easy enough to cheat, so that the time gained could be used for the benefit of the sick and weak or the truly devout.

I walk up the stairs and find everything the same as when we left yesterday.

Dead silence reigns. Various objects, iron buckets, valises and other boxes stand on the ground, lined up in the same order as when they sat here at their work. They sat on these things instead of on chairs,—chairs were hard to sit on because you had to bend your head too low. All is in place just as it was yesterday when the men sat here—and it makes you feel that the objects are waiting sadly for those who sat here yesterday to come back. In that space one feels what is missing, all is cloaked in sadness and melancholy. You go up to a place where someone sat and you find hidden a *sidur*, a *tallis* and *tefiln*[11]—yesterday at this time they were being used and now they lie abandoned, there is no hand to put on the phylacteries, no mouth to say the prayers, no body to be wrapped in the prayer shawl.

Before my eyes swims an image of those mornings, when one would stand guard and look out to make sure no one was coming, while the religious Jews, false to their oppressors and true to their god, trembled as they sent a prayer up to the heavens. More than once they had to tear off their phylacteries in mid-prayer and go back to work as if nothing had happened. More than once, "they" had burst in, and he—the cynical, bestial *Oberscharführer*, the chief of all the crematoria—pretended to scream at them for having created a "Bible-commando" here. But deep down he was pleased that in the heart of Hell, by the same chimney through which pass hundreds of thousands of Jewish lives, there are Jews who sit with their backs against the bricks, warmed by the fire of the burned Jewish victims, of their burned fathers and mothers, their burned wives and children—and in this place they pray, study or recite Psalms. If they can still recognize here in this corner that everything is governed by the higher power of God, then such Jews must be allowed to believe and to practice their faith and even here and now to deepen their faith. It is better, safer, to have such an element, they can rest easier with such an element. That was why they showed a certain tolerance, and treated the matter as unimportant [...]

[*several lines missing—yellowed and decayed*]

[...] yesterday they had brought food with them for today and did not foresee that by this time today they would be taken away—in a locked and barred train—on a road [...]

Still hanging on the wall is a list with the names of the five comrades who were to take turns watching the gate. Five names, each name as if a living, moving being is here before your eyes. From each name floats the familiar face of a good comrade. It feels as if he's speaking to you, saying: "Look, brother, see the error in our calculation. Yesterday I thought and calculated that I would stand today, down there by the gate, and today the devil has carried off my body in his arms! Remember, brothers, remember, that tomorrow is not in your hands." The list hangs on the wall, a living witness to our insignificance and worthlessness.

The slip of paper exudes sorrow, fear and terror. It tells of what once was and is no more. Vanished and who knows where? An invisible hand reaches out from it to seize our being and draw it into a world of sorrow and melancholy. The five names, the five beings, seem to look out at you from a deep abyss to wake, call and warn. And the menacing voice grows stronger with each minute, it shouts into the now-deaf ear and storms its way into the numbed heart. In the tumult of the voices I hear the echo of the words: "Remember! Remember tomorrow." I leave shattered, downcast and resigned. The sound persecutes me like the voice of doom, it leaves me no rest, it forces me to think. This day has stretched out like an eternity. I could barely wait for the whistle to signal our return. I began to breathe easier. How symbolic this day has been of the general situation, of the usual mood.

Friday Night

Many of the comrades looked with mockery and contempt at the few dozen Jews who assembled to welcome in the Sabbath and to say *maariv*, the evening prayer. There were also those who looked at them with bitterness, for the dreadful reality, the horrendous tragedies that take place daily before our eyes can in no way arouse a feeling of gratitude or make one want to sing praises to the Creator who has allowed a people of barbarians to murder and exterminate millions of innocent men, women and children, whose only fault is to have been born Jewish, to have recognized as the Almighty the same God to whom he now prays, to have brought monotheism to humanity. And because of this they now fall as victims. And they should still praise Him? Why? Songs of praise over a sea of our own blood? Pray to Him who will not hear the cries and screams of innocent little children, no! And this Jew walks away bitter, angry at the others, who do not understand as he does.

Even Jews who were once religious now stand coldly off to the side. For a long time now they have not been at peace with their God. They are bitter about His ways. They cannot understand how a "Father" can hand over his children into the hands of bloodthirsty killers who mock Him and laugh at Him. They don't want to speculate too much, for fear of losing their last support, for fear of destroying their last consolation. So they sit quietly, they do not demand a reckoning from Him, nor do they offer any reckoning to Him. Sometimes they would like to pray, pour out their hearts, but cannot. They don't want to be false, false to Him and to themselves.

And yet despite the general atmosphere, there exists a group of stubborn and observant Jews who repress any bitterness, drown out any protest that daily assaults their heart and soul, and wants, demands a reckoning—wants to ask why? No! They allow themselves once more to be caught in the net of naive faith. No reckoning, no theorizing. They believe, they are even now convinced, and show it every day, that all that transpires, all that happens to us is governed by the higher power, whose reasons we cannot grasp, that we, with our simple human understanding, cannot comprehend. Even now they cling to their God. They are imbued with this deep belief, even when they see, feel, sense that they are drowning in the sea of their own faith. And maybe, maybe deep in their hearts "something" weighs upon them, will not let them rest, but still they hold fast, so as not to lose their last consolation, not to lose their last support.

And from the family of 500—believers, non-believers, embittered or indifferent—a group came into being of those who prayed, small at first but that grew larger with time, a group who said all the daily prayers with a *minyan*.[12]

Sometimes it would happen that one of us who didn't pray would be drawn in by the prayers and the singing. He would hear a sound, an air from a traditional Friday night prayer, and it would tear him away from the horrible tragic reality. On stormy waves of remembrance he was carried back to a world of yesterday. He swims back to the years gone by. And sees himself in his home once more.

Friday night. In the great synagogue it is warm and bright as if lit by several suns. Jews stand in their Sabbath clothes, in their holiday mood. They have left behind their weekday preoccupations along with their weekday clothing. When they locked up the shop or closed the business, they broke the link with a world in which the soul is a slave to the body. They had freed themselves of the weekday cares and worries, both individual and collective. They are happy and care-free, and feel fortunate to enter a world where you needn't bring the burdens of the week.

Now in the synagogue a voice rings out, announcing to the congregation that the time has come to go out to welcome in the Sabbath Queen.[13]

Magnificent songs rise in the air, touching melodies resound. In the air blends the harmony of gladness and spiritual exaltation. With wings of sanctity they rise to the highest heavens, float in a world of divine elevation. Every word, every song fills them with courage and hope. From time to time a deep sigh desecrates the holiness. A Jew has suddenly thought about his weekday life, has seen himself burdened by all his cares, individual and collective. He sees before his eyes his tragic reality. He feels himself trampled under the feet of his oppressors. He feels his insignificance and worthlessness. He falls from a great height, feels himself sinking back into the deep abyss of despair. A minute ago he thought he had found salvation in the stormy sea of troubles and now it's vanished. He searches, would like to hold on to something that will not let him sink into the abyss. Another wave crashes before him. But now he hears a new sound that uplifts and encourages him. *"Vehoyu limshisso shossoyikh."*[14] Be not afraid,—your enemies, your oppressors, will be stamped out, annihilated. Do not fall into despair, you son of ancient martyrs! And the Jew is again filled with courage, faith and the certainty that tomorrow will be brighter than today. He forgets today, is already living in tomorrow, whose shining rays he has just glimpsed. Renewed hope has flowed into his blood and made him strong. He sings once more with the whole congregation and returns to the lofty, spacious skies of the spirit.

He remembers that magical stroll with his father and brother, with many other Jews. They walk homeward with measured steps, calm and carefree, their souls filled with the peace and joy they carry with them out of the great synagogue. The street is calm and quiet, Sabbath candles glow in the windows. They are the only pulse of life moving through the silent streets. All the shops are closed, the sanctity of the Sabbath rests everywhere, and the majesty and holiness streaming out of God's day has spread its reign over the entire *shtetl* and penetrated every corner of human life.

Everyone feels uplifted by an inner happiness.

He arrives at home to an idyllic warmth, a wave of holiness wafts over the entire space and everything present in the house. Everywhere rests the holiness of the Sabbath. From every object rings a note that creates the harmony of holiness. He remembers the sounds of hearty Sabbath greetings as he and his father enter the house. With their coming, a wave of joy flows into the home imbued with Sabbath peace and the Divine Presence. He remembers, he sees now how the eyes of his mother, his wife, his sisters and brothers shone with holiness.

The hearty sounds of *"sholem aleichem"*[15] rang through the air, as father greeted the holiness that came down from the heavens to rest amid the four walls of our house, and now floats over the heads of his beloved family.

He sees himself amid his whole happy, satisfied family. They eat, drink and sing, all feeling so good, so happy, satisfied, carefree and safe, full of courage and hope. An idyllic world is spread before them, their world, of which they alone are the masters. They feel threatened by no one. The[y] go their way boldly and in safety in the newly revealed world.

And all at once, a stormy, roiling wave cruelly tore him away, ripped him away from that world.

Gone was the home, gone the Sabbaths, vanished the world and drowned his happiness. His father, mother, sisters and brothers, his wife—no one is left in that world.

Gut shabes, gut shabes!—they say to each other. It pounds at the heart, pierces the very soul—*gut shabes!*—for whom? Where are the smiling faces? Where are the beloved parents? Where are the dear sisters and brothers? Where are you, my darling wife?—*gut shabes!*—To whom, for whom? I see before me the horrible abyss of my shattered world. And from the abyss I hear the voice of my family burned in the flames. I flee, flee as from a ghost. I want to free myself as quickly as I can from the nightmare—drown out the fire that has flared up in my very core.

But there are other moments when you want to recapture the stirring of the spirit, you want to thaw the numbness, warm the icy cold. There are times when you want to remember, remember in order to endure again, feel the suffering again, bleed again with the pain that until now we have not been able to feel, because the work we do, seeing the horrible death of those millions of people passing before your eyes, the sea of blood in which we drown every day, the waves of collective suffering, all these constantly dilute and numb the individual misfortune.

And sometimes you yearn for the "pleasure" of being able to go back, to penetrate into your own world, to relive the past, and then today, to swim through the years, to reach the past and stay as long as possible on the surface of that distant life, distant joy, and then, only then, let yourself down into the abyss of this hellish world. To seize a ray of that bright sun and carry it down to the depths of darkness, to see the awful, horrendous, unbounded misery in which we sink.—Then, then I would run there, to that spot, to that corner where a few *minyans* of Jews stand and pray in saintly piety, and from there I would seize the light, take a spark and run away with it, and run to my bunk. And in its warmth the frozen stiffness of my heart would melt. And then I could have a joyous Friday night. I was carried through the stormy waves of my vanished years, and when I reached the shore of my Sabbath of today, my heart broke into tears. I was content, I had a tearful Sabbath, a cup of tears. Long, long I had yearned to see in my fantasy my beloved mother, my father in holiday mood, my dear sisters and brothers, my dear wife singing, relive with them the Sabbaths of joy, Sabbaths of carefree happiness and then to mourn for them. To mourn for my family, my near and dear ones who are gone forever. To cry for my Sabbaths, which will never, never come back, to cry for my misfortune, which I have only now felt, only now realized . . .

I long for the brothers because they are my brothers, I long for them also because a piece of my hellish life is bound up with them. I look now toward that corner where they used to stand in prayer. A dead and frozen numbness emanates from that place. No one, no one is left there. Vanished the lives, extinguished the sound.—Yet another yearning and a new grieving came to me in my deep sorrow.

We long for our brothers because they are our brothers.

We long for them also because we miss the light, the warmth, the faith, the hope that flowed out of them.

With their disappearance the last consolation vanished.

The Czech Transport

Preface

Dear reader, I write these words in moments of my greatest despair and I do not know and do not believe that these lines written here I will myself one day after the "storm" be able to read. Who knows if I will have the good fortune to be able to reveal to the world the deep secret I carry in my heart? Who knows if I will some day see a free man once again and be able to speak to him? It may be that this, these lines I write, will be the only witness of my past life. How happy I will be if my writings do reach you, free citizen of the world. Perhaps a spark of my inner fire will ignite in you, and you will fulfill just a small part of our will in life, and you will take revenge, revenge on the murderers!

Dear finder of these writings!

I make one request of you, and this is indeed the essential aim of my writing, that this life I live under sentence of death should at least have a meaning. That these days in Hell and my hopeless tomorrow may in the future reach a goal.

I give you here just a small part, a minimum of what took place in this Hell called Birkenau-Auschwitz. You can only imagine how it was in reality. I have written a great deal more than this. I believe that you will certainly find its traces and from it all you will form a picture of how the children of our people perished.

Now I have for you, dear finder and publisher of these writings, a personal request: that through the address written here, you will discover who I am! And then, through my relatives, you can obtain a photo of my family and one of my wife and myself. You should use these pictures as you see fit in this book. By means of this I hope to preserve their dear beloved names, those for whom I cannot now shed even a tear! For I live in a Hell of death and cannot even properly evaluate the extent of my loss. And I myself have also been sentenced to death. Can the dead weep for the dead?! But you "free" stranger, free citizen of the world, I beg of you to grant them one more tear, when you have their pictures before your eyes. To them I dedicate all my writings—that is my tear, my sigh for my family and for my people.

I wish to enumerate here the names of all my family:

My mother—Sarah
My sister—Libe
My sister—Esther-Rokhl
My wife—Sonja [Sarah]
My father-in-law—Raphael
My brother-in-law—Wolf

They perished on December 8th, 1942, gassed and burned.

I also had news of my father, Samuel, who was captured by "them" on the day of Yom Kippur 1942, but after that I know nothing. Two brothers, Eber and Moyshl, were captured in Lithuania. My sister Feigele was captured in Otwock.

That is the sum total of what I know about my family.—

I do not believe that any of them are still alive. I ask you, and this is my last wish, that under the portrait of us alive you should inscribe the date of our deaths.

What will be, what will become of me, has already been shown me by reality. I know the day is drawing near, the day before which my heart and soul are trembling. Not so much for life—although one wants to live, for life has its power of seduction, but one reason to live still remains, which does not let me rest: to live, to live for revenge! And to perpetuate the names of my loved ones. I have friends in America and in Eretz-Israel. Of those addresses I remember one, which I give you here — and from them you can learn who I am and who is my family. Of my five uncles in America, here is one address:

J. Joffe
27, East Broadway, NY
America[1]

All that is written here I myself lived through in the 16 months of my "*Sonderarbeit*."[2] My accumulated sorrow, the horrendous pain and suffering I endured, I could not, because of the "conditions," express in any "other" way but, unfortunately, only through writing.

Z.G.

Night

A deep blue sky, adorned with bright, sparkling stars, spreads out its arms over the entire world. A serene moon, carefree and happy, sets out on her majestic course to survey her kingdom, the world of night. She lets her springs flow out so that man can drink his fill of love, happiness and joy.

In those days people could sit in peace, without bars or fences, people on whom the pirate's boot had not yet trampled, whose eyes had not yet seen barbarity's ugly face. They could sit quietly in their homes and, from the intimate shadows of their room, look out upon the splendor, the magic, of the enchanted night as they wove sweet dreams of future happiness.

In streets, in gardens they stroll, carefree and happy, looking up with dreamy eyes at the broad realm of the sky and smile lovingly at the moon, who enchants and intoxicates their hearts and souls.

Young people sit in the dark lanes, on benches cloaked in shadows. [...] and confide to their friend the moon the secret that they are in love. Their eyes gleam in the moonlight and onto his breast and throat falls a tear of joy from his beloved's eye, for their hearts overflow with love.

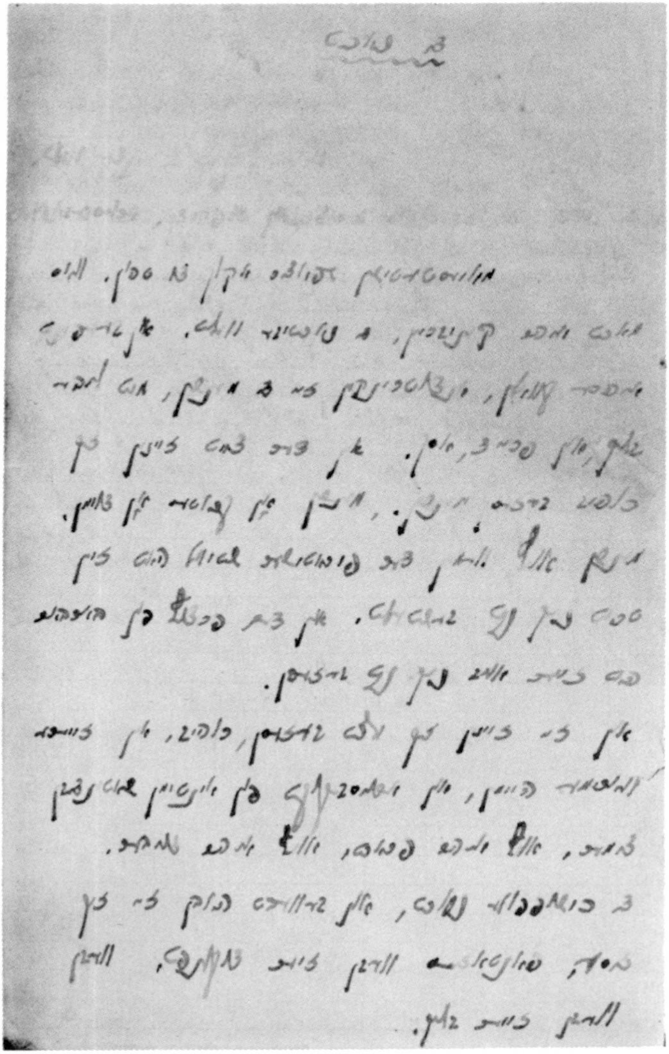

FIGURE 6 The beginning of "Night."

On the waters now they float, lost in their dreams and filled with longing, as the gentle ripples carry them to new worlds they dream of and they sing sweet songs and play yearning melodies. And the air now carries to the heavens the harmony of song and love. Mankind sings its praise to Her Majesty the Queen of Night, in thanks for the love and joy she has inspired in the world.

Just so did the night look down, that horrible and brutal night of Purim[3] 1944 in which they, the murderers of the world who had prepared the slaughter, sacrificed to their god the quivering, trembling young lives of the Czech Jews, 5,000 in number.[4]

They prepared it well, the slaughter. All preparations were ready days before the great event. It even seemed that the moon and stars and heavens were in league with the devil and now dressed in their finest so that the great celebration would be rich and imposing.

They turned our Purim festivities into a *Tishe-b'ov*.[5]

It seemed to us that the world had one sky for all the nations and another one for us. For them the sky and stars scintillate with life and splendor, and for us, for us Jews, the same dark blue starry sky, but then the stars go out and fall deep into the abyss.

Of the moon as well there are certainly two. For the nations, a kind and gentle moon that smiles down tenderly on the world and hears its song of happiness and joy. And a moon for our people, cruel and brutal, who stands calmly by when she hears the cries and lamentations of millions of hearts as they struggle with death, death who is advancing toward them.

The Mood in the Camp

In the camp there reigns among the Jews a mood of sorrow and mourning. They move about depressed and broken. All now lives in tense expectation.

Days ago we had been told that "they" would come to "us" and the ovens burned for three days straight, ready to receive their guests. Yet it was put off from day to day, which is a sign, an indication, that something is certainly preventing it from happening. And who knows what consequences will come from this. And this will be the impulse, the dynamite, the spark in the powder keg, which has been waiting, long been waiting for the explosion. This is what we believed, this is what we thought. For they are part of the camp, the Czech Jews. They have been living seven months in this cursed place, the most unfortunate corner of the world, and they know everything, understand everything.[6] Every day they see the massive, black fiery smoke that rises from the depths of Hell up to the highest heavens, with its daily toll of victims.

They know, no need to tell them, that this is the place, this is the site that was specially built and destined to eliminate our people through gassing, shooting, slaughtering or through pain and suffering, sucking from them the marrow and blood, through hard labor accompanied by blows, until they drop helpless in the deep mud and their emaciated bodies remain lying motionless forever. But they, the Czech Jews, did believe and hope that perhaps the fate of our people would not fall upon them, that the nation of Slovakia would act in their favor. And the fact is indeed that this is the first time that transports of Jews, whole families, did not go directly to the fire, but rather were brought together into the camp. This was a consolation for them, a sign that the "power" had singled them out from the general "Jewish law" and they were not destined for the same end as the Jews from the rest of the world, to be sacrificed to their god. But they, poor naive victims, could not know, could not understood, could not penetrate into the dark and evil thoughts of the vile sadists and criminals, that if their lives had been spared until now it was for a specific goal, a particular diabolical purpose. The barbaric deception demanded that they should still remain alive. And when through that deception their aim had been attained, then their lives were no longer needed and they became the same as all the Jews, whose final destination is death.

Sudden and unexpected, the news reached them that they would be "sent out" of the camp. Their hearts were filled with fear and foreboding, an intuition told them that some awful fate has been prepared for them, but still they did not want to believe. Only on the last day of their lives did they realize that they were not being taken to work in another camp, that what awaited them was death and to death they were being sent.

Now the camp is tense, though it is not the first time that they have taken thousands at a time from the camp, people who know for a fact that they will go straight to their death. Yet today is still an exceptional case, for today's victims are whole families, who thought they were coming to live here and hoped to be liberated—they did indeed stay for seven full months—and return to their brothers still living there in Slovakia. All now feel for them, the thousands of vibrant lives, now sitting locked in cold, dark barracks with boarded doors, locked up as in a cage.

Once the families were separated, torn apart, they led them in. A lone woman weeps in one barrack, her husband in another is sunk in sorrow and the grown children in a third grave sit and cry in longing for their parents.

Here in the camp all walk around in deep melancholy and look instinctively in that direction, to that corner, there beyond the barbed wire, beyond the fences, to the full barracks that now hold the thousands of worlds, those whose last night is now being written. They sit there now, the unfortunate victims, sunk in pain and torment and fearfully await the coming minutes. They know, they feel, that the last hours are drawing near, the last hours of their lives. Through the cracks in the barrack walls the moon shines in and lights the victims waiting for their death.

All the hearts and souls there have been broken, bloodied, ripped ragged. They would so wish to be together now, husbands and wives, fathers and mothers with their children, at least in the final hours, to hug and kiss and pour out their hearts with weeping and with a shared lament!

Fathers and mothers would be supremely happy if they could only press their child to their hearts, kiss and lovingly caress the child and cry for their misfortune and cry for their child, so young, who must now in bloom of youth, in innocence and for no reason— except that he was born a Jew—leave the world a sacrificial victim.

The victims would so wish now to cry over their misfortune, cry over their fate, but there is no harmony there. They would like, the whole family together, to lament and mourn their destruction. But even this, this last pleasure, to go their final dreadful way together, to go as one till the last step, to be together to the last breath—even this the vile beasts have not permitted them. They sit now separated, divided, torn apart. Each is cloaked in deep melancholy, drowning in a sea of pain and suffering, and makes his final reckoning, closes out his accounts with the world.

They weep, they groan and sob, this final reckoning rocks and shatters their being.

The world is so beautiful, so magnificent and appealing. Through the cracks of their living graves, they look out on the splendid, enchanted world. They remember times gone by, how lovely, how happy were their lives. The bygone years, now vanished forever, run like a film before their eyes, and then appears the horrible reality. Now weighed down and broken by atrocious suffering, they await the coming of a painful and horrible death.

Each feels himself tossed on the successive waves of his life, from beginning to end.

Even the children, the little ones with their mothers, they too can sense the approaching destruction. Their childish intuition foretells horrors to come. The overall sorrow has instilled a deep depression in their childish hearts. They are frightened by their mothers' passionate kisses and caresses. They cuddle up, press closely to their mother's heart in fear, they cry quietly, not to trouble their mother in her deep sorrow.

Over there sits a young girl, not yet 16 years of age. Before her eyes swim visions of her childhood years, carefree and good. She goes to school, learns her lessons well. She comes home happily every day and tells her mother that today she's won a prize. The mother gives her a warm kiss. From her mother's eye a teardrop falls on her rosy cheek. In the evening the father comes home from work. She shares with him too the news of her good work at school. The father takes her tenderly on his lap, presses her to his heart and plants a multitude of fatherly kisses on her face, her eyes. He gives her sweets and plays with her as if they were both children.

The waves of childhood carry her to another shore. It has been a happy, magical evening. She has finished school with a prize, and a great celebration is now being held with all her friends and loved ones. All the guests wish her and her dear parents great success in life and in learning. People kiss and are joyful, they sing and dance. She is the center of attention, the reason for the day's festivities. She is happy, proud and pleased with her success.

Now she sits at her piano and plays a song for her guests. All sit quietly, intent and still, all entranced by the music. She herself is in heaven. With each note she feels another wing added to her body. And just as she reaches the highest heights, the misfortune occurs. In the middle of the grand celebration, the door bursts open and the arrogant faces of the vile bandits appear before them, to tell them they must get ready, prepare to be on their way, to join the transport that will leave tomorrow, early in the morning. A horrible nightmare takes place before her, as they are torn from their home and brought to this death camp. They have already spent seven months here and now she is alone, no father or mother by her side. Sad and lonely, fearful and trembling, she waits for the dreaded death and cries bitterly over her fate. If at least she could have her father and mother near her and kiss them tenderly and be together with them. Ah, how happy she would be.

A golden thread was spun and now in the middle has been cut short.

Another young woman sits and mourns. Twenty years she has lived. Young, beautiful, splendid. Great success she has achieved, loved by many, worshipped and revered. She met a young man and won his heart and she loved him too. Both were so happy, so content. She remembers that evening, a magical one, like today. They walked together in the shaded lanes and neither spoke though they had much to say to one another. But he was not bold and neither was she. They sat together on a lonely bench and the moon and stars shone magically into that very corner where they sat. In their loving eyes tears appeared, and then it happened, he took her passionately in his arms and quietly revealed the secret of his love for her. A long, sweet kiss united their burning lips—and their enamored hearts beat rhythmically in time and spun out the dream that both had so long dreamed.

And suddenly, unexpectedly, from the highest heavens they sank into the deepest abyss. They were at the threshold, about to reach the highest joy, all preparations made, ready for the wedding, when suddenly the great misfortune came.

They were torn away from their ideal home, she taken by the transport and he remained alone. She had news of him, received his parcels too. In contact once again, they continued to spin their thread and hoped and believed that the happiness they dreamed of would soon come true.

And now all is lost, all the dreams, all the fantasies have run out, disappeared forever, no more hope, no more luck.

She feels, she senses that the thread has snapped. She sees the awful abyss into which she will soon vanish. She wants to live, the world taunts and beckons, and she is young, strong and beautiful. How wonderful, how carefree her life had been. She can still feel, still breathe the heady aroma of yesterday, and today! Ah, how dreadful, how horrible. She sits alone now captive in a dead world, and waits together with the others, the victims, the unfortunates, for horrendous death.

And where is he, her beloved, now? If only he could be with her in the moments of her pain, how happy she would be if she could share with him her pain-filled heart. They would wrap their arms around each other and press their hearts together. And they would cry together over their destruction, their misfortune, and go together deep into their grave. Where is he, where is she? The thought will not let her rest, her feelings grow more turbulent, more stormy from one minute till the next. She is going to her death alone and miserable, and he, her beloved, her happiness and joy, will remain alone in the world. For whom? If she now leaves the world. The thought drives her mad, the nightmarish chaos breaks her spirit. All at once, she screams: No! I won't go, without you I won't go. Come with me, my beloved. And in minutes, her wild, hysterical laughter rings out. She stretches out her arms to him, then draws them back, uttering mad words to herself: Ah, my love, you have come back to me.

A golden thread two hearts had spun and in mid-spinning the pirate came and cut it short.

Over there another young woman sits in sorrow and despair, a child pressed to her breast. She is still young. A first child she bore in this world, full of life and charm. She too must now say farewell to the world and to herself. The past swims before her, the good years. How long ago was it? She remembers clearly, how vivid is the image still today before her eyes. Her entire life is concentrated around this image. She cannot separate herself from it. It was her wedding day. She was then the happiest woman in the world. All the dreams, all the fantasies of her life had come true. United now forever with him, with her true love. How happy, how contented she was that day. Like an idyll those magical years float by. She had just taken the first steps in her new life.

Her path was strewn with flowers, roses of many colors, intoxicated she was by their scent, carefree and happy she swam through these newfound waves.

She recalls the day the secret was revealed to her, that beneath her loving heart a new future was being woven. Just today she felt the palpitating fruit of her love. She will never forget those minutes. In the suspense of those minutes she wants to linger. She remembers how she stood facing her husband, timidly lowered her eyes and told him the secret, that she will soon be a mother. She can still feel his arms around her, and the hot kisses he gave her then along with his tears. And when the longed-for day arrived and the child, the unfortunate child she now holds pressed to her breast, came into the world and they heard its first quavering cry, how much joy, how much happiness it brought them. A new source of life had appeared before them. The sound of a new song filled their home and turned it into an idyll. Their parents, friends and acquaintances, all came to the celebration, all were delighted, enjoyed themselves and wished the parents well. They were both so proud, he had become a father, she a mother. There was new meaning, a new aim in their lives. How happy she was as she pressed the child to her heart and her dearest husband would then kiss them both. And suddenly the storm broke through and dragged them from their home and drove them here to this place.

She sits now solitary and alone, her husband just yesterday torn from her and she alone, broken and in despair, brought here with her child, among these people who would soon be dead. She is frightened, afraid to be alone. She feels, senses, that she is drowning, together with them, the victims, sinking in a sea of death. And where is he, her beloved husband, could he perhaps stretch out his hand to rescue her.

She feels their life has been destroyed forever. She kisses her child passionately and the hot tears fall. She knows, senses that she, along with her unfortunate child, must soon go to their death. She cannot sit still in one place. She weeps in despair, tears pieces from her flesh. Oh, how awful she feels, how horrible. If at least her beloved husband were near her, her suffering would be so much lighter. Their awful fate they would have shared together. She and he and their child, they would have held each other close and walked together in one row. But now she is here alone, she cannot, she is too weak to bear so much pain, so much suffering. Her only child, her joy in life, she cannot bring him there as a sacrifice.

She moans and weeps over her misfortune. And the child cuddles to his mother's heart and a deeper groan bursts from his little heart, and in his little eyes the sparkle of a tear remains fixed. Mother and child both feel the beginning of their end.

Just as she took her first steps into a happy world, this Jewish mother from Czechoslovakia, the bandits came and seized her on her path.

Sitting there too is an old mother, old not in years but in suffering. She is not yet 50 years old. She weeps bitterly at her fate. She thinks now not of her own life, which is already in the grave. She is now with them, with her children, who yesterday were torn apart, the son taken from his wife and child. Her daughter left without her husband. They sit there, as she does here, locked in a prison, waiting, waiting for death.

Oh, if only they would—the bandits—take her for a victim and spare the lives of her children, young blossoms, still in early bloom, how happy she would be. With joy she would run to death, knowing that for the price of her life, she had saved a child.

But who hears her cries, who hears her scream, who has a heart for her suffering? It is drowned in the sea of pain and trouble, of mothers by the thousands who mourn the same misfortune. And she doesn't know that she, and the child too, the devil wants them for his victims.

From all the women's graves comes a deep wail, the cry of a mass of victims, still clinging to the edge of life . . . and cannot let it go, for all are still young, torn from life in mid-bloom. They want to live, for that were they born, and do not know through whose fault they are all here sentenced to death. And why, why did the deepest depths open their mouths like wolves to swallow them up. And here stand the green-uniformed bandits who forcibly tear them from the edge of life and throw them, hurl them, deep into the grave?

And why does the moon taunt them so, these victims sitting in the dark grave, and her rays, like so many devils, spread over them and shine as if for spite with more magic and more splendor than ever?

Just as life shows itself to them, so splendid, so beautiful, they see waving before them in the moonlight the sharp sword in the hand of the great executioner who has long been waiting so impatiently for them.

Beyond the boarded-up women's graves stand new prisons, where the great mass of men now sit locked up and wait. Like the women, they too were chosen today to be victims. The men sit there sunken deep in sorrow, and a nightmare of mingled thoughts runs through their minds. They too are settling final scores with the world and with themselves. And though they know and feel deep down the end is drawing near,—they still don't want to believe, for nearly all are still young and strong and healthy, they can work and be productive. And weren't they "assured" by the criminals and murderers that they are being sent to work, and they want to believe in the illusion that they have been brought here in order to live and they will not be sent over there, to those large buildings that spew out each day the smoke of thousands of victims. No, it is not meant for them.

For some of the serious thinkers, realists who have understood the devil's swindle and do not believe in "their" word, a new idea is being woven, that they will not give up their lives lightly [...] there will be victims among the devils too, but there was no one they could speak to of these ideas, for the great mass are captive to quite other kinds of thoughts.

Strong young men sit there and think of their fathers and mothers, who were torn from them. And their hearts tell them that no good awaits them, and they, the healthy children who have strength and energy, would like to be with them now and help them in their pain. Their minds, their heart and soul are with their fathers and mothers there. Their only desire now is how to help them, how to get news of them.

Over there a young man sits with bowed head and longs in sorrow for his sweetheart, his promised one, who just yesterday was with him still. The sound of her last words still rings in his ears. And suddenly they were torn apart. Not even the time to say a word of farewell. His heart is filled with dread for her fate, her future. Who knows? Who knows? Will he ever see her again?

Oh, if he could only have one last look at her and send her one word of comfort in her sorrow, how happy he would be. Oh, if he could only be with her there, to go their way together. He feels, senses, sees before his eyes the suffering she endures as she waits and longs for him.

A young father too sits sunk in melancholy. In their former "graves" his young wife and child are dying in torment. And he suffers with her, his wife, his beloved, with whom he was once so happy.

One body, one heart, one soul they formed, the two of them. He knows, he feels, his look breaks through the many prison walls that separate them. He sees his helpless wife in her despair and sorrow, holding their child, his child, pressed closely to her heart as she weeps over him. From her cries, her screams, he hears a call to him: Come, my beloved husband, come to me. I cannot stay here alone any more. See, I hold him in my arms, our child, our joy. I cannot go on alone. I have no strength left. Come here with me and with our child, and let us all together fall into the grave.

He sees, he feels her break under the heavy load of pain, and it drives him mad, he can find no rest, no place to be. His arms stretch out to her. He wants to run, to throw himself at her, though he cannot rescue them, and yet, how happy he would be if he could embrace his helpless wife in his steely arms and hold her close and press her to his heart and cover all her limbs with kisses. And their child, their only consolation, he would clasp in his now-trembling arms and kiss his dear little eyes, his soft cheeks, his little head with golden curls — how sweetly and tenderly he would caress him. Oh, how happy he would be if he could drink his fill of them, his wife and child, and free her from her burdens. He would take them both in his strong muscular arms and run away with them.

A mother sits broken with her child and sinks into the deep sea of sorrow and in another prison sits a warmhearted father who wants to bring them help but cannot.

The vile beasts and devils have cleverly thought out their game. They deliberately tear apart the families so as to bewilder the victims, to burden them with a new worry before death.

From all the prison-graves rings out now a great lament. In the air a harmony of prayer comes together, from thousands of unfortunate victims, waiting now in fear of death. Like a symbol, a bolt of lightning flashes before them. For our unfortunate people a great miracle took place this day. For this day is Purim for our people and perhaps another miracle will happen, even at the edge of the grave.

But the heavens remained still. They were not moved by the cries of the little children, nor of fathers and mothers, nor of old or young. Dumb and motionless, the moon remained quiet and carefree, and awaited, along with the murderers and criminals, the holy celebration. The five thousand innocent lives to be brought as a sacrifice to their god.

And the wild beasts and criminals celebrated their success in turning our beloved Purim into a *Tishe-b'ov*.

The "Power" Prepares

Three days earlier, on Monday, March 6, 1944, three men came. The camp commandant, cold-blooded murderer and bandit *Oberscharführer* Schwarzhuber,[7] the *Oberrapportführer Oberscharführer* . . . and our *Oberscharführer* Voss,[8] the chief of all four crematoria. Together, the three of them circled the entire crematorium area and worked out a "strategic" plan, whereby the guards, a strengthened security force, would be in a state of military readiness on the day of the great celebration.

This caused great amazement among us, for in the 16 months of our tragic and horrible "*Sonderarbeit*" it was the first time that the power had taken such precautions. Before our eyes had already passed hundreds of thousands of strong, young, full-blooded lives, more than once transports of Russians and Poles and also Gypsies, who knew they were being led to their death, and no one tried to resist or to wage combat, all went like sheep to the slaughter. Only two exceptions can be noted in those 16 months. One was in a transport from Białystok, when a bold and courageous young man threw himself at the guards with knives and stabbed several of them, drawing blood, before being gunned down as he fled. The second case—to which I bow my head in deep respect and honor—was the case of the "Warsaw transport." Jews from Warsaw who had become American citizens and some who were American by birth, had been kept all together in an internment camp in Germany and were to be sent to Switzerland and put under the protection of the Red Cross. But the great and "highly cultured" power, instead of sending them to Switzerland, brought the American citizens here to the fires of the crematorium. It was then that the heroic act took place, when a courageous young woman, a dancer from Warsaw, grabbed the revolver of *Oberscharführer* Quackernack[9] of Auschwitz's "political section" and shot the "*Rapportführer*," the notorious bandit, *Unterscharführer* Schillinger.[10]

Her deed inspired courage in the other brave women, who slapped the faces of the enraged, savage beasts, the uniformed S.S., and pelted them with bottles and other such objects.

Those were the only transports where there were cases of resistance, for those were people who knew they had nothing to lose. But hundreds of thousands went knowingly like sheep to the slaughter. That was why today's preparations caused us such amazement. We assumed that "they" had certainly heard rumors concerning the Czech Jews who, having already spent seven months in the camp together with their families, surely knew by now what was taking place here and would not let themselves be taken so easily. That is why they were preparing with all the technical means at their disposal to combat these people, who might have the audacity to refuse to go to their death and pose some resistance to the "innocent" criminals.

Monday at noon they send us back to the block to rest so we could return to work with renewed energy. Nearly the whole block—140 men (after the "separation" of the 200)—will have to handle this transport today, as both crematoria, I and II,[11] will be working at full speed.

The plan is set forth with full military precision. We, the most unfortunate victims of our people, are to be thrown into the battlefront against our own sisters and brothers. We are to be in the front line, so that if the victims do resist, they will throw themselves at us, while the "heroes and fighters of the great power" will stand behind us with machine guns, grenades and rifles—and shoot from there.

One day passed, then a second and a third, and Wednesday came and today is the day finally chosen for the arrival of the transport. The transport had been put off for two specific reasons. It seems that in addition to strategic preparations, a certain moral assurance was also needed. The other reason is that the "power" intentionally seeks to carry out the greatest killings on Jewish holidays—that was what caused them to murder the victims on Wednesday night, when Jews were celebrating Purim. In those three days, the "power," cold-blooded murderers and criminals, well-trained and bloodthirsty cynics, used every possible ruse in order to mask the reality, to confuse their minds so that they should not "realize" what was happening and penetrate into the dark and evil thoughts of the smiling, so-called "cultured" representatives of the power.

And the deception began:

The first rumor "they" spread was that the five thousand Czech Jews would be sent to another "work" camp[12] and had therefore to prepare their identity papers. Each according to his profession or vocation, without distinction between men and women up to 40 years of age. As for the rest, the older people, also without distinction of sex, and women with young children, would remain together as they had until now, families would not be torn apart. Those were the first opium pills, which deceived the frightened mass and diverted their attention from the tragic reality.

The second deception was that all the possessions people owned must be taken with them on the trip, and the "power," for its part, gave double rations to all those who were going on the trip.

Then they thought up yet a third hoax, sadistic and diabolical. They let out a rumor that until March 30, for various reasons, there could be no correspondence with Czechoslovakia, and anyone who wanted to receive packages, as they had until now, had to write letters to their friends, predated up until March 30, and hand them over to the "power," who would send them on so that they could continue to get their packages as before. None of them realized, none could have imagined, that a "power" could be so vile, so shameless as to invent these abject criminal swindles, and in combat against whom? Against an unprotected, unarmed mass, whose only strength is their own will, empty-handed, weaponless.

This whole well-planned scheme was certainly the best way to lull the victims, to paralyze these clear-sighted and realistic people. All, with no distinction of age or sex, let themselves be captured through the illusion that they would be taken somewhere to work and then—when the bandits felt that the "chloroform" had worked "properly," only then did they proceed to the first phase of the extermination operation.

They separated the families, ripped them apart, men separate and women separate, old apart and young apart, and in this way lured them into the trap, into the nearby camp still standing empty. Into the cold wooden barracks they were lured, the naive victims, each group led in separately and then locked in behind the boarded-up doors.

The first phase of the procedure was successful. They were disturbed, confused, incapable of logical thinking, for even when they had found their bearings, realized that they had been brought here to die, they were still helpless, without even the strength to think of struggle and resistance. Every brain, every mind—once they sobered up from the opium of illusion—now had a new problem. A full-blooded vigorous young man, a full-blooded young woman, now began to think of their father and mother. Who knows what is happening to them. The young men full of strength and courage, now also numb with sorrow, sat there and thought about their young wives and the children who just today had been torn away from them. Every impulse of struggle and resistance was instantly drowned out by each one's individual pain. Each was a prisoner of his own family misfortune, and this dulled and paralyzed any thinking or reasoning about the general situation that he himself is a part of. And those who when they were free had formed a young, energetic and combative mass now remained sitting motionless and resigned, dejected and shattered.

On the first step to the grave, these five thousand victims made the step with no resistance.

The diabolical deception, long practiced and well thought out, was here once again a success.

Led to Their Death

Wednesday, March 8, 1944, the night of Purim, when the fortunate Jews in those countries where they still live were in their synagogues and prayer houses or other places to celebrate the great holiday, the national symbol, the eternal miracle of Purim, they exchanged wishes that a speedy end should come to the Haman of modern times.

At the same time in Auschwitz-Birkenau 140 Jews of the *Sonderkommando* marched out, also headed for a place, but not a synagogue, nor a place of celebration, to observe the holiday, to honor the great Purim miracle.

They went like mourners, with heads deeply bowed in sorrow. There emanated from them a deep sadness and woe that also affected all the other Jews of the camp. For the path they walk is the way to the crematorium, to the Hell of the Jewish people. And the holiday they will soon celebrate is not that of the Jews returning from death to life—but the holiday of a people of pirates carrying out the age-old sentence, now renewed and strengthened by their god.

Soon we will be witnesses, with our own Jewish eyes we will have to watch our own destruction, as five thousand full-blooded, glowing, quivering lives of women and children, men, old and young, people with no distinction of sex or age, will soon be driven by hardened criminals, armed with rifles, grenades and machine guns, and with the aid of their constant companions, their wild four-footed partners, the mad dogs, will be chased and murderously beaten until, stunned and confused, they run unthinking into the arms of death.

And we, their own brothers, will have to lend a hand to this, to take them off the trucks, lead them to the bunker, strip them naked. And then, once they are completely ready, help accompany them to the bunker—to the grave—of death.

When we arrived at that great Hell called Crematorium I,[13] they, the representatives of power, were already there and preparing for battle. A great many S.S. arrived, in a state of readiness for war. Fully loaded rifles and grenades at their sides. Round and round the crematorium they walked, the well-armed soldiers, placed in such a position that whatever happened, all would be ready for battle. Trucks were positioned in every corner, their lights shining on the great battlefield. And a special truck with ammunition also stood by, in case they needed more bullets against the enemy, their mighty enemy . . .

Ah, if you, citizen of the great free world, could see this scene, you would stand in amazement, thinking that there in that building with the big, tall chimneys are men as big as giants who can fight like the devil, so heavily armed are they. Men who can conquer whole worlds, decimate strong armies. You would think that surely they are getting ready, those great heroes who have challenged the world power, to do battle with the enemy who wants to rob them of their land, their people and all they possess.

You would surely be disappointed if you were to wait a little longer and see with your own eyes just who that great enemy, that mighty adversary, is, against whom they will pit their brutal strength today.

Do you know against whom they are preparing for battle? Against our people of Israel. Soon they will come, Jewish mothers with babes pressed to their breast, or leading grown children by the hand and, frightened and helpless, they will look up at the "chimneys." Fresh young girls will jump from the trucks and they will wait for a mother or a sister, to go together into the bunker.

And men too, young and old, fathers and sons, will come here or to that other Hell, Crematorium II, also to be driven to their death.

This is the great enemy on whom the pirate has declared war. They are "afraid," the bandits, that one among the thousands of victims may refuse to fall like a fly, will perhaps have the courage to commit some deed before dying. It is this unknown, unidentified hero that they are afraid of, against him have they armed themselves with their "cultured" rifles.

Everything is ready. Seventy men from our commando have also been positioned as guards in the area of the fenced-off crematorium. And behind us—outside the fence—they stand with their guns ready, barrels pointed at the victims.

Autos and motorcycles speed back and forth, rush "here" and "there," making sure everything is still in order. Dead silence reigns in the camp. Every living thing has vanished, disappeared into the wooden graves. Now in the still of night new footsteps are heard. Helmeted soldiers are now marching, fully armed as if they were on a battlefield. For today is the first time that military troops have come into the camp at night, when all are asleep, lying guarded behind barbed wire, behind fences. A state of war has been declared in the camp.

All the living must now sit perfectly still in their cage, though all are aware—for it has happened often, and lately all the time—that victims are led to their death in full daylight, openly for all to see, and everyone sees, everyone watches as they go to their death. Only today have they chosen to do it this way, out of fear, out of terror. Only the night, the sky and stars, the shining moon—their eyes the devil cannot mask. And they alone will witness what the devil does here tonight.

In silence, in the secret silence of the night, the sound of trucks is heard. They are entering the camp, bringing the victims. The dogs bark, vicious, savage. They, the constant partners, are ready to throw themselves at a victim. Loud shouts ring out from the drunken officers and soldiers who stand at readiness.

There were also prisoners who came, Germans and Poles, common criminals who willingly offered their help for the celebration, and all together, the gang of devils and the criminals, will load them onto the trucks and take them to the crematorium.

The victims are locked in mortal fear, their hearts beating wildly. Sitting in great tension, they hear everything that is happening. Through the slits of their graves they see those murderers, those robbers, waiting with the trucks to rob them of their lives. They know it will not be long now, that even here in the dark graves where they would now be willing to live forever, they will not let them stay. They will rip them violently from this place and take them somewhere, send them off to the devil in his Hell.

All at once, the desperate mass is seized by a terrible shudder and in stunned tension they all remain dumb. Rooted to the spot as if dead. They hear the footsteps coming closer and their hearts gave a bound. The nailed-on board of the first grave is ripped off. Until now, that nailed-on board has been for them, the victims, a barricade, a means of protection. For as long as that board was still in place, they were still separated from death, and there beat somewhere deep down a hope that they would remain forever in that cage—until freedom would come to them here in their prison.

And now the doors open wide and the victims remain standing motionless, looking in terror at the beasts and instinctively they begin to draw away, as from a ghost, deeper into the grave. They would have liked to run away somewhere, to flee to where the barbaric eyes will not find them.

They are terrified seeing face-to-face those who have come to take their lives. But the dogs began to bark ferociously and to throw themselves at the victims, while another wild beast, a Pole, a German, brings down his club and cracks open the head of a young Jewish girl. And the desperate mass, which has been pressed together in one solid clump, now gradually began to separate—until it falls to pieces. Resigned, dejected and shattered, they began to run toward the trucks to avoid being bitten by a mad dog or beaten by an enraged beast. And more than one falls, while running with a child, and already the cursed earth began to drink the warm blood of a young Jewish child.

The victims stand in the trucks, ready to leave, and look around, searching as if for something they had lost. One young woman has a feeling, perhaps her beloved husband will come to her from somewhere—a mother searches in the tragic night, perhaps her young son will come. A young girl in love searches too, looks around at the densely packed trucks, perhaps in one of them she will see her loved one.

They cast nervous glances at the beautiful world, at the stars and moon moving majestically across the skies. They look back at the grave, empty now, in which they were once enclosed. Ah, if only they would let them go back there! They know, they feel, that the truck is unsteady ground and will not hold them long. Their eyes wander over there, through the barbed wire of the camp, where they still were yesterday. Back there still stand the frightened Czech families, who look out through the slits, watching their sisters and brothers being led off somewhere. In the glow of moonlight their eyes meet. Their hearts beat rhythmically in fear and terror. In the still of night is now heard a word of farewell from the sisters and brothers, friends and acquaintances who still sit in the camp and wait for the end, to the sisters and brothers, fathers and mothers already standing in the trucks, soon to go to their death.

This second procedure the devil has also carried out successfully and it has placed the victims on the second step to the grave.

The Victims Arrive

They move off. All is still tense . . . They, the murderers, still have the last orders to give. Our eyes turn now to that corner, to the point to which the sound of the wheels is drawing near.

We hear again the familiar sound of motorcycles moving and the trucks driving rapidly in pursuit. The front lines of the victims have already arrived. We can see from afar the bright headlights of the trucks, moving ever closer to us.

They are on the move. They are coming. We can see, see from afar, the shadows of human lives. To our ears come the soft moans and cries that escape from their hearts.

Now the victims see the truth, the reality—they are being taken to their death. The last hope, the last ray, the last spark has been extinguished. They look around at the world, watching it like a film passing before their eyes. Their gaze wanders in every direction, they would like to capture it all.

There from afar glitters to them their native land, so near they could see it every day. From the distance the high mountains adorned with white crowns brought them every day a greeting from their beloved home. Oh, you dearest mountains. You lie there sleeping peacefully and dreaming carefree in the light of the moon, and we, your loving children, whose lives were bound with yours, must perish from the world. How many golden days, how much joy and happiness, how many magical pages you have written in our lives. How much love and tenderness we enjoyed through you. How many nights like this one we spent in your arms and drank from the springs that will forever bubble forth—and for whom? Now they are taking us away from you.

And there, far beyond the mountains, stands a home, lonely and forlorn, and waits in solitude, for them, her unfortunate children, to come back.

Ah, their home, their warm and loving home, winks to them, calls out to them, her devoted children.

And here! Where are they being taken? The world is so beautiful, so splendid, so tempting, she calls them to her, she rouses them to life, wakes the desire to live. With thousands of threads they are bound to her, the wonderful, the great wide world. She stretches out her arms to them and in the still of night a call is heard from her to them: my children, my devoted ones! I love you so deeply, come to me. There is room enough here for everyone, great treasures I have long hidden for you. My springs bubble up forever, to nourish all equally with no distinction of strength or power. For you and because of you I was indeed created.

And they, the dear devoted children, now yearn for you, beloved world, they cannot take leave of you, for they are all young, healthy, fresh and courageous, full of life and charm. They want to live, for that indeed they all were born.

All the victims hold on tenaciously with hands and teeth, clasp their arms around the world, sink their teeth into life, like a child who clasps the mother they are tearing away from him. And here, with no fault and for no reason, they want to tear them violently away from their dear devoted world.

If only they could stretch out their arms until they were huge, and with those huge arms hug the whole world, with sky and stars and moon, with the wonderful mountains, the cool earth, the trees and grass, all that exists in the world, hug it and press it close to their hearts — how happy they would be.

If they could stretch their bodies over the whole vast world and warm the cold earth with the fire of their hearts and soften her hard spine with their hot tears and kiss all the limbs of their vast and beautiful world.

Ah, if they could only drink her in all at once, drink in the world and life, and sate their hunger and slake their thirst and forever still the hunger, the thirst for life. Ah, if they could embrace the shadow children, the unfortunate victims who still sit in the graves and wait their turn for death to come to them — how good it would feel, how good! In these last minutes they will spend on the earth, they yearn to kiss, caress and love all that lives, all that exists.

They feel, they sense, that these trucks that speed so quickly, and the autos and motorcycles that surround them, all are slaves of the devil, rushing now with noise and clamor to bring the victims they have captured to their god.

Now they are leading them before the world, slinking with them through life, for the way to death — it must go through life. They feel the last minutes are approaching, the film will soon reach its end, they look anxiously in all directions, their gaze reaches into every corner. They look for something in this world, they want to take something from her, to snatch up one last small thing before their death.

And perhaps one of them has a thought — a bolt of lightning through a darkened brain — a thought of escape, and the eyes look into the night for a way out, a way somewhere to escape from death.

The noise grows louder, the headlights already shine on the huge building that is Hell.

They Are Here

The unfortunate victims have arrived. The trucks come to a stop. Their hearts are frozen. They stand in helpless terror, resigned, and dejected and look around at the space, at the building, in which their world, their young lives, their quivering bodies will soon vanish forever.

They cannot understand what they want from them, the dozens of officers with silver and gold epaulets with shiny revolvers and grenades at their side.

Why must they stand here like condemned thieves, surrounded by helmeted soldiers, and from behind the trees and barbed wire by the light of the moon they see shining gun barrels pointed at them. Why? Why? Why are so many headlights shining? Is it too dark tonight? Is the light of the moon too dim?

They stand stupefied, helpless and resigned. They have seen the actual truth before their eyes, the abyss stands open and they are already sinking into it. They feel, they sense, that all, this life, these fields, trees, all that lives and exists — is vanishing, sinking into the depths together with them. The stars go out, the skies grow dark, the moon ceases to shine, the world is ending with them together. And they, the unfortunate victims, all they want is to sink, to vanish as quickly as possible into the sea.

They throw away their bundles — all that they took on the "trip," they have no need of any more things.

They let themselves be taken down from the truck without resistance — and fall fainting like mown grass into our arms. Here, take me, brother dear, take me by the hand and lead me down the short path that is left between life and death. We lead them tenderly, our beloved sisters, we hold them by the arms, we go in silence step by step, our hearts beating in rhythm. We suffer and bleed along with them and we feel that each step we take is a step further from life, a step closer to death. And before going down into the deep bunker, before they take the first step to the grave, they give one last look at the sky and moon—and a deep sigh escapes instinctively from both our hearts together. And in the moonlight you can see tears shining on our sisters being led to their death and a tear freezes on the brother who leads her.

In the Undressing Room

The large underground room, with twelve columns supporting the weight of the building above, is now brightly lit with electric lights. Around the walls, around the columns—they long ago installed benches and nailed on hangers for the victims' belongings. On the first column, a plaque in several languages explains that they are in a "bath" and must undress to disinfect their clothing.

Now that we are here with them, we stand stock-still and look at them. They know all, understand all, know that this is not a bath, but a corridor that leads to the grave.

The room fills up more and more. Trucks arrive with new victims, and the "room" swallows them up. We stand around in confusion and cannot find a word to say to them, though this is not the first time. We have had many transports before this one and scenes like this we have seen many times before. And yet we feel weak and powerless, as if we too could easily fall, together with them.

We are all stunned. Under the old and tattered clothing their bodies are full of charm and enchantment. Heads with curly hair, black, brown, blond and a few gray also and from them, large deep dark eyes look out at us full of magic. We see before us bubbling, quivering, passionate lives, all in full bloom, brimming with sap and nourished with the waters of life like flowers, like roses still growing in a garden. Swollen with rain, damp with morning dew. In the sunlight the sparkling drops of their flower eyes wink to us like pearls.

We do not dare, cannot find in ourselves the courage, to tell these dear sisters of ours that they must undress completely. For the clothing they wear is still the coat of armor within which their lives reside. The moment they take off their clothes and stand there naked, they will lose their last protection, their last foothold, the last thing they still have to hold on to. We haven't the heart to tell them they must undress quickly. Let them stand one moment more, one instant longer, in their armor, in their mantle of life.

The first question on everyone's lips is whether their men have come here yet. They want to know if their husband, father, brother or loved one is still alive. Or are their stiff dead bodies already lying somewhere where the flames are burning them until not a trace remains. And she herself is left abandoned, alone with her orphaned child. Has she already lost forever her father, brother, lover. Why then, for what reason should she go on living? Tell me, brother—says another, who in her mind is already resigned to loss of life and world. In a courageous voice she asks us boldly: "Tell us, brother, how long does this death last? Is it hard, or does it come easily?"

But we don't let them stand there very long. The murderous beasts make themselves felt. The air is filled with the screams of the drunken bandits who cannot wait to sate their bestial eyes that thirst for the nakedness of these, my beautiful beloved sisters. Blows rain down over shoulders, over heads. The clothing falls quickly from their bodies. Some are ashamed and want to hide somewhere not to show their nakedness. But here there is no corner, here there is no shame. Morality and ethics—together with life they go to the grave.

Some fling themselves at us, throw themselves into our arms as if drunk with love and beg us with shame in their eyes to undress them. They want to forget everything, to think about nothing. With the world of yesterday, with her morals and principals and ethical concepts, they have settled their accounts, said their goodbyes on the first step to the grave. Now, on the threshold of annihilation, while they are still on the surface of life and the body alone still feels, still senses, still has the impulse to find one more time some joy in life, they want to give it everything, the last pleasure, the last joy that can still be had from life—they want before death to give it some satisfaction, some gratification. This young body, quivering with life's blood, they want the hand of a strange man, the nearest, the most beloved here, to touch, to caress their body now. They want to feel in that caress the hand of a husband or lover who would have touched or caressed the body burning with passion. They want to feel that intoxication now, my dear, my lovely sisters. And their flaming lips stretch toward us with love and want to kiss with passion as long as the lips still live.

More trucks arrive and more victims pour into the large room. From the naked ranks, many tear themselves away and fall wildly screaming and crying on those who have just arrived—these are children who have caught sight of their mothers, who kiss them, hug them, rejoice that they are here together again. For a child is glad that a mother, a mother's heart, will go with her to death.

They all undress completely and stand together in rows, some crying, others still, unmoving. One tears out the hair from her head and talks deliriously to herself. When I go up to her I hear only these words: "Where are you, my beloved, why don't you come to me, I am still young and beautiful." Those standing nearby say that she went mad yesterday in the prison.

Others talk calmly and quietly to us: "Oh, we are so young. We want to live, we have taken so little from life." They do not try to ask us for anything, for they know, they understand, that we too are victims like themselves. But they do talk, just for talk's sake, for their hearts are overflowing and before their death they want to tell their pain to a living person.

A group of women sits kissing and hugging, they are sisters who have found each other and now they pour themselves together to form one knot, one mass.

Over there, a mother sits naked on a bench with her daughter on her lap. A child, a girl not yet fifteen. She holds the child's head to her breast and kisses all her limbs. And hot tears stream down on the young flower. A mother mourns her child, whom she will soon lead with her own hands to death.

In the room, the vast grave, now shines a new light. On one side of the great Hell, they stand in lines, the women's bodies alabaster white, and wait, wait for the doors of Hell to open and give them passage to the grave. We the men stand facing them, fully clothed and motionless, and watch. We cannot comprehend, is this scene a reality or is it merely a dream? Have we somehow fallen into a world of naked women, where the devil will soon play his devilish game with them? Or are we in some kind of museum, in an artist's studio, and the women, of various ages and all sorts of expressions, with their quiet tears and soft moans, have come here specially for the artist, to serve as models.

And we all wondered why these women, unlike so many other transports, are so calm. Many even seem courageous and carefree, as if nothing were about to happen to them. It amazed us that they can look death in the face with such bravery, such calm. Don't they know what awaits them? We look at them with pity, for we see before our eyes a new and horrific picture, how all these palpitating lives, vibrant worlds, all the sounds, the noise that emanates from them, in a few hours all will be dead and still. Their mouths forever mute. Their sparkling eyes that now enchant with their magic, will stare blankly in one direction—looking for something in the eternity of death.

All these seductive bodies, now abloom with life, will soon be lying stretched out on the ground in dirt and filth like repulsive creatures, their pure alabaster bodies covered in human filth.

From the pearly mouth—teeth and flesh together will be ripped out and much blood will spill.

From that chiseled nose—two streams will run, red, yellow or white.

And that face, all pink and white—will turn red, blue or black from the gas. The eyes will be so red with blood that you will not recognize that it's the same woman who stands here now. And from that head with locks of wavy hair, two cold hands will cut off the hair and from the ears and hands remove the rings and earrings.

Then two strange men will put on gloves or wrap cloths around their hands, for these snow-white forms that shine so brightly here, will be so repulsive to look at—they will not want to touch them with bare hands. They will drag her, this lovely young blossom, over the cold, filthy cement floor. And the body will sweep with it all the dirt it finds along the way.

And like some disgusting carcass, it will be heaved and thrown aside. And tossed onto the lift and sent up to the fires of that Hell and in minutes these bodies, fat and fleshy—will be reduced to ash.

Already we see and feel their final end. I look at them, the throbbing lives that here take so much space, each one a whole world—and in minutes—another image passes before my eyes—I see a comrade pushing a wheelbarrow full of ashes toward the vast grave. I stand now near a group of women—ten or fifteen in number—and all of them, their bodies and their lives, will soon be in a single wheelbarrow. No trace, no substance will be left of all those standing here, all those who once made up entire cities, who had a place in the world, will soon be eradicated, pulled out by the roots—as if they had never, never been born. Our hearts are torn with pain. We feel, we suffer the torment of the passage from life to death.

Our hearts swell with sympathy. Oh, if we could sacrifice pieces of our own lives for our beloved sisters, how happy we would be. We want to press them to our aching hearts, kiss all their limbs, drink up all this life that is about to vanish. We will engrave deep in our hearts how they look now, all these palpitating lives, and deep in our hearts forever carry this image of these lives extinguished before our eyes. We are all prisoners in a nightmare of thoughts that hold us captive. They, the dear sisters, look at us bewildered, why are we so "upset" while they are so calm. They would so like to talk with us now: what will happen to them after this, after they are dead, but they are too shy, too hesitant to ask—and the secret remains concealed from them until the end.

All are standing now, the entire great naked mass, looking fixedly in one direction, and clearly a dark thought takes form in their minds.

There on the far side of the room lie all their possessions in one pile, all jumbled together, all the clothing they have just now thrown off. These belongings will not let them rest. Although they know they will have no need of them, still they are bound to them by many threads. They feel attached to them still—these garments that still hold the warmth of their bodies. There they lie, strewn about, here a dress, there a sweater, things that once warmed and clothed them. Ah, if only they could put them on once more, how good it would feel, how happy they would be. Is this really the way it is—is the situation so tragic, that their bodies will never again wear these things?

Is it true that they will really be forever abandoned here? That their owners will never come back to them?

Ah, these garments, already abandoned like orphans. Like witnesses, like an evil sign, an omen of the death that is coming soon.

Ah, who knows who will wear these garments next. One woman steps out of the ranks and picks up a silk scarf from under the foot of another who had stepped on it. She picks it up it quickly—and disappears back into the ranks. I ask her: Why do you need that scarf—it's a souvenir for me, answers the girl in a low voice. And will go with it to the grave.

The Death March

The doors open wide and Hell stands before the victims. In the small room leading to the grave stand aligned, as if for a military parade, representatives of the great power. The whole political section has come today to be present at the festivities. High-ranking officers whose faces we have not yet seen in the past sixteen months. Among them is also a woman, a woman S.S. officer, commandant of the women's camp. She has also come to attend the great "national celebration" where the children of our people will die.

I stand at one side and observe the two groups, the bandits, mass murderers—and my sisters, the unfortunate victims.

The march, the death march has begun. They walk bravely, proudly and with steady step, as if they were walking toward life. They do not break down even when they see the last place, the last corner, where the last act of their lives will soon play out. They stand firm, do not lose their footing—even when they see that they are already captives in the heart of Hell. They settled their accounts up there, with the world and with life, long before they arrived here. Back in prison all the threads that once bound them to life were cut.

That is how they can walk with such calm and composure and not break down even as they near the end. They march without pause, the naked full-blooded women. It seems an eternity that the march goes on, an eternity.

It seems that worlds, whole worlds have stripped naked here to walk this diabolical walk.

Mothers walk holding young children in their arms, leading others by the hand. They kiss their children now—a mother's heart has little patience, all along the way she kisses her child. Sisters walk arm in arm, fused into a single entity. In their walk to death they want to be together.

They cast sidelong glances at the officers standing there, not wanting to grant them one real look—no one begs, no one seeks pity for herself. They are conscious, the victims, they know that in them and in their hearts there is not a single drop of human conscience. They will not give them the satisfaction of begging in despair that they should spare the life of any one of them.

Suddenly the long train of naked bodies comes to a halt. A child walks out, a pretty nine-year-old with long blond, neatly plaited braids, hanging down her childish back like two golden straps. Behind her walks her mother, still quite bold, and now she stops and, looking at the officers, boldly and bravely begins to speak: Murderers, bandits, shameless criminals! Yes, today you will murder us, innocent women and children. On us, unarmed and unprotected, you cast the blame for this war, on me and on my child, it is we who brought the war on you.

Remember, bandits, with our blood you hope to cover your own defeats on the front. You have lost the war, it's certain now. You surely know of the huge setbacks you suffer daily on the eastern front. Remember, bandits, today you can do all you want, but a day will come, a day of vengeance. Great victorious Russia will avenge us and will cut your living bodies into pieces. Our brothers from the whole world will not rest until they have avenged our innocent blood.

Then, turning to the woman she says: You bestial woman, you too came here to see our misfortune. Remember! You too have a child, a family, you will not enjoy them for long. Living chunks we will tear from your body, and your child, like mine, will not live much longer. Remember, bandits! you will pay for it all—the whole world will wreak vengeance upon you. And she spit in their faces and ran with the child into the bunker. They stood there numb, not daring to look at one another. They had just heard a great truth that cut and tore and plucked at their bestial souls. They let her speak, although they knew what she would say, but they wanted to hear what she thought, what she had to say, a Jewish woman going to her death. Solemn and deep in thought they stand now, the murderers, the bandits. This woman, here in the grave, had torn the mask from their faces and shown them what the future, the very near future, held in store for them. They had all thought of this more than once, more than one black thought had clouded their minds, and now this Jewish woman had told them the truth. Unafraid, she had revealed to them the whole truth, the full reality.

But they are afraid to think too long, lest the truth they heard should penetrate too deep. And then, what would they have to live for? But no! The Führer, their god, has explained it otherwise, that victory is not on the battlefields of east and west, but . . . here in this bunker, here is victory. Here is the mighty enemy because of whom their blood is being shed now on all the fields of Europe. Marching here are our enemies, for whose sake the English planes are dropping bombs day and night and killing young and old.—Because of them, because of these naked women here, he has to be far from his home, and his child had to give his life there on the eastern front. No, the Führer, the god, is right. We must eradicate, exterminate them. When the naked women with their children are lying dead, that will be the decisive, the certain victory. Ah! if we could only do it faster, round them up, herd them together more quickly from the whole world, and drive them naked, like these naked women here, drive them into Hell. Ah! how good it would be. The cannons would stop their awful roar—the planes would no longer drop their bombs—and the war would come to an end. All would be peaceful in the world. The children would come home from far away and a new, happy life would begin for them. Just one obstacle still remains—these naked women here—the children of this people that are hidden somewhere, whom we cannot find to bring them here and strip them naked like these women, these enemies walking past us now. And the hand of a beast raised a whip and struck with murderous rage the naked bodies of the women.

Run faster, enemies, quickly into the bunker, into the grave, for your every step to the grave is a step closer to our victory. For the victory must come soon, must come quickly. We are paying too much on all the fronts,—run faster, you devil's children, do not linger on the way, for you are hindering our victory.

And row upon row they march, the naked young women. And the march stands still again. Now an attractive young blond girl speaks further to the bandits: You black criminals! You look at me with your thirsting animal eyes. You feast on the nakedness of my shapely body. Yes, it is your time now. In your civilian lives you could not even dream of such a sight. You criminals of the underworld, here you have found the perfect place to satisfy your sadistic eye. But not long will this pleasure last. Your game is over, you will never be able to murder all the Jews. And you will pay heavily for all this.—And all at once she springs out toward them and slaps three times the *Oberscharführer* Voss, the chief, the commandant of the crematoria. Clubs rain down upon her head and shoulders. She has entered the bunker with a broken head, from which the warm blood flows. The warm blood caresses her body, her face glows with joy. She is happy and content, feeling in her hand the pleasure of slapping the face of the notorious murderer and bandit. She has reached her final goal. And walks serenely to her death.

The Song from the Grave

In the large bunker stand thousands of victims, waiting for death. All at once, spontaneously, a song rings out. Once again the clique of superior officers stand transfixed. They cannot understand, they cannot grasp, how is it possible, that there in that bunker, in the heart of the grave, on the threshold of extinction, in the last moments of life, that people—instead of moaning, instead of weeping over their young lives about to be snuffed out—can raise their voices in song.

Perhaps the Führer is right after all, that they are devils, for how can a mere human be so carefree, brave and calm in the face of death.

The notes, the melody that now rises from that place is well known to all. Especially to them, the bandits, these sounds are like knives, like spears slashing into their hearts. What this mass of dead are singing now is the famous, the everywhere familiar, "*Internationale.*"

The *Internationale*, the anthem of the great Russian people — what they are singing now is the song of the powerful and victorious army.

The song tells them, reminds them, of the victories on the fronts won not by themselves, but by the others, by the Red Army. Against their will they find themselves carried away by the melody. Like a furious wave, the song sobers their muddled brains, clears their minds of their superstitious fanaticism and reminds them of all that is happening here.

The song forces them to leaf through the pages of a not-so-distant past and see the tragic and horrible reality. It reminds them that at the start of the war, the Führer-god explained and assured with his "ego" that in six weeks, all of Russia would lie under their boot and in Moscow the black swastika would be flying over Red Square. And they believed that the end would be as certain as the beginning.

And what happened, what suddenly came to pass?

The victorious European armies that had so quickly enslaved powerful peoples, armed with the greatest technical means and military skills, armies led by seasoned strategists, imbued with the profound belief in the almighty victory, proud of their ancient dream of Germany, "*Deutschland Über Alles*" — now lie broken, running in full retreat. From the highest peaks they fall into the deepest abyss. And all the earth is soiled by their blood and flesh. Where is their strength? Where their art, technique and strategy? How could they defeat all the others, but not these, not the Russians, a backward Asian people? Was it the force of internationalism that inspired them with supernatural strength, that forged their muscles into steel and turned their will into a storm that can destroy the world.

The melody of the song does not let them rest, it troubles them, shatters the certainty they felt up to now. Through the notes they hear the sounds of the marching armies who now with pride and strength stamp on the graves of their brothers over there. Through the notes they hear the shooting of the armies, the explosion of the dropping bombs. The melody grows stronger, the notes reach higher and higher. All are now carried away by the song which, like a stormy wave, breaks out of this place to pour out over the entire world, and in its might to wash away everything in its path.

Now they feel, now they perceive, this officer clique, representatives of the great strong power, how small, how worthless, how futile they are. It seems to them that the musical sounds are living beings that represent the two battling armies—one side winning with strength and greatness and the other, the one they represent here, standing numb and speechless, shivering with fear and dread.

The sounds come ever nearer to them, they feel them reaching, pushing into every corner, and wherever the sounds reach, the ground trembles beneath their feet. Soon there will be no place for them. And the ground, the only thing that was certain up to now, will also soon be drowned by the wave. Ah! The sounds, the melody, they speak of victory, they tell of a magnificent future. Already they see before their eyes, the victorious Red Armies running drunk with triumph through the streets of the Reich, cutting, trampling, burning, destroying everything that exists. Black thoughts run through their minds. Is that not the message of the song, that the vengeance that the Jewish woman here just now announced will become reality? Will they not soon have to pay for the singers of the song whose lives they are about to take? Who knows . . .

Hatikva

They breathed more freely, the gang of high-ranking officers, now that the echo of the last note had faded. But it didn't last long. A new song of faith and courage comes pouring out of their hearts. The mass now sings the national anthem. They sing the *Hatikva*. This song too is known to "them." More than once have they heard it. Now with pride and happiness the mass is singing the national anthem. Again they stand motionless, the officers' gang. This song too tells a story. It wakes, calls out to remember. The mass of the dead speak to them through this song, for with this song they have become bolder: You bandits, murderers of the world! You thought, you believed—you let yourselves be misled by your *Führer*, your god—that you would wipe out the people of Israel, that their extermination would be your victory. But now comes this song to tell them, to remind them, that victory over the people of Israel, this too they will never attain.

There are Jews living all over the world—in lands where their foot was unable to reach, but even in lands where their influence is still great, they can no longer have their way, for those people have sobered up and will no longer sacrifice innocent victims to your savage barbarity and bestial cruelty. The song reminds them that the long-martyred people of Israel will go on living and will build a future, build a home in that ancient land far away. The song reminds them, the song tells them that the illusion that so easily misled them, that "no Jew will exist in the world except in a museum," that no one will be left to demand revenge—or himself take revenge—this song comes to recall that Jews do live in the world, after the storm they will come together here from all corners of the world and each will look for his mother, his sister and brother and they will ask us—where were they murdered, the children of our people?! They will ask, where are the sisters and brothers, those who are soon about to die, those who now sing this song? They will assemble huge armies whose sole aim will be revenge. They will exact payment for all the victims, for the innocent blood that you are about to spill and for the blood you have already spilled.

The *Hatikva* will not let them rest, it wakes, it calls, it weaves around them a deep melancholy.

The Anthem of Czechoslovakia

Today's transport stretches on interminably for them. Hours have turned into years. Dejected and broken they stand, the great bandit-gang. They had hoped and believed that this day would fill them with emotions of pure joy, to see a mass of thousands of young Jewish victims struggling in pain and torment. And instead they found a mass singing, practically carefree, laughing death in the face. So where is the revenge? Where is their punishment? They hoped that they could sate their thirst for Jewish blood with terrible suffering, and instead the mass stands there bold and calm, singing these songs which have become for them like punishing rods that penetrate their flesh, that cut deep into their bestial hearts and will not let them rest. It seems to them that they, the strong and mighty bandits, are now the accused, and the naked mass is taking revenge on them—revenge through song.

Now they sing the anthem of the enslaved Czechoslovak people. They were citizens of that nation. They had lived like all the citizens of that nation, in peace and security, until the barbarians came and enslaved the entire people. They have nothing against the Czech people, they know they bear no guilt for their misfortune, for their destruction. They feel great sympathy for them, for their pain and suffering, and together with the whole Czech nation they await the freedom soon to come, though they know they will not see or hear it. But in their imagination they foresee how it will look, the near future of a reawakened Czech people. And now they sing that anthem that will soon be heard over the entire land. From high mountains and deep valleys will ring the echo of the new life, the reawakened freedom. From the deep grave they send a greeting to the Czech people, that with renewed energy they should stand ready for the fight.

The song reminds them, the song tells them, that all the peoples of the world will soon be liberated and among them Czechoslovakia. Everywhere the flags of freedom will fly for all the peoples. And what will become of them, the oppressors and persecutors, who in all of Europe have shed so much blood of so many innocent people? On that day when all the small, enslaved nations will reawaken to life, then the great and powerful nation will lie enslaved and broken under the yoke. That day, when the world celebrates universal freedom—will be the day of their enslavement. On that day of peace when on the streets of all of Europe, people will kiss and hug, on that day they, the criminals and murderers, will sit in hiding somewhere in fear and terror of the great day of Judgment—the day of reckoning with the world. At that time, when all the peoples will rebuild the ruins, then will they feel even more deeply their misfortune.

That future day of universal freedom will be for them a day of great destruction. All the shattered and ruined nations will come to them and demand that they should pay for everything, for they alone and no one else brought this misfortune on the world.

Ah! these terrible songs that will not let them rest—they have spoiled their great celebration.

The Partisan Song

The last buses begin to arrive. The women's transport is almost over. A minor "incident" has taken place. She won't let herself be undressed, a well-developed young woman from Slovakia. She refuses to enter the bunker with the deadly gas. She shouts, she screams, she calls the other women to battle. "Shoot me!"—she cries out to them and they, the bandits, willingly oblige. They do her that favor. They took her back up to the moonlit earth and two men with yellow armbands twisted her arms behind her back. And the fresh vibrant young girl fought hard, with convulsive movements of all her limbs. In the still of night a brief crack rang out and a wild beast with a highly cultured bullet quickly robbed her of her life. A young tree was felled, a dull thud was heard and her heavy body hit the cold earth. A stream of blood spread over the ground and her eyes looked fixedly toward the moon, who continued on her course.—There was a life and is no more. A few minutes ago she strained, shouted, cried out and called for struggle and resistance, and now she lies stretched out, arms spread outward as if she would embrace the entire world.

Down below in the huge bunker they are still singings songs. Their voices shout down all anxiety, drown out every fear that tries to take possession of their heart and soul. Now they sing the Partisan song, which like a spear pierces deep into their hearts. For the partisans are the heroic freedom fighters from whose ranks many martyrs fall each day. In the future they will be the heavy hand of punishment, when the defeated armies flee in terror to hide in fields and woods, somewhere in a pit, in valleys amid thick trees and bushes, and they will come from their hiding places and pay them back for everything. They will take revenge for the suffering and hardships that they themselves endured because of them. With bloody cruelty they will take revenge for the innocents, fathers and mothers, sisters and brothers, who are being murdered here. For these, these thousands of lives, wiped out here today. And then, when the storm is over, they will come from everywhere, will come to the surface from all the earthen graves to form great battalions of revenge, revenge-takers. And they will be witnesses before the world of the horrific, sadistic, barbaric deeds that they inflicted on millions of people all over the world. They will lead the victorious armies to the fields and woods and show them the places where the hundreds of thousands of innocent victims lie, those who were buried alive in deep graves or those burned alive in fire. And may they for all, for all, take revenge.

Barely has the last woman entered the bunker when the door slams shut and is hermetically locked and bolted so that no air can enter. The victims stand as if stuffed into a cask, already suffocating from heat and thirst. They feel, they know, that very soon, one more minute, one more instant, and the end will come. And yet they go on singing. Now they want to forget it all. On the waves of music they want to hold themselves afloat, on those sounds and through those sounds, through those high sweet notes they want to swim the short distance from life—to death.

And they, the high-ranking officers still stand and wait, wait until they have breathed their last breath. One more act, the last, the noblest, they still have left to see, when the thousands of victims will sway like grasses in a storm and when the last, the very last trace of life is gone—then they will see the "most beautiful" scene of all, when the 2,500 victims will fall like chopped down trees, each interwoven with the others. And that will be the last act of their lives, of their world.

Pouring in the Gas

Now in the stillness of the night, the sound of two pairs of footsteps. Two silhouettes stand out in the moonlight. They put on their masks to pour in the mortal gas.[14] The two cans they carry will soon kill the thousands of victims there. With quiet steps they walk toward the bunker, toward the depths of Hell. They walk calmly, cool and sure of themselves, as if they were about to carry out a holy task. Their hearts cold as ice, their hands—never a sign of trembling, they walk with guiltless steps to each "eye" of the deep bunker and pour in the gas and cover the open "eye" with a heavy lid so that the gas cannot escape. Through the peepholes they can hear the deep, agonized groans of the mass inside now wrestling with death, but their hearts are not moved. Deaf and dumb, cold, frozen they walk to the second "eye" and once more pour in the gas. Up to the last "eye" they walk and then the masks come off. And they walk back, proud, brave and happy to have performed an important duty for their people, for their nation. They are now one step closer to victory . . .

The First Victory

Already they are going up the stairs, the gang of high-ranking officers, happy and satisfied that an end has come at last to their "singing," to their "life." They can breathe freely once again. Now they will flee from this place, flee the ghosts, and the sense of doom that torments them from the depths of Hell. This was the first time in their "death-practice" that they experienced such psychological depression, being under such tension for hours on end and feeling as if they were criminals, being punished with fiery rods whose pain they still feel now. And punished by whom? By that cursed diabolical band of Jews. But thank God, it is over at last and they are free. The mood of threat and punishment has finally abated. The victims lie now rigid in death. And they begin gradually to free themselves from the deep spiritual nightmare and to feel the pleasure of the great victory. They walk proudly from their first battlefield here, happy and in good spirits. Twenty-five hundred lives of the formidable enemy who hinders them in the combat for their land, for their people, now lie dead and rigid. Now they have "enabled" the combat forces on the eastern and western fronts to advance more easily to victory.

The Second Front

Now they all move over "there," to the other crematorium.[15] The officers, the guards, and we go, too. The front line is put in place once again. All stands again in military readiness. And here even stronger security measures have been established, for if the first encounter with the victims came off calmly with no fighting and no resistance, if the battle was won without a casualty, here on the second front something could go wrong, for the victims who are about to arrive are, after all, a mass of strong young men. In a short while we hear the familiar sound of the truck wheels. "Here they come!" shouts the commandant. Now everything must be ready. In the still of night we hear the soldiers, for the last time before battle, cocking the rifles and verifying the machine guns, to make certain they will function properly when the time comes that they may have to do their "work."

The glaring headlights once again light up this place of death. And by the shine of their lights and the shine of the moon, we see again the gleam of many gun barrels, held in the hands of the "great power" that is waging battle against the helpless and unarmed people of Israel. From behind the trees and barbed wire, fierce-looking faces peer out. The moonlight casts a terrifying glow on the "death's head" helmets of the "heroes" who wear them with such pride. Like devils, like demons, like murderers and criminals, they stand in position in the still of night and wait, wait with fear and hunger for the prey that is about to come.

Disappointment

Everyone is tense, "we" as well as "they." The representatives of the power stand in fear and terror. They tremble lest the desperate mass of men should choose, at the threshold of the grave, to fall as heroes. If that happened, a misfortune might befall one of them, too. And who knows who it might be? Perhaps he himself could be the victim!

We too feel anxious as, with beating hearts, we take them off the trucks. We hope, we believe, that it could happen today, that this could be the decisive day that we too impatiently await. That this could be the moment when the desperate mass will, at the threshold of the grave, raise the flag of battle and we, hand in hand with them, will enter into this unequal combat. We will not look to see if it is useless or if we might thereby gain our freedom or our lives. It would be for us the greatest chance to reach a heroic end to our unhappy lives. For an end must surely come to the horror and tragedy. But we just stood there disappointed. Instead of throwing themselves like wild animals at us and at them, for the most part they came down from the trucks calmly and peacefully, looking around at the broad space. They fixed their gaze upon that building—that vast Hell—and with arms hanging and heads bowed in resignation, they walked quietly toward the grave. They all ask about the women, if they have already been here. Their hearts beat only for them, to whom they are still bound by thousands of unbreakable threads. Their flesh and blood, their heart and soul are still bound in one organism and they still don't know, the father, husband, brother, lover or friend, whether their wife and child, sister, bride, loved one or friend, the thousands of lives they still think about, worry about, to whom their lives are still so attached—already lie in that same building, in that deep grave dead and motionless, forever still. They don't want to believe, when we tell them the truth, that the thread binding them to their women has already long been severed.

Some quickly throw their parcels to the ground. They know, they recognize the building that spits out victims every day, from the chimneys up to the heavens high above. Others stand motionless or whistle a little tune or look thoughtfully and longingly at the moon and stars, then walk straight down to the deep bunker with a sigh. And before long they all were standing naked in the bunker and they went quietly to their death without struggle or resistance.

He and She

Heartrending scenes like this took place only at those times when a number of women, for whom there was no room in Crematorium I,[16] were brought to the men. Naked men run madly to the women, each one searching, looking for his wife, or mother, or a child, a sister, a familiar face. The few "happy" ones who found each other here, hold one another closely pressed and kiss each other passionately. In the middle of the large room you see horrendous sights, like that of a naked man embracing his wife, or a brother and sister who stand ashamed and kiss as they weep and walk "happily" together into the bunker.

A great number of women remain sitting all by themselves. Their husband, brother, or father was among the first to enter the bunker. A man thinks about his wife, child, mother, sister and does not know, poor soul, that somewhere in this same bunker, his wife stands naked among strange men, and searches their faces to see if among them she can find his beloved face. And so, seeking with longing, her eyes roam wild around.

Longing and seeking, a woman lies stretched out amid the mass of men. Her body is stretched out with her face toward the mass, and she searches among them till her last breath, looking for her husband.

And there by the edge, by the bunker wall, stood her husband who could not rest. He rose on tiptoe, he too searching for his naked wife, there amid the mass of men. And when he noticed her and his heart began to beat faster and his arms stretched out to her and he tried to make his way to her and loudly called her name—then the gas poured into the room and so he remained, frozen in place, his arms stretched toward his wife, with open mouth and staring eyes. With her name on his lips, his heart gave out and his soul left his body.

Two hearts had beaten there in time, and in longing and seeking they expired.

Heil Hitler

Through the small window in the door of the grave, they, the "masters," can see for themselves the mass of men lying dead, felled by the deadly gas.

Happy and satisfied that the final victory is in their pockets, they walk out of the grave. Each of them can now calmly and safely go back home. The great enemy of their land and people has been wiped out, erased. Now everything will be possible once again. Their great god the Führer himself had said: every Jew killed is a step closer to victory. And here, in a few short hours, five thousand with one blow were brought to their death. Such a victory, such a triumph, without a victim, without a single casualty. Who else but these brilliant officers here can boast of such a glorious deed?

They take their leave with the raised hand salute, their "*heilig*"[17] greeting, and climb into their autos and head for home.

The autos hurry now, joyous and insolent, as they carry home from victory the great heroes of the world. Soon telephones will start to ring, each one will tell another about the great victory and triumph.

Until it reaches him, the Führer and god, the great news of the victory and triumph that was won here today. "Heil Hitler!"

At the Place of Death

The area has grown still. There are no more guards, no trucks full of ammunition, no searchlights. All at once everything has vanished. A dead silence has returned to God's world as if, from the depths of Hell, a silent wave of Death had spread over the world and lulled it to sleep, rocked the whole world to an eternal sleep of death. The moon again pursues her nightly course. The stars sparkle magically in the deep blue sky. Calm and still, the night floats into eternity as if nothing had happened in the world this day. The night, the moon, the sky and stars have swallowed deep into themselves the secret of what the devil accomplished this night, leaving no sign nor trace of the atrocities for the world to see.

In the moonlight nothing is visible on this place of death but some little shadowy mounds, abandoned bundles strewn about, witness to the life that once was. We see the outline of human shadows dragging a heavy burden along the ground to an open door. They heave the body in and walk back with quiet steps, to drag over another one and vanish with it through the open door. In the still of night is heard the bolting of a door, now they have been locked in, our brothers, our unfortunate brothers who will soon have to return to their work of death. Then footsteps are heard in the silence. It is the guard walking around the graveyard, keeping watch over the unfortunate brothers who go about their work in Hell, the work with their dead sisters and brothers. And the guard watches them so that they cannot run away from death.

In the Bunker

With trembling hands the brothers now turn the screws and lift the four bolts. The two doors open onto two vast graves. The air carries a wave of hideous death. They all stand numb as their eyes refuse to believe what they see. How long? How long had it taken? Before our eyes still hover the fresh and vibrant young men and women, our ears still ring with the last sound of their words. The look in their deep tear-filled eyes still follows us.

And what has suddenly become of them? The thousands of bubbling, bustling, singing lives now lie frozen in death. No sound, no word is heard, their mouths now mute forever. Their eyes transfixed, their bodies motionless. In the dead and frozen silence all that is heard is a faint, barely audible sound, that of a liquid trickling from all the openings of the dead bodies. It is the only moving thing in this vast dead world.

Our eyes are glued to the scene, hypnotized by the sea of naked dead bodies that has appeared before us. A naked world is there before our eyes, lying collapsed, entwined together in a tangled ball as if before their death the devil had deliberately led them in some diabolical game and laid them out in these poses. Here sit two bodies against a wall, their arms wrapped around each other. There only a piece of shoulder protrudes from the mass, the head and legs buried, squeezed between the other bodies. Here only an arm or leg is visible, sticking up in the air, the rest of the body submerged deep in a naked sea. You see only chunks of human bodies on the surface of a naked world.

In the great naked sea, heads now float into view. They lie on the surface of the naked waves. They look as if they are swimming in the deep vast sea and only the heads are seen above the abyss of nakedness.

The heads, black, brown or blond, are the only details that stick out from the naked mass.

Preparations for Hell

The sensitive heart must be deadened, numbed to every painful feeling. We must drown out in ourselves the horrible suffering that washes like a storm over every limb. We must transform ourselves into automatons that do not see or feel or understand.

Arms and legs set to work. There stands a group of comrades, each at his assigned task. With force we tug and pull the bodies from the tangled ball, one by a leg, one by an arm, whichever is more convenient. It looks as if they will fall apart from all the constant tugging. The body, once alabaster white, is then dragged across the cold dirty cement floor and like a broom it wipes up all the dirt, all the filth it picks up on the way. We take the smeared body and lay it face up. The frozen eyes look at you as if to ask: Brother, what will you do with me now? More than once you recognize a familiar face, someone you spent time with before coming here to the grave. Three men stand and prepare the body. One holds a cold pair of tongs and shoves it into the lovely mouth to look for gold teeth and if he finds one he rips it out taking some flesh with it. A second cuts the hair—tosses away the wavy tresses, the women's crown. And the third tears out the earrings, often drawing blood as they are ripped off. The rings that do not let themselves be taken easily are also torn off with tongs.

Next the body is given to the lift. Like logs, each held by two men, the bodies are thrown onto the lift. And when they number seven or eight, a signal is given with a stick and the lift goes up.

In the Heart of Hell

Up at the top of the lift stand four men. Two on one side of the lift place the bodies in the "reserve"-room, and two who drag the bodies straight to the ovens. They are laid out two by two at the mouth of every oven. Small children lie off to one side, thrown together in a heap—to be added to two adult bodies. They are placed on the iron "purification-board,"[18] then the mouth of Hell is opened and the board is slid into the oven. The hellish fire sticks out its tongues like open arms and swallows up the body like a treasure. The first to catch fire is the hair. The skin swells with blisters, which burst in a matter of seconds. The arms and legs begin to twitch—for the tightening blood vessels make the limbs move. The whole body is now aflame, the skin has burst, fat drips out and you hear the hissing of the burning fire. Now you can no longer see a body but a blaze of hellish fire with something inside it. The stomach explodes quickly. The intestines and entrails run out and in minutes no trace of them remains. What burns the longest is the head. From its eyes blue flames now sparkle—the eyes are burning and the marrow, and from the mouth the tongue burns too. The whole procedure takes twenty minutes— and a body that was once a world is now turned into ash.

You stand and gaze as if rooted to the spot. Two bodies are loaded onto the board. Two people, two worlds, who had their place among mankind, who lived and existed, built, created, achieved for the world and for themselves, laid a brick for the great edifice, wove a thread for the world and the future—and soon, in twenty minutes, no trace of them remains.

Now two more are lying there, washed. Two beautiful young women, once they were magnificent. Two whole worlds they had been on earth, how much joy and pleasure they brought to the world, every smile was a comfort, every look a joy, every word held enchantment like a heavenly song, wherever they posed a foot, they brought joy and happiness. Many hearts loved them and now they lie together on the iron board and soon the mouth of Hell will open and in minutes no trace of them will remain.

Now three more lie there. A child pressed to its mother's breast, what joy, what happiness the mother and the father had at the birth of the child. Built a home, wove an idyllic future for them, and soon in twenty minutes no trace of them will remain.

The lift goes up and down, carrying its countless victims. Like in a great slaughterhouse stacks of bodies lie waiting their turn to be taken away.

Thirty hellish mouths are flaming now in the two large buildings and swallowing up countless victims. It won't be long before the five thousand people, the five thousand worlds, will be devoured by the flames.

The ovens burn with turbulent waves, their fires lit long ago by the hands of the barbarians and murderers of the world, who hope by their light to drive away the darkness of their world of horror.

The fire burns powerfully, steadily, no one disturbs it, no one puts it out. It is constantly fed by its innumerable victims, as if the ancient people of martyrs had been born specially for them.

You vast free world, will you ever notice that great flame? And you, man, will you one evening stop and stand where you are and raise your eyes to the deep blue heavens, masked with flames — know then, you free man, that these are the fires of Hell that burn here, endlessly fed with people. Perhaps your heart will one day be warmed by their fire, and your ice-cold hands will some day come here and put the fire out. And perhaps your heart will be infused with boldness and courage and you will change [replace] the victims of this fire, this Hell that goes on burning here forever and may those who lit the fire be devoured in its flames.

The Reuniting

Down there, on the accursed earth, they were separated, ripped apart, torn asunder by the barbarian.

Down there, in the graves, in the prisons, there they sat, each separate. And each heart bled, yearned for the other.

Down there, to their death they went, each separate, here a woman, here a man, here a mother, here a father, here a sister, here a brother.

Down there, in the bunkers, they are dragged, each separate. Here a woman, there a man, to the lift they are dragged now, divided and apart.

Down there, to Gehenna, to its open mouths, each completely alone, they are flung into the fire. In Crematorium I burns a woman with a child. And her husband is devoured in Crematorium II.

Down there, from two chimneys, tall and deep, tongues of fire shoot out now in black columns of smoke.

Down there, through the smoke of one chimney, lives stream out now, the life of a woman, a child, a mother, a sister, friends. And from the second chimney, opposite, the lives of those torn away, a husband, father, brother or friend, through the black columns of smoke now rise to the skies.

Down there, they were separated, ripped apart, torn asunder, but here above, to the clouds they soar now together. The sundered families to the heavens soar, now reunited, and vanish into eternity together.

Down there, where the reign of the barbarians has its stronghold still, thousands of lives are now driven from the earth. To the highest heavens now they soar, to the sisters and the brothers, the millions who just yesterday were murdered there.

There above, the skies and the glittering stars are veiled, and darkened grows their shine. A black cloud like a mourning coat now moves toward the moon on high.

It is the victims now who want to dress the moon in mourning clothes.

There above, the moon now wants to disappear. She does not want to dress in mourning, she wants to escape somewhere. But the great black cloud pursues her relentlessly and holds her enveloped in his arms.

There above, from the deep blackness there, are heard the cries of millions, sobbing and groaning, voices of the murdered children, millions of innocents, burned to death on earth. We will pursue you forever. Your light will not shine down upon this earthly world, not until we here above can have an answer for our blood.

K.L. Auschwitz-Birkenau 1944
Birkenau map

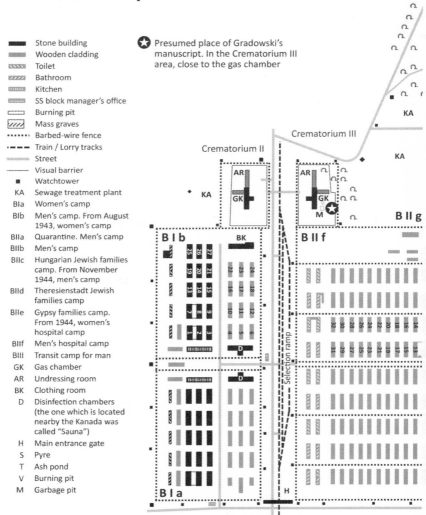

Stone building
Wooden cladding
Toilet
Bathroom
Kitchen
SS block manager's office
Burning pit
Mass graves
Barbed-wire fence
Train / Lorry tracks
Street
Visual barrier
■ Watchtower
KA Sewage treatment plant
BIa Women's camp
BIb Men's camp. From August 1943, women's camp
BIIa Quarantine. Men's camp
BIIb Men's camp
BIIc Hungarian Jewish families camp. From November 1944, men's camp
BIId Theresienstadt Jewish families camp
BIIe Gypsy families camp. From 1944, women's hospital camp
BIIf Men's hospital camp
BIII Transit camp for man
GK Gas chamber
AR Undressing room
BK Clothing room
D Disinfection chambers (the one which is located nearby the Kanada was called "Sauna")
H Main entrance gate
S Pyre
T Ash pond
V Burning pit
M Garbage pit

⭐ Presumed place of Gradowski's manuscript. In the Crematorium III area, close to the gas chamber

FIGURE 7. Map of the Auschwitz-Birkenau death camp.

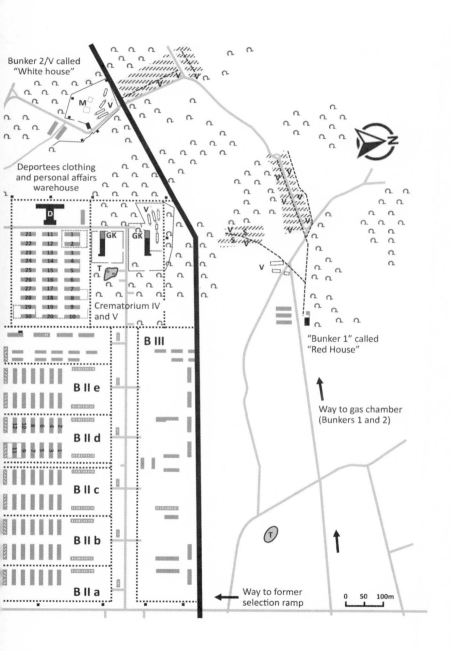

Bunker 2/V called "White house"

Deportees clothing and personal affairs warehouse

Crematorium IV and V

B III

B II e

B II d

B II c

B II b

B II a

"Bunker 1" called "Red House"

Way to gas chamber (Bunkers 1 and 2)

Way to former selection ramp

0   50   100m

AFTERWORD

Desolation without Consolation: Living with Zalmen Gradowski

Arnold I. Davidson

Zalmen Gradowski's voice is unlike any other, and reading him is, quite simply, an unprecedented experience; it pierces us in a way that we cannot and should not ever fully recover from, transforming us from historical observers to present participants. We are not prepared to accompany Gradowski, and he knows it. The beginning of his first manuscript, after the dedication, sounds like this:

> [Come] here to me, you fortunate citizen of the world who lives in a land where happiness, joy and pleasure still exist, and I will tell you of the abject criminals of today who took an entire people and turned their happiness to sadness, their joy into eternal sorrow—their pleasure forever destroyed.
>
> Come here to me, you free citizens of the world, where your life is made safe by human morality and your existence is guaranteed by law, and I will tell you how these modern criminals, these vile bandits, expunged all morality from life, wiped out the very laws of existence . . .
>
> Come now, while the destruction is still in full progress [. . .]
>
> Come even now, as the annihilation still zealously goes on.
>
> Come even now, when the Angel of Death still has all his power.
>
> Come now, while in the ovens the funeral pyre still blazes with its great flames . . .
>
> Tell them, your wife and child, that if you never return from the

journey, it is because your human heart was too weak to withstand the weight of the horrific, bestial acts your eyes observed.

Tell them, your friends and acquaintances, that if you do not return, it is because your blood froze and could no longer flow, at the sight of the horrific, barbaric images, of how they died, the innocent, helpless children of a poor and forlorn people . . .

Do not fear, when in the wet earthen graves you see living, vibrant children, for you will see them later on in worse conditions yet.

Do not fear, when in the middle of a freezing night you find a large mass of Jews, driven out of their graves and pursued in its journey, on its unknown, unfamiliar way. Let not your heart tremble at the sound of the children's cries, the woman's screams, the groans of old and sick, for you have yet to see crueler and more horrible.

Do not fear, when after such a march, when the day begins to break, you will find old couples lying on the road amid red and purple stains — these are the sick and weak, shot to death when they could not endure the march.

Do not worry about those already dead, save a groan for those who for the time being are still alive . . .

Come, my friend, now we will descend into the camp where my family and I, and tens of thousands of Jews, lived for a short time. I will tell you what they lived through in those horrible times until they reached their final destination.

Listen, my friend, and learn what takes place here.[1]

I have quoted these opening passages at length in order to emphasize that they are the response to an acute and lacerating question that Gradowski had to confront: How do you prepare someone to face the unimaginable? Gradowski fully realized how nearly impossible this task was, but he felt it incumbent upon him to at least attempt to prepare us to take part in his personal and cosmic trauma. With our historical hindsight, we have some idea of what is to come; we can grab on to some (no doubt inadequate) points of orientation as we accompany Gradowski. However, for Gradowski's contemporaries, who did not have available the benefits and harms of hindsight, Gradowski's unmediated or uncrafted address could not help but produce crushing disorientation. How can one go on when we are told that we "will want to erase [our] name from the family of man and will regret the day that [we] were born" (8)? Many people will be tempted to think that this opening is a melodramatic example of rhetorical exaggeration. Yet as we proceed, we will come to feel that these apparent excesses were, in the end, not enough to prepare us for the tragedy that we are undergoing. In Gradowski's circumstances, the idea of excess is empty—nothing is enough. In effect, Gradowski's opening serves more as a warning than as a preparation.

Gradowski is not asking for our empathy. Empathy, whatever its virtues, is too distant from his experience, not forceful enough to allow us to partake of this experience. Empathy is experience once removed. Primo Levi's two masterpieces, *If This Is a Man* and *The Drowned and the Saved*, appeal to a kind of intellectual/moral empathy, addressing us with a dispassionate language that asks us for a sober intellectual examination of Levi's experience, and a moral judgment based on reason. Elie Wiesel was masterful in being able to provoke a type of emotional/moral empathy, relying on a passionate language whose unabashed arousal of our emotions inexorably culminated in a moral conclusion. Gradowski's language, although appealing to both intellect and emotion, is a different genre of expression than one finds in Levi or Wiesel. It is not a language of empathy, but of direct participation. Neither reason nor affect in themselves are sufficient for Gradowski. He wants us, as literally as possible, to be with him in Auschwitz, that is, he is not satisfied with our empathy toward him and his fellow condemned, all smothered by brutality and waiting for death—such empathy is too removed, too unstable. He demands that we be present with him at Auschwitz, going through, hour by hour, what he is going through as he experiences it. Empathy becomes superfluous; Auschwitz is, as it were, happening to us at the same time that it engulfs Gradowski. Gradowski's peculiar style expresses itself in a language of demonstrative immediacy, of deixis, and pulls us into his world so that we are lying, sitting, and standing next to him, our distance diminished. He is not merely our narrator, but our companion, not someone with whom we empathize, but someone whose experience we directly share. If Levi's writing exhibits anthropological detachment and Wiesel's prose exemplifies psychological engagement, Gradowski's writing creates a participatory lamentation, a singular lamentation that sometimes even overflows with lyricism. Is Gradowski looking for our friendship? Friendship is the art of compassionate people. But our compassion is too late for Gradowski, our friendship too abstract and nebulous. What Gradowski wants is our participation, and participation is the art of making one present. Gradowski's prose is a magnet of presence, and he draws us in, the separation between us shattered by his words.

Gradowski's poetic, philosophical, even theological insistence on participation is an element of, and makes reference to, a longstanding Jewish tradition. A classic example can be found in Maimonides' discussion of the laws of Pesach. Basing his interpretation on several passages from *Deuteronomy*, in the *Mishneh Torah*, "Laws of Chametz and Matzah," chapter 7, Maimonides writes:

> In every generation a person shows himself that he personally had come forth from Egyptian subjugation, as it is stated, "God freed us from there . . ." (Deut. 6:23). And regarding this, the Holy Blessed One commanded in the Torah, "Remember that you were a slave in the land of Egypt . . ." (Deut. 5:15, 15:15, 24:22), that is to say, as if you yourself had been a slave, and you came forth into freedom, and were redeemed.[2]

It is clear that for Maimonides, Pesach is not only a festival of commemoration, but a festival of participation. It directly concerns each of us as Jews—"as if you yourself"—and without the phenomenological texture of our participation, we cannot experience the genuine force and the true significance of the holiday. Exempting oneself from participation in the Exodus is a failure to recognize the unity of the Jewish people, a unity that is not only historical but, so to speak, metaphysical, the meta-historical continuity of the people of Israel. Projecting oneself into the event is a theological requirement.

The Passover Haggadah is itself unambiguous about the required perspective:

In every generation it is one's duty to regard himself as though he personally had gone out of Egypt, as it is written: You shall tell your son on that day: "It was because of this that Hashem did for 'me' when I went out of Egypt." It was not only our fathers whom the Holy One, Blessed is He, redeemed from slavery; we, too, were redeemed with them . . .[3]

As the Lubavitcher Rebbe, Rabbi Menachem Mendel Schneerson, emphasizes, quoting the Haggadah, personal involvement "is considered fundamental to the Seder experience."[4] The Exodus is, first and foremost, an experience, not merely a faded memory.

The great twentieth-century philosopher and Talmudist Rabbi Joseph B. Soloveitchik takes up and extends Maimonides' point of view:

Distant events address themselves to us directly; there is in their appeal a note of immediacy and urgency; we experience their full emotional impact upon us and somehow identify ourselves with them. . . . The Halakhah has helped develop such a peculiar time-awareness. We are enjoined to rejoice on Passover not for the sake of celebrating an ancient exodus, but mainly because this drama is being reenacted time and again. We observe our own liberation. "In each generation one is obligated to see oneself as if he himself had been freed from Egypt" (*Pesachim* 116b). We mourn every year the destruction of the Temple, and the halakhic dictum has prescribed mourning after this distant event equal in scope and intensity to the emotional distress caused by the untimely death of a beloved member of the family. "This was the custom of R. Yehudah the son of R. Illai: On the afternoon before Tish'ah be-Av, they would bring him dry bread, and he would drink with it a container of water—and he resembled one whose deceased relative is lying before him" (*Ta'anit* 30a–b). Personally feeling the presence of a nineteen-hundred-year-old calamity is required by the Halakhah.[5]

Gradowski uses all of his resources to try to ensure that we experience the "full emotional impact" of the events of the Shoah and "somehow identify ourselves with them." We are not called upon to identify with Gradowski the individual in order to be able to feel empathy toward him; Gradowski puts *us* in Auschwitz with all of its "immediacy and urgency." If we experience Auschwitz with Gradowski, we will never be able to forget it, just as the survivors have been fated to live with their indelible, never-ending experiential memories. Those who have lived through Auschwitz know that this memory is reenactment. And Gradowski demands that we be part of this reenactment, with all of the recurrent trauma that it involves.

However, despite his extraordinary literary descriptions, Gradowski cannot fully close the distance, the gap, between himself and us: we did not, it goes without saying, live through Auschwitz, and Gradowski knows that this difference between him and us will never vanish. His goal is to bring us as close to the abyss as our imagination, fueled by his prose, will allow. One of the most powerful symbols of this remaining distance is expressed through our ability to cry, in stark contrast to Gradowski's loss of the capacity to shed tears. Each of Gradowski's introductions to the parts of his manuscripts focuses on his loss of this human capacity, as if being unable to weep definitively separates Gradowski from those who did not suffer Auschwitz. Speaking of his family, Gradowski exclaims:

> Alas! I, their child, here in this Hell, cannot even cry, for I drown each day in a sea, a sea of blood. Each wave chases the others. There is not a moment when you can huddle in your own corner and sit and cry, cry over the Destruction. The continual and systematic death, which is here the only life of one's whole life, drowns out, bewilders, numbs your feelings. You cannot feel, you cannot perceive even the greatest pain. The individual destruction has been swallowed up by the general one.
>
> Yet sometimes the heart is stabbed, the soul is pierced—why do I sit so "calmly," why do I not cry, not mourn, over my tragedy? Is all feeling frozen, numb, atrophied? Sometimes I hoped, sometimes I consoled myself that a time would come, a day when I will have earned the right to cry—but who knows . . . the ground is shaky, already it trembles under our feet.
>
> What I want now, and this is my only wish, since I cannot cry for them, may a stranger's eye let fall a tear for my loved ones. (58–59)

The murder of Gradowski's family should have provoked an abundance of tears; however, faced with the murder of millions of Jews, Gradowski's individual tragedy, his personal loss, is but a drop in the sea of mourning, no longer distinctive, not of any general significance. To focus on his own family would be a kind of (understandable) egoism, elevating himself and his loss to some special status. In Auschwitz, it was as if there were no individual tragedies, as if individuality was itself erased by a number tattooed on one's forearm. And, as Rabbi Soloveitchik is reported to have said:

> ... however tragic our national mourning is, it is extremely difficult to relate to the death of millions. However, it becomes meaningful when we read about the tragic death of an individual. Indeed, we are then moved to tears.[6]

Genuine national mourning arises through a series of acts of individual mourning. Without a space for individual loss, meaningful tears do not flow; they have nothing specific to attach themselves to, and thus they have no particular force. Any so-called general tears are but inert abstractions.

In the next introduction, in "Separation," Gradowski continues this theme:

> Let my dear loved ones also benefit from a sigh, a tear—from someone's eye. For I, their most unfortunate child, accursed man, I "cannot," I am unable to let out even a groan, a tear for them. In this hellish life in which I find myself, for nearly 16 months now, I have not yet had a day, a day in which I can withdraw into my own world, to know, to feel, to get a sense of my own misfortune. The constant systematic extermination process of our people, which I live through every day, drowns out the individual misfortune and numbs all feeling. And there is another factor here: that my own life already hovers under the wings of death. And who knows if I will one day be able to cry, to feel my horrendous pain, who knows?
>
> My family, burned here on December 8, 1942 ... (69)

From a physical, moral, and spiritual point of view, in Auschwitz one no longer inhabits one's own world. Gradowski's tears are dry with anonymity—Why *me*? is no longer an intelligible question.

In his final introduction, in "The Czech Transport," speaking of a photo of his family, Gradowski pleads with his readers:

> By means of this I hope to preserve their dear beloved names, those for whom I cannot now shed even a tear! For I live in a Hell of death and cannot even properly evaluate the extent of my loss. And I myself have also been sentenced to death. Can the dead weep for the dead?! But you "free" stranger, free citizen of the world, I beg of you to grant them one more tear, when you have their pictures before your eyes. To them I dedicate all my writings—that is my tear, my sigh for my family and for my people. (102)

If Gradowski were to begin to weep, justice would require that he never stop—how much weeping does one have to do to mourn millions of deaths, each death obliterating a world. Some early words of the book of *Lamentations*, commemorating the destruction of the Temple, read as follows:

> Over these do I weep; my eye continuously runs with water because a comforter to restore my soul is far from me. My children have become forlorn, because the enemy has prevailed.[7]

Here, unlike in Auschwitz, the capacity to cry is intact; and the references to a comforter (who consoles) and to the presence of children (even forlorn) have no sense whatsoever in the face of the gas chambers and crematoria. The tragedy of *Lamentations* is more human than the catastrophe of Auschwitz. And who would weep for Gradowski, already on his way to death? The answer, of course, is that we will weep for him and his individual losses. Yet that response just emphasizes our distance from Gradowski; when we weep, we demonstrate that we were not in Auschwitz, that we still inhabit our individual worlds, that we are not physically and spiritually enclosed in the chambers of death. Gradowski never asks us to weep in general. His plea is for us to weep for his mother, his two sisters, his wife, his father-in-law, and his brother-in-law, and he names each one of them—their names give back to them their individuality. And we have remained individuals, called on to shed tears for other individuals, each one with his or her own (destroyed) world. Tears restore and reveal humanity; they recover lost worlds. So *we* cry, while Gradowski almost always remains dry-eyed.

—

Gradowski's chapter "A Moonlit Night" is a stunning example of what I would call a "lyrical lamentation." His lyrical prose vibrates with life, even in this place of suffering and death. Indeed, this lyricism can be profoundly disconcerting—how can one describe such horrendous events in such poetically vital prose? How can the desolation of a lamentation coexist with the beauty of his poetic pathos? Even Gradowski's description of what happens to a burning body in the crematorium makes use of adjectives, images, metaphors, rhythms, and turns of phrase that embody the aesthetics of lyricism, an affective, physical stirring of the emotions whose moving musicality seems completely out of place as we are surrounded by the sight and scent of thousands of burning bodies:

> . . . the mouth of Hell is opened and the board is slid into the oven. The hellish fire sticks out its tongues like open arms and swallows up the body like a treasure. . . . What burns the longest is the head. From its eyes blue flames now sparkle—the eyes are burning and the marrow, and from the mouth the tongue burns too. The whole procedure takes twenty minutes—and a body that was once a world is now turned into ash. . . .
>
> Thirty hellish mouths are flaming now in the two large buildings and swallowing up countless victims. It won't be long before the five thousand people, the five thousand worlds, will be devoured by the flames.
>
> The ovens burn with turbulent flames, their fires lit long ago by the hands of the barbarians and murderers of the world, who hope by their light to drive away the darkness of their world of horror.

> The fire burns powerfully, steadily, no one disturbs it, no one puts
> it out. It is constantly fed by its innumerable victims, as if the ancient
> people of martyrs had been born specially for them. (149–50)

Immersed in the intensity of Gradowski's prose, we are liable to
be distracted from the scene that he is describing: the dissolution of
human beings into ash. We are moved and transported by the lyricism of Gradowski's writing, but we arrive at a place of inexpressive
horror, a point of aphasia, devoid of poetic exaltation or excitation.
We end up overcome by lamentation, and the very lyricism of this
lamentation is a stylistic technique that helps to thwart our catharsis.
We are not purified, but paralyzed. There is no catharsis in Auschwitz. We have often posed the question of whether lyrical poetry is
possible after Auschwitz. Gradowski shows us that lyrical lamentation is indeed possible during Auschwitz. And the lyricism of his
lamentation (rather than an unadorned language) leaves us all the
more confused, unable to orient ourselves in this world of destruction. Lyricism and lamentation pull us in opposite directions, the
vitality of life and the motionlessness of death.

The moon, no doubt, is a more natural object of lyrical description than is a burning body. Yet even here Gradowski's evocative
language can be disorienting, misleading; the lyrical invocation of
and address to the moon is, beneath the surface, a moment of rad-
ical theological critique. Let me juxtapose the lyrical with the lamentation in this section of Gradowski's manuscript, starting with his
initial poetic invocation:

> I loved her and with trembling I awaited her coming. Like a faithful ser-
> vant I would stand hours long and admire her splendor and her magic.
> Like one riveted to the spot, hypnotized, my eyes would gaze at her
> kingdom, the deep blue night skies, adorned with bright glittering stars
> and wait in solemn suspense for the moment of Her Majesty's arrival.
> And she, the Queen, arriving in all her splendor, in the company of her
> retinue, was calm, carefree, happy and joyous, as she came out for her
> mysterious rounds, to have a look at her realm, the world of night, and
> bestow on mankind a ray of her light. (60)

We begin in the realm of Romantic prose poetry. Yet we are, almost immediately, lyrically drawn into the suffering of lamentation:

But now, now that I am alone, left solitary here, my home, my family, my world, my people wiped out by the pirates cruelly and for no reason, and I, alone among millions, under sentence of death, sit enchained in my prison and suffer the pain and fear of death, today when I see her, I run from her as from a ghost.

. . . I no longer want to see her shine, for she causes me more grief, makes my pain deeper, my torment stronger. I feel better in the darkness, in the reign of the dead and mournful night. She, the night, is in harmony with the feelings in my heart and the torments of my soul. The dark of night is my friend, the weeping, the screams, they are my song, the fire burning the victims is my light, the atmosphere of death is my perfume, this Hell is my home. Why, for what purpose, cruel moon, do you come to disturb people in their unconscious misfortune? Why do you wake them from their frightful sleep and show them a world that is a stranger to them now, a world to which they can never, never in their lives again return? . . .

Why do you send your rays, which here turn into spears that pierce with pain the bleeding hearts and suffering souls? Why do you let your light shine on this accursed hellish world, here where the night is lit by gigantic flames—by the fire of the burning victims, innocents who are murdered here? . . .

Here you ought not to shine!!! Here in this horrible corner of the earth, where people are tortured with savage atrocity, constantly sinking in a sea of blood and affliction, and wait in fear of inescapable death, here, here you ought not to shine!!! (61–62)

The moon's realm has now become a world of suffering and torment, of fire and extermination, of blood and death—its world of "magic and beauty" has been transformed into a place where no light has a right to shine, and so the world should "forever be in darkness," "veiled in eternal sorrow" (64). However lyrically described, this world is symbolized by a permanent scream, the unending, piercing sound of lamentation. The selfish and sadistic moon is told to "clothe

yourself in black," to shroud yourself in "clouds of mourning"—
mourning has replaced morning (65).

By the end of this lyrical lamentation, absence of movement and
virtual darkness are all that is left, the lamentation is complete:

> Let just one ray fall on the earth, a ray for them, a moonbeam for the
> victims, the victims of my people . . .
>
> Come here, moon, and remain here motionless forever. Sit down on
> a mourner's bench at my people's grave and shed at least a tear for them,
> for no one else is left here to weep, to mourn for them. You alone, sole
> witness to this misfortune, to the destruction of my people, of my world.
>
> May your only ray, your mournful light, burn forever at my people's
> grave. May that be their *yortsayt-likht*, their mourners' candle that only
> you can light for them! (65, 67)

In the end, the lyrical light of the moon has been replaced by a single
ray of lamentation, a ray that must burn forever, an eternal, single *yar-
tzeit* candle that endlessly reminds us of the darkness of death. Vibrant light—bright and diffuse—has undergone a metamorphosis
to become a diminished, indeed solitary, ray of desolation.

How did we move from the lyrical moon to the desolate moon—as
unexpected as it may seem, Gradowski gets there by way of theology.
Jewish tradition obligates one to perform a very particular liturgical
ritual known as "the sanctification of the moon" (*Kiddush Levanah*).[8]
And I will try to show that this ritual is the most immediate context for
understanding Gradowski's "A Moonlit Night." The ritual begins with
praise of God, the first six verses of Psalm 148, hardly a compelling
beginning from Gradowski's point of view. In Auschwitz, the opening
liturgical praise of God cannot help but seem, at the very least, discor-
dant. Following an initial general imperative to praise God, the sun
and the moon are commanded to praise Him for having created them
and, as the Talmud emphasizes, for setting "a law and a time, that they
should not deviate from their task."[9] The moon is "joyous and happy
to perform the will of [its] Creator";[10] the moon is essentially the joyous servant of God. Thus, as we praise the moon, and the moon per-

forms God's will, we are in effect also praising God. When one performs this ritual, it is "as if he greets the Face of the Divine Presence":

> The school of Rabbi Yishmael taught: If the Jewish people merited to greet the Face of their Father in Heaven only one time each and every month, it would suffice for them, since in the blessing of the moon there is an aspect of greeting the Divine Presence. Abaye said: Therefore, we will say the blessing while standing, in honor of the Divine Presence.[11]

The entire atmosphere of this ritual reinforces the poetics of divine praise. As befits the blessing of the moon, our encounter with the Divine Presence, this is a joyous occasion, preferably recited "at the conclusion of the Sabbath while people are dressed in their finest clothes." Moreover, "it is also customary to defer *Kiddush Levanah* until after Tishah B'Av [the day that commemorates the destruction of the first and second Temple] ... because the sadness of Av ... [is] inappropriate to the joy required during *Kiddush Levanah*."[12] If joy is the emotional framework of this ritual, thus excluding its performance on Tishah B'Av, the saddest day of the Jewish liturgical calendar, then what should we say about Auschwitz? The desolation of Auschwitz deadens any praise, blots out any joy. And if we want to say that Tishah B'Av is also a time of desolation, then Auschwitz is a time of absolute or hyper-desolation, that is, desolation that leaves no room for consolation. However genuinely tragic was the destruction, twice, of the Temple, there is a bewildering discontinuity between the suffering of Tishah B'Av and the suffering in Auschwitz. How can we allow ourselves to joyously bless the moon and praise God in the midst of the utter horror of Auschwitz? The destruction of the Jewish people is a tragedy unto itself.

The waxing and waning of the moon is taken to symbolize the waxing and waning of the Jewish people, and the ritual should be performed when the moon is waxing: "just as the moon is reborn after a period of decline and total disappearance, so too Israel's decline will end and its light will once again blaze to fullness."[13] In Auschwitz the light of Israel is overtaken by the blazes in the crematoria. How could

Gradowski, after being forced to watch many thousands of bodies burn, sincerely recite the following prayer:

> May it be the will before You, Hashem, my God and the God of my forefathers, to fill the flaw of the moon, that there not be in it any diminution; and may the light of the moon be like the light of the sun and like the light of the seven days of Creation, as it was before its diminishment . . .[14]

If the moon mirrors the status of the Jewish people, how can we even hope that "there not be in it any diminution"? Such a wish strikes us as more like delirium than hope. The decline of the moon, like that of the Jewish people in Auschwitz, ought to go beyond diminution to the point of nearly vanishing. In these circumstances, the moon, like the presence of God and the future of the Jewish people, can, at best, be little more than a flicker. After the fires of the ovens go out, what remains is the darkness of desolation, not the light of creation, but the utter blackness of destruction, of ash.

In one of the most theologically interesting discussions of the sanctification of the moon, the Talmud considers the specific blessings that should be recited:

> Rav Aha of Difti said to Ravina: And they should bless the blessing of: Blessed are You, Lord our God, King of the Universe, Who is good and Who does good, for the benefit that people derive from the light of moon. Ravina said to him: Is that to say that when the moon is shrinking, we bless, as we do for other disasters: Blessed are You, Lord our God, King of the Universe, the true Judge, so that we should conversely bless: Blessed are You, Lord our God, King of the Universe, Who is good and Who does good, when the moon is growing? Rav Aha of Difti said to him: You are correct, and we should say them both: The blessing of the true Judge, when the moon is waning, and the blessing of Who is good and Who does good, when the moon is waxing.[15]

Although from a cosmological standpoint, the moon still waxes and wanes, even in Auschwitz, from an axiological standpoint, both moral and theological, the moon has no right to grow and should remain in a state of continuous decline. We cannot, nor should we be able to, imagine Gradowski, after emerging from the gas chambers and crematoria, standing under the moonlit sky and praising God, "Who is good and Who does good." Those words, in this context, would be a kind of mockery, blasphemy not praise; they would make the idea of the good completely incomprehensible from a human point of view. The moon, God's joyous servant, should not be permitted to shine, and God has, so to speak, forfeited his right to praise. In Auschwitz, those words, if uttered by Gradowski, would be a defilement of the memory of the murdered. As has often been repeated by survivors, many of the best people did not survive, but were annihilated under the shining light of the moon, a light neither earned nor beneficent. "Who is good and Who does good" is inconceivable to Gradowski and thus it is vacuous as a blessing.

The second blessing, "Blessed are You, Lord our God, King of the Universe, the true Judge," is appropriate to the waning moon, and, by analogy, to the diminishment of the Jewish people. This blessing is said when one hears of the death of an immediate relative; on hearing of the death of another person in general, one responds by pronouncing the second half of the blessing, "the true Judge," omitting the name of God. In either case, this blessing acknowledges that God's judgments are beyond our comprehension, and affirms our faith in the justice of His judgments. Indeed, *Berakhot* 54a enjoins us to bless God not only for the good, but also for the bad that befalls us. However, to call Auschwitz "bad" is a form of conceptual and moral laziness. The death camps stretch the idea of bad beyond its limits, and it is a concept no longer applicable to understanding the specificity of Auschwitz. Do we really want to say, for example, that the brutal murder of babies and children is "bad"? "Bad" is so weak here that it only reveals a thoroughly confused mind. And could we really imagine that God's judgments in Auschwitz were just, the judgments of "the true Judge"? Being beyond our understanding should not imply violating and destroying our understanding. We will never understand, I hope, how millions of innocent deaths could be justified, and Gradowski's account radically undermines the description "the true Judge."

Gradowski is not in a position to say either blessing. The moon has no right to shine, so "Who is good and Who does good" is excluded; the diminution in Auschwitz cannot be the result of just judgments, so "the true Judge" is not at all pertinent. Indeed, death in Auschwitz was arbitrary, not even the object of judgment. Judgment requires evidence and deliberation; the movement of a hand, indicating to go to the right or to the left, is not a judgment: it is an outburst of baseless hatred.

The justification of Gradowski's attitude is strengthened by these further words of the ritual, addressed to the moon:

> Just as I dance opposite you, but I am not able to touch you, so may they not be able — all my enemies — to touch me for evil. Let there fall upon them terror and fear; at the greatness of Your arm, let them be still as stone.[16]

Dancing signifies joy, but the moon, as a heavenly body, cannot be touched. So much more so is God, the symbolic referent of the moon, beyond our reach. We can, however, receive the light of God, despite his metaphysical distance from us. To parallel and balance this distance, we pray that our enemies will be unable to touch us for evil, that they will feel terror and fear at the greatness of God and "be still as stone." Yet Gradowski already knows that his enemies have not only touched him for evil, but have proudly crushed him beneath it. The only human beings still as stone in Auschwitz are the tortured and murdered Jews. The continuous presence of these enemies, their undiluted and uninterrupted evil, undercuts the idea that the moon and God, although distant and untouchable, will continue to protect us. Gradowski lives daily with the relentless, numbing evil of his enemies; he cannot discern the protection and safety of God. In Auschwitz, protection and safety are illusions, sometimes even delusions.

In reciting Psalm 121, another portion of the ritual, we are told that our "help" comes from God, that God "neither slumbers nor sleeps," that He will not allow us to falter. God is our "Guardian," our "protective Shade," and we are directly assured that the moon will not harm us. In summary, "Hashem will protect you from every evil; He will safeguard your soul." The Psalm concludes: "Hashem will safeguard your departure and your arrival, from this time until eternity."[17] Help, protection, safeguard—these promises have no content for Gradowski; they have been repeatedly betrayed, and Gradowski could not bear the hypocrisy of reciting these verses. And the last verse is especially chilling for anyone who had been deported to Auschwitz. No one could forget their departure to Auschwitz, sealed in cattle cars, crushed together, with no food or drink or bathroom, people sick and dying all around one—a voyage with *no* safeguards. Then one arrives at the destination, a place which is nowhere; one is immediately brutalized, stripped of one's everyday humanity and, for many, sent immediately to the gas chambers. Where was God during this departure and arrival? How could Gradowski sensibly utter the words of this Psalm, given what he has experienced and suffered? His faith, a genuine faith, has arrived at its limit. Departure and arrival in Auschwitz transport one to the limits of the world. A voyage to death undoes any prayer of protection.

In order to emphasize that the sanctification of the moon is addressed to God (it is in no way whatsoever a worship of the moon as such), the ritual is typically followed by a recitation of the *Aleinu* prayer, which affirms that "He is our God and there is none other."[18] In light of all of these details about the blessing of the moon, I think it is clear that Gradowski's overarching gesture in this chapter is to perform a kind of desanctification of the moon, a critique of and challenge to God's sovereignty, even goodness. Yet Gradowski's desanctification takes place within a theological perspective. He carefully undoes each phase of the ritual—there is no joy, no praise, no greeting of the Divine Presence, no hope for protection; we are in the grip of overwhelming evil and God's sanctification would be but a hollow ritual. Indeed, Auschwitz is a paradigm of desanctification, and Gradowski has the courage, pushed forward by degradation, to undertake a profound theological critique, one that is a distinctively Jewish theological critique.

Despite this critique, we should not underestimate the significance of Gradowski's theological orientation. His faith has not vanished but is, let us say, markedly diminished. Indeed, he struggles to retain the possibility of faith, but without naïveté, without ignoring the reality of his situation. Steadfast faith, in Gradowski's circumstances, would not take seriously the difficulty of faith. Auschwitz was constructed to destroy faith, to annihilate the Jewish faith by torturing and exterminating the Jews. Gradowski is, against all odds, still alive and his faith is not yet definitively dead. Let us read again, in this new context, Gradowski's words of confrontation to the moon. This new reading will focus in on Gradowski's theological tone, now heard from within a theological ritual. After telling the moon, "Here you ought not to shine . . . in this horrible corner of the earth," Gradowski continues:

> Why do you still shine today with such magic and splendor? In clouds of mourning you should shroud yourself. And no more bestow your light to anyone on this earth. You should mourn together with the victims, flee from the world, vanish into the highest heavens and show yourself no more to accursed mankind. Let the world forever be in darkness. Let it be veiled in eternal sorrow just as my people were led into eternal sorrow. (64)

After this plea for permanent darkness — a symbol of the complete loss of faith — as Gradowski brings his challenge to a provisional conclusion, he envisions the presence of a single ray of light, and this single ray alerts us to the fact that Gradowski is still living under the shadow of faith, not yet ready to abandon the tradition that has nurtured his life:

> Moon, gather up all your light, come here with your splendor and enchantment. Stay here forever with your magic and your charm. Then clothe yourself in black as you go your way across the tragic unfortunate horizon, and in sorrow and mourning you should also clothe the heavens and the stars, that your kingdom should forever be in mourning. Let dark clouds be drawn forever across the heavens. Let just one ray fall on the earth, a ray for them, a moonbeam for the victims, the victims of my people, for they have loved you to their last breath and

could not part with you even by the grave, and their last farewell they sent to you as they had already sunk deep into the abyss, and from those depths too, their last song, their last living sound they sent to you . . .

May your only ray, your mournful light, burn forever at my people's grave. May that be their *yortsayt-likht*, their mourners' candle that only you can light for them! (65, 67)

No more moonlit night, just a single ray "shining" on the grave of the victims. And when we read the moon as also standing in for the Divine Presence, we can see this last mournful ray of light as inevitably provoking the question of God and faith, a question still alive, but under great pressure, for Gradowski. The last living sound that the victims send to the moon—that is, to God—is, of course, *Shema Yisrael*. And Gradowski, too, knows the power of these words. Yet after what he has witnessed, one ray of light is his maximal theological gesture. Gradowski is desperately hanging on to this sorrowful ray of light, in spite of, or because of, the assault on his faith. In the horrors of Auschwitz, this is a profound theological stance, one that exemplifies all of Gradowski's heart-searing theological struggles.

In the final lines of his second manuscript, Gradowski's moon reappears and she is confronted one last time by the victims. After describing the still-shocking deaths—of men, women, and children—in Auschwitz, Gradowski tells us that "the sundered families to the heavens soar, now reunited, and vanish into eternity together" (151). Yet before they vanish, they must reiterate their lamentations, directed again to the theology of the moon:

There above, the skies and the glittering stars are veiled, and darkened grows their shine. A black cloud like a mourning coat now moves toward the moon on high.

It is the victims now who want to dress the moon in mourning clothes.

There above, the moon now wants to disappear. She does not want to dress in mourning, she wants to escape somewhere. But the great black cloud pursues her relentlessly and holds her enveloped in his arms.

There above, from the deep blackness there, are heard the cries of millions, sobbing and groaning, voices of the murdered children, millions of innocents, burned to death on earth. We will pursue you forever. Your light will not shine down upon this earthly world, not until we here above can have an answer for our blood. (151)

In this atmosphere of darkened shine and deep blackness, of diminution, the moon does not want to confront the victims again. If only she could disappear, without having to give any answers . . . However, she cannot escape—she is relentlessly pursued—and, against her will, the victims will dress her in mourning clothes. These are also the mourning clothes of God. He is no longer shrouded in a *tallit*, but is covered in the black clothes of lamentation. And in this symbol we may see a tormenting theological ambiguity: we do not know if God is mourning the victims or if they are mourning His diminution. Perhaps there are multiple levels of mourning, piled up on one another like the piles of victims in Auschwitz. Without "an answer for our blood," mourning can only continue, and, if need be, it will continue for an eternity. Neither the human nor the divine can escape Auschwitz. Now the last living sounds, of the victims and of Gradowski, are cries, sobbing, and groaning.

—

The most religiously intense section of Gradowski's manuscripts is entitled "Friday Night." As Gradowski acknowledges, welcoming the Sabbath in Auschwitz was treated by many Jews with mockery, contempt, and bitterness. Surrounded by unending murder and extermination, praise of, and prayers to, God seemed senseless:

> And they should still praise Him? Why? Songs of praise over a sea of our own blood? Pray to Him who will not hear the cries and screams of innocent little children, no! And this Jew walks away bitter, angry at the others, who do not understand as he does. (96)

Also present were once-religious Jews, who for a long time "have not been at peace with their God." They are bitter and do not understand, cannot reconcile their God with this massacre. Yet they do not walk away, but "now stand coldly off to the side," unable to pray, since "they don't want to be false, false to Him and to themselves." And in a remarkable statement, Gradowski observes: "They don't want to speculate too much, for fear of losing their last support, for fear of destroying their last consolation" (96). Even an ambivalent, perhaps incoherent, consolation may provide some support, and its loss could provoke a total collapse. Although coldly distant, they grasp, with their very lives, any semblance of consolation, and thus they do not demand or offer a reckoning.

Finally, there is a group of "stubborn and observant Jews" who repress their bitterness, drown out their protests, and are once again "caught in the net of naive faith. No reckoning, no theorizing" (96). Although they cannot comprehend God's reasons, they realize that speculation, reckoning, theorizing will further weaken their religious practices:

> Even now they cling to their God . . . imbued with this deep belief, even when they see, feel, sense that they are drowning in the sea of their own faith . . . but still they hold fast, so as not to lose their last consolation, not to lose their last support. (96)

Better to drown in a sea of faith than in an ocean of blood. Naive faith is still faith, and it draws them back into their lost lives, providing moments of consolation.

From within this "family" of Jews, Gradowski tells us, a group came into being, growing larger with time, "who said all the daily prayers with a *minyan*." Sometimes even those who "didn't pray would be drawn in by the prayers and the singing." The Sabbath prayer service would "tear [them] away from the horrible tragic reality" (97); Gradowski describes someone who would join this prayer group with these wrenching, nostalgic words:

> On stormy waves of remembrance he was carried back to a world of yesterday. He swims back to the years gone by. And sees himself in his home once more. (97)

Gradowski goes on to recount these happy Friday nights of the past. His account exploits memory to engage in an extraordinary spiritual exercise of self-transformation, an exercise that transports him out of Auschwitz and brings him back to his family and the joys of the Sabbath.[19]

The "holiday mood" of Friday night leaves behind one's daily preoccupations; it is a "happy and carefree" mood, one of "gladness and spiritual exaltation," a moment of "courage and hope." However, these Jews cannot help but be plunged back into their "tragic reality," feeling themselves trampled, insignificant, and worthless. They find themselves "sinking back into the deep abyss of despair." Salvation has now vanished, and they search to "hold on to something." Yet this despair does not become total desolation. A verse from *Jeremiah* comes to mind (30:16), reminding them that their "enemies, your oppressors, will be stamped out, annihilated." This verse fills them with courage, faith, hope, and strength. "Tomorrow will be brighter than today" and, thanks to Jeremiah, the whole congregation sings and "returns to the lofty, spacious skies of the spirit." Then Gradowski's memory turns to the peace and joy of the Sabbath evenings with his family, and his memory produces a stunning phrase: "Everyone feels uplifted by an inner happiness." This memory of inner happiness transforms Gradowski. He remembers the walk home from the great synagogue, the "majesty and holiness" of the Sabbath penetrating "every corner of human life." He returns home, surrounded by an "idyllic warmth," greeted by the eyes of his family that "shone with holiness." He re-creates, through this spiritual exercise of memory, a scene of him eating, drinking, and singing with his family, "carefree and safe," inhabiting a world of which "they alone are the masters. They feel threatened by no one" (98). Could we ever have imagined Gradowski as being able to reproduce these moments of inner happiness while a Sonderkommando in Auschwitz? Suffering often produces a spiritual desert; Gradowski's memory is sufficiently spiritually intact to produce a spiritual oasis. These exercises are a metamorphosis; they alter Gradowski's self-consciousness, re-creating his status as a human being, even if only temporarily, and allowing him to overcome the dehumanization of Auschwitz. His memory of past

Sabbath evenings with his family is a mode of rehumanization. This momentary resurrection is directly linked to his religious sensibility. Yet, however extraordinary it is, there is also a price to be paid, and the price is paid in further suffering.

Remembering and reliving these times of family peace and happiness, Gradowski's spiritual exercises are suddenly interrupted:

> And all at once, a stormy, roiling wave cruelly tore him away, ripped him away from that world.
>
> Gone was the home, gone the Sabbaths, vanished the world and drowned his happiness. His father, mother, sisters and brothers, his wife—no one is left in that world. (99)

There is nobody to whom Gradowski can say *gut shabes*. Instead of seeing himself sitting at the Sabbath dinner table, a new terrifying image emerges:

> I see before me the horrible abyss of my shattered world. And from the abyss I hear the voice of my family burned in the flames. (99)

Gradowski is now torn between wanting to flee this theater of images and wanting to remember, to "recapture the stirring of the spirit" (99). His memories bring painfully to life his own individual misfortune, a fate that had previously been diluted and numbed by the endless collective suffering that he witnessed every day. Yet despite his individual pain, Gradowski emphasizes the "pleasure" of being able to go back, of experiencing and reliving the past. The sparks of the Sabbath, remembered in the present with all of their spiritual pleasure (and distress), are a kind of theological therapy. They do allow him a reprieve, but he then tells us—it is the force of his spiritual exercise—that when he reached the shore of his "Sabbath of today," his "heart broke into tears":

> I was content, I had a tearful Shabbat, a cup of tears. Long, long I had yearned to see in my fantasy my beloved mother, my father in holiday mood, my dear sisters and brothers, my dear wife singing, relive with

them the Sabbaths of joy, Sabbaths of carefree happiness and then to mourn for them. To mourn for my family, my near and dear ones who are gone forever. To cry for my Sabbaths, which will never, never come back, to cry for my misfortune, which I have only now felt, only now realized ... (100)

Crying and mourning cannot be taken for granted; in Auschwitz they were typically submerged by suffering, a suffering that made the very acts of crying and mourning seem superfluous or superficial. Gradowski reminds us that these acts, like remembering, are modalities of (re)humanization. These spiritual exercises (even though they have their stark limitations) return him to his former self. They cannot, however, liberate him from Auschwitz; the desolation of Auschwitz always reappears. And Gradowski will stop remembering, crying, and mourning. He looks to the corner of his barracks, where Jews usually pray in *minyanim*, but "no one, no one is left there. Vanished the lives, extinguished the sound." He longs for these fellow Jews because they are his brothers, and because he misses "the light, the warmth, the faith, the hope that flowed out of them" (100). All he finds is emptiness and silence, permeated by his suffering. And thus Gradowski concludes this chapter with the most devastating words in his manuscripts. Speaking of these Jewish brothers and their *minyanim*, Gradowski exclaims:

With their disappearance the last consolation vanished. (100)

This could well be one of the few times that a religious Jew has made such a devastating declaration, but it is, all things considered, a statement that matches the devastations in Auschwitz. What does it mean, from within the Jewish tradition, to claim that the last consolation vanished?

This is the appropriate place to consider Gradowski's writing against the backdrop of the book of *Lamentations*, the Jewish model of desolation. Desolation in *Lamentations* is omnipresent, and the conclusion to this book implicitly but clearly raises the problem of consolation. *Lamentations* opens with destruction, solitude, and bitter weeping . . . and without comfort. As the desolation persists and grows, as the feeling of loss and disorientation deepens, a kind of desperation begins to take hold. At the end of the last chapter, in the darkness of this desolation, the question of our future relation to God comes to the forefront. The harsh final verses of this scroll seem to leave no obvious room for consolation, and therefore threaten our relation to God:

> Why do you ignore us eternally, forsake us for so long?
> Bring us back to you, Hashem, and we shall return, renew our days as of old.
> For even if You had utterly rejected us, You have already raged sufficiently against us.[20]

If God ignores (literally, "forgets") us eternally, forsakes us for the length of days, what can we ask of Him, what can we say to Him? It is God who must bring us back to Him; as forgotten and forsaken, our pleas go up in smoke; it is up to Him to initiate a new relationship; we can only affirm that if God, as it were, reaches out, we will return to Him and our days will be renewed. There is a definite note of optimism in this verse. We are ready to return to God, if only He will let us return. We need the consolation of knowing that, as in days of old, we can serve and be pleasing to God and He will safeguard us. Hope has not been extinguished, and we wait for His initiative. Nevertheless, the immediately following final verse seems to undo the hoped-for, the longed-for, consolation of the penultimate verse. Indeed, an alternative translation of this last verse would drop the conditional and translate the first part of the phrase as an assertion: "For You had utterly rejected us."[21] The second half of the phrase should then be read as a final lament—"You have already raged sufficiently against us"—as if we are warning God that His rage is becoming excessive. The theological divergence between the penultimate and ultimate verses revolves around the possibility of consolation. To complicate matters even further, rabbinic tradition did not accept a public reading of this book that ends on such a desolate note. The tradition instituted the practice of concluding its reading by chanting again, aloud, the penultimate verse, restoring the hope of consolation, a promise of return necessary to the theological future of the Jewish people. After all of the mourning and despair of *Lamentations*, the relationship between desolation and consolation remains unresolved. And this very lack of resolution maintains a space of hope—a space, I will argue, that is gradually closed in Gradowski's account of Auschwitz, a space now completely filled by suffering.

In grappling with the ambiguities of *Lamentations*, a number of commentators have put great weight on a distinction between anger and rejection. Anger, however frightening, is not rejection. Anger can be appeased and overcome; rejection terminates a relationship. Rabbi Bachya ben Asher (also known as Rabbeinu Bachya), moving within the framework of the more consoling interpretation, relates anger to the penultimate verse and rejection to the ultimate verse:

> Rabbeinu Bachya writes that the latter [final] verse relates to the former [penultimate verse]: Bring us back to You, Hashem—and we will return. For if You do not bring us back, it will *seem as* if You have *utterly rejected us*—but this is not true. You have **raged** *against us*—and justifiably so. True You were enraged with us, but rage can be reversed. Only rejection is final, but God never rejected His people.[22]

However unconvincing this interpretation may be, its theological motivations are evident. We must find a way to maintain our relationship with God; desolation cannot have the last word. Is it at all plausible to claim that this kind of interpretation could work in and for Auschwitz? If God's anger was behind the destruction of the Temples, anger without rejection, how are we to understand the horrors of Auschwitz? These horrors go beyond *Lamentations* to become what can easily be seen as utter rejection, forsaking the Jews in a way that destroys any further relationship. If the destruction of the Temple is an event of maximal anger, the gas chambers and crematoria are far beyond this maximum; all that seems left in the camps is rejection without consolation. If Auschwitz is not a place of divine rejection, what could be? There is no 'beyond Auschwitz.' And yet Gradowski moves between anger and rejection, never fully settled; anger may not be enough, but rejection may be too much. For the religious Jew like Gradowski, there is no theological stability in Auschwitz. And Gradowski possesses the virtue of never making things easier than they are.

Yet what could consolation look like in Gradowski's circumstances? Is consolation in Auschwitz humanly imaginable? Suppose that you have witnessed the torture, gassing, and burning of an uncountable number of Jews. Suppose that, as a Sonderkommando, you have been forced to work inside the gas chambers and crematoria. Suppose your entire family has been murdered. These kinds of suppositions have no limit, and yet Gradowski's faith has not collapsed. He searches for consolation. Attracted to the *minyan* in the corner of his barracks and returning in memory to his joyous Sabbath evenings, Gradowski is open to, and ready for, consolation. Turning toward the space where his fellow Jews pray, Gradowski is stunned, shocked to see that no one remains there. All has vanished, been annihilated, and there is only deathly silence. At this moment, he writes, "With their disappearance the last consolation vanished." I have often asked myself: If I were standing in Gradowski's place, what image of consolation could I bring to mind? Or is consolation, there and then, unthinkable? Any expected, previous form of consolation would be too weak to comfort, counterbalance, or compensate for Auschwitz. Auschwitz is unprecedented. The specific suffering in Auschwitz is outside of the bounds of historically known forms of consolation. As the suffering is unprecedented, so must be the consolation. How do we find consolation for these millions of murders? Could any attempted consolation match, or even approach, this almost indescribable tragedy? It is clear, I think, that any consolation in Auschwitz must come from God. Here it is beyond the power of human beings to initiate any effective and transformative consolation; so what can God do? Does the Jewish tradition provide the resources to imagine genuine divine consolation in Auschwitz?

After initially thinking that consolation in Auschwitz was impossible, unfathomable, that Gradowski himself could never have found true consolation, I realized that a central moment in the Jewish liturgy provides a picture of how Gradowski and his comrades *could experience* this supernatural consolation. The core of the Jewish liturgy is the prayer known as the *Amidah* or *Shemoneh Esrei*, a series of blessings consisting of praise, supplication, and thanksgiving; it is repeated by the religious Jew three times a day. The second of the *Amidah* blessings is praise of God's might, an eternal might exemplified by his revival of the dead. We are told that God "maintains His faith to those asleep in the dust" and that it is a principle of our faith to know that He "restores life." This second blessing closes with the words: "Blessed are You, Hashem, who revivifies the dead."[23] Now I ask you to imagine Gradowski, looking toward the *minyan* of praying Jews, who are perhaps about to recite the *Shemoneh Esrei*, and discovering that no one is there, that he is facing, yet again, the emptiness of death. Gradowski is overtaken by the most acute desolation, ready to proclaim that the last consolation vanished. And then, miraculously and with no warning, the dead start to be reanimated, restored to life. All of the dead in all of the camps are revivified, transformed from dust and ash into flesh and blood. Gradowski's family, his neighbors, his friends are standing next to him, perhaps forming a *minyan*, so that they can enthusiastically recite the second blessing of the *Amidah*. Everyone lost is returned, and millions of Jews are reunited, overwhelmed by the joyful consolation of being together again. Instead of the "sundered families" soaring to heaven, reunited, only to "vanish into eternity together," they are now arising from the earth, drawn together to live together once more, to continue their lives . . . and desolation recedes. A union that is reunion, with their families and with God, is the beginning of a new, resurrected life. This revival may not fully be "an answer for our blood," but it would have been a supernatural gesture of faithful consolation (151). And, crucially, it shows us what consolation would have looked like in Auschwitz. Anything less dramatic would not have consoled. Alas, Gradowski did not witness any resurrections and so—how could it be otherwise—the last consolation vanished.

Consolation was not theologically impossible in Auschwitz, but it was not forthcoming. As Gradowski faces endless waves of desolation, he becomes more confrontational, more aggressive, even impudent, toward God. To proclaim that the last consolation vanished is tantamount to openly criticizing and challenging God. These challenges, however, demonstrate Gradowski's persistent connection with God. He is not indifferent. His theology of protest is a theology of connection, of intellectual and especially affective connection. Even as his intellectual doubts create more distance from God, his emotional attachments to Him do not yet yield. We all know that intellectual hesitation and affective necessity are not incompatible. Pulled apart by his need for consolation and its felt absence, Gradowski's experience of God's *hester panim* is such that his attitude swings between, on the one hand, ritual supplication and religious practice, and, on the other, rebuke and distance. When Gradowski's theological patience ends and he is compelled to assert that the last consolation vanished, his impudence can shock and distress a religious Jew. Is he not succumbing to outrageous arrogance? Yet this impudence is itself an element of a venerable Jewish tradition. In *Sanhedrin* 105a, considering God's ties to, and the severing of His ties to, the Jewish people, an astonishing remark appears:

Rav Nahman says: Impudence is effective even toward Heaven.[24]

Gradowski's impudence is nobly motivated, not arbitrary. It is the kind of impudence expressed by a religious Jew, trying to hold on to his religiosity in a place completely devoid of spirituality. One might ask, parallel to a previous set of questions: Where does one draw the line between impudence and blasphemy? Is Gradowski challenging God or chastising Him? However we draw this distinction, I think that it is fair to say that Gradowski's impudence is theologically necessary in Auschwitz; his loss of consolation is much more devastating than his impudence. And his impudence is a dispute with God that, as *Pirkei Avot* puts it, is for "the sake of Heaven."[25]

With the vanishing of consolation, we know that Gradowski then actively turned to armed resistance. He became one of the leaders of the movement and was killed in the revolt at Auschwitz on October 7, 1944. Lacking divine consolation, he concentrated on human revenge. And feeling the need for revenge was a first stage in overcoming the inhuman passivity demanded and required in Auschwitz. The very fact that Gradowski seeks vengeance lifts him out of this stagnant passivity—automatons do not dream of revenge. Most of those deported to Auschwitz could not even think about vengeance; all they could focus on were their most immediate needs and their suffering. Vengeance would have been an existential luxury. The future was made to be empty in Auschwitz, yet Gradowski filled his future with resistance: If there was not to be supernatural intervention, then only human initiative could be relied upon. And Gradowski wanted revenge to be as extreme as the divine consolation of resurrection. In the penultimate chapter of his second manuscript, Gradowski presents a frightening vision of vengeance. Following his detailed description of burning bodies and suffering souls, Gradowski pleads for the "free world" to notice the "great flame," and for free men to "put the fire out" (150). This is the beginning of revenge, but Gradowski, in his desolate and impudent rage, goes much further. Most people will be shaken, perhaps repulsed, by the final sentence of this chapter:

> And perhaps your heart will be infused with boldness and courage and you will change [replace] the victims of this fire, this Hell that goes on burning here forever and may those who lit the fire be devoured in its flames. (150)

"May those who lit the fire be devoured in its flames" assaults our moral sensibility. I will not try to give a moral justification of this vision, but I will ask you to acknowledge its existential or anthropological value. The power of imagining that those who lit the fire will be consumed by it allows Gradowski to return to the realm of human emotion and desire. A thirst for such revenge is humanly understandable in Auschwitz; Gradowski has not succumbed to what we so easily call "dehumanization"; he is, despite everything, human, all too human. And what human being would not have thoughts of revenge were they in Gradowski's place? Auschwitz without revenge is like Auschwitz without consolation—a place frozen by dread, suffering, and death. Taking revenge, or finding consolation, are signs of humanity, traces of a former life, a life of action and aspiration.

Revenge and consolation are both elements of our philosophical anthropology. Furthermore, Gradowski's grenades, guns, and his pen have become protagonists in the same struggle, a struggle to maintain one's human identity in the face of human inhumanity, a constant effort not to lose one's self. A self lost in Auschwitz may never be found again. Gradowski's manuscripts show us that his self never deserted him, and after reading his words, we, too, shall never be able to abandon him. Zalmen Gradowski is one of us, and we must live with him.

─

Every paragraph of Zalmen Gradowski's manuscripts merits the meticulous attention appropriate to a singular voice. In a very real sense, every Shoah memoir is singular, but Gradowski's perspective, attitude, tone, phrasing, modes of expression, and so on are truly *sui generis*. Toward the end of her first memoir, *Une petite fille privilégiée*, Francine Christophe, deported to Bergen-Belsen as a child, writes:

> No, I am no longer from your world. I am from a world apart, I am from the world of the camps.[26]

Gradowski brings us into this world, makes us present with him. We are traumatized, but we cannot let ourselves be paralyzed. This is a trauma that we must confront. Zalmen Gradowski's writing is a form of resistance; our reading should be nothing less. With respect to Auschwitz, where resistance was heroic, his writing and our reading are resistance pursued by other means. God may not have provided him with consolation, but Gradowski has consoled us, left us a written consolation of courage, determination, and posthumous victory. Zalmen Gradowski was and remains a hero.

Notes

Foreword

I would like to first acknowledge Carlo Saletti and Batia Baum, who for more than a decade accompanied me on the journey to publish Sonderkommando and other clandestine manuscripts. Carlo Saletti was my co-editor, along with Georges Bensoussan, of the Sonderkommando manuscripts that were published in the *Revue d'Histoire de la Shoah* in 2001, and he was also my co-editor of Zalmen Gradowski's manuscripts. I have learned so much from his extensive historical knowledge. Batia Baum translated Gradowski's manuscripts from Yiddish to French. She introduced me to the world of Yiddish literature and taught me just how vivid and meaningful it is. All my gratitude to Avichai Zur and Yossi Wolnerman, who both gave me crucial information about Gradowski and these manuscripts of his, which had never been published before. Moreover, I am extremely grateful to Elizabeth Branch Dyson for supporting this editorial project. —Philippe Mesnard

1. Franciszek Piper, "Die Vernichtungsmethoden," in *Auschwitz, 1940–1945: Studien zur Geschichte des Konzentrations- und Vernichtungslagers Auschwitz*, vol. III (Oświęcim: Verlag des Staatlichen Museums Auschwitz-Birkenau, 1999), 140ff.

2. Jean-Claude Pressac, *Auschwitz: Technique and Operation of the Gas Chambers* (New York: Beate Klarsfeld Foundation, 1989), 132.

3. See Raul Hilberg, *Documents of Destruction: Germany and Jewry, 1933–1945* (Chicago: Quadrangle Books, 1971); Saul Friedländer, *The Years of Extermination: Nazi Germany and the Jews, 1939–1945* (New York: HarperCollins, 2007); Randolph Braham, *The Politics of Genocide: The Holocaust in Hungary*, 3rd ed. (1981; repr., Boulder, CO: Social Science Monographs, 2016). Based on research done by Piotr Setkiewicz of the State Auschwitz Museum, the French historian Jean-François Forges puts the figure at 423,500 Hungarian Jews deported and around 300,000 murdered in Birkenau. See J.-F. Forges, "Afterword," in *Qui t'aime ainsi*, by E. Bruck (Paris: Points Seuil, 2022), 146.

4. Dori Laub begins a short chapter of *Testimony*: "On the basis of the many Holocaust testimonies I have listened to, I would like to suggest a certain way of looking at the Holocaust that would reside in the following theoretical perspective: that what precisely

made a Holocaust out of the event is the unique way in which, during its historical occurrence, the event produced no witnesses." See Shoshana Felman and Doris Laub, *Testimony: Crises of Witnessing in Literature, Psychoanalysis, and History* (New York: Routledge, 1992), 80, and chapter 3: "An Event without a Witness: Truth, Testimony and Survival," 75–92.

5. Giorgio Agamben, *Remnants of Auschwitz: The Witness and the Archive*, trans. Daniel Heller-Rosen (New York: Zone, 1999), 41ff.

6. Simha Guterman, *Le Livre retrouvé* [The recovered book], trans. Nicole Lapierre (Paris: Plon, 1991).

7. Itzhak Katzenelson, *The Song of the Murdered Jewish People*, trans. Noah H. Rosenbloom (Tel Aviv: Hakibbutz Hameuchad, 1980).

8. See *The Collection Auschwitz*, in *YIVO-Bleter*, no. 27 (Spring 1946): 194–98. People can find an English translation of this text by David Suchoff, accompanied by an introduction, in "A Yiddish Text from Auschwitz: Critical History and the Anthological Imagination," *Prooftexts* 19, no. 1 (January 1999): 59–69.

9. See Nicholas Chare, Ersy Contogouris, and Dominic Williams, "Disinterred Words: The Letters of Herman Strasfogel and Marcel Nadjari," in *Testimonies of Resistance: Representations of the Auschwitz-Birkenau Sonderkommando*, ed. Nicholas Chare and Dominic Williams (New York: Berghahn, 2019), 111–30.

10. "Wotchłani zbrodni (Kronika oświęcimska nieznanego autora)" [Amidst the horror of murder (chronicle of Auschwitz from an unknown author)], *Biuletyn Żydowskiego Instytutu Historycznego*, nos. 9–10 (1954): 303–9.

11. Unknown author's manuscript [Lejb Langfus] in *Biuletyn Żydowskiego Instytutu Historycznego*, nos. 9–10 (1954); Zalmen Lewental's manuscript in *Biuletyn Żydowskiego Instytutu Historycznego*, nos. 65–66 (1968); Gradowski's first manuscript in *Biuletyn Żydowskiego Instytutu Historycznego*, nos. 71–72 (1969).

12. His name has been spelled Marcel Nadjari, Nadzari, or Nadsari; in Greek, it is Μαρσέλ Νατζαρή (January 1, 1917–July 31, 1971).

13. Marcel Nadjari, "Handschrift von Marcel Nadsari," in *Inmitten des grauenvollen Verbrechens: Handschriften von Mitgliedern des Sonderkommandos* (Oświęcim: Verlag des Staatlichen Auschwitz-Birkenau Museums, 1996), 270–74.

14. See *Inmitten des grauenvollen Verbrechens*.

15. *The Scrolls of Auschwitz* (Tel-Aviv: Am Oved, 1985).

16. See Primo Levi, *The Drowned and the Saved* (1986), trans. Raymond Rosenthal (London: Abacus, 1989), esp. "The Grey Zone," 31–72.

17. David Roskies, *The Literature of Destruction: Jewish Responses to Catastrophe* (Philadelphia: Jewish Publication Society, 1988), 548–64.

18. Philippe Mesnard, Carlo Saletti, and Georges Bensoussan, eds., "Des Voix sous la cendre," *Revue d'histoire de la Shoah: Le Monde juif*, no. 71 (January–April 2001), republished as *Des Voix sous la cendre: Manuscrits des Sonderkommandos d'Auschwitz-Birkenau* (Paris: Memorial de la Shoah/Calmann-Levy, 2005).

19. Ota Kraus and Erich Kulka, *Továrna na smrt* (Prague: Čin, 1946); Ota Kraus and Erich Kulka, *Die Todesfabrik*, trans. Zora Weil-Zimmerling (Berlin: Kongress Verlag, 1957).

20. For complementary information, see Robert Jan Van Pelt, *The Case for Auschwitz: Evidence from the Irving Trial* (Bloomington: Indiana University Press, 2016), 185–86.

21. Léon Poliakov, *Auschwitz* (Paris: Julliard, 1964).

22. Miklós Nyiszli, *Auschwitz: A Doctor's Eyewitness Account*, with a foreword by Bruno Bettelheim (1960; repr., New York: Arcade, 2011).

23. Raul Hilberg, *The Destruction of the European Jews* (New York: Quadrangle, 1961); Hermann Langbein, *People in Auschwitz* (Chapel Hill: University of North Carolina Press, 2004).

24. Gitta Sereny, *Into That Darkness: From Mercy Killing to Mass Murder* (New York: McGraw Hill, 1974); Filip Müller, *Eyewitness Auschwitz: Three Years in the Gas Chambers*, ed. and trans. Susanne Flatauer (New York: Stein and Day, 1984).

25. Gideon Greif, *"Wir weinten tränenlos…": Augenzeugenberichte der jüdischen "Sonderkommandos" in Auschwitz* (Köln: Böhlau Verlag, 1995); Gideon Greif, *We Wept without Tears: Testimonies of the Jewish Sonderkommando from Auschwitz* (New Haven, CT: Yale University Press, 2005). The Sonderkommando members interviewed are Josef Sackar, Abraham and Shlomo Dragon, Ya'akov Gabai, Eliezer Eisenschmidt, Shaul Chazan, Leon Cohen, and Ya'akov Silberberg.

26. Eric Friedler, Barbara Siebert, and Andreas Kilian, *Zeugen aus der Todeszone: Das jüdische Sonderkommando in Auschwitz* (Munich: Deutsche Taschenbuch Verlag, 2005).

27. Shlomo Venezia, *Sonderkommando: Dans l'enfer des chambres à gaz* (Paris: Albin Michel, 2007); Shlomo Venezia, *Inside the Gas Chambers: Eight Months in the Sonderkommando of Auschwitz* (Malden, MA: Polity, 2009).

28. Sila Cehreli, *Témoignage du Khurbn: Résistance juive dans les centres de mise à mort* (Paris: Kimé, 2013).

29. Nicholas Chare and Dominic Williams, *Matters of Testimony: Interpreting the Scrolls of Auschwitz* (New York: Berghahn, 2016). Chare and Williams also edited *Testimonies of Resistance: Representations of the Auschwitz-Birkenau Sonderkommando* (New York: Berghahn, 2019) and *The Auschwitz Sonderkommando Testimonies: Histories, Representations* (New York: Palgrave Macmillan, 2019).

30. Witness accounts on Państwowe Muzeum Auschwitz-Birkenau website: http://70.auschwitz.org/index.php?option=com_content&view=article&id=20&Itemid=136&lang=en; University of Southern California Shoah Foundation: https://sfi.usc.edu/; "Dario Gabbai Remembers the Sonderkommando Uprising," USC Shoah Foundation, https://www.youtube.com/watch?v=I9hLniDfxjE.

31. Olga Lengyel, *Five Chimneys: The Story of Auschwitz* (1946; repr., Literary Licensing, 2011), 132; André Lettich, *Trente-quatre mois dans les Camps de Concentration* (Tours: Imprimerie Union Coopérative, 1946), 30.

32. Tadeusz Borowski, *This Way for the Gas, Ladies and Gentlemen* (New York: Penguin Classics, 1992).

33. David Olère, *Un peintre au Sonderkommando à Auschwitz* (New York: Beate Klarsfeld Foundation, 1989).

34. Rudolf Vrba (Walter Rosemberg) and Alfred Wetzler, *London wurde informiert: Berichte von Auschwitz-Flüchtlingen*, ed. H. Swiebocki (Oświęcim: Verlag des Staatlichen Museums Auschwitz-Birkenau, 1997), 229.

35. Charlotte Delbo, *Aucun de nous ne reviendra* [None of us will return] (Paris: Minuit, 1970); my translation.

36. Wiesław Kielar, *Anus mundi: Five Years in Auschwitz* (1972; repr., New York: Viking, 1981), 191.

37. Langbein, *People in Auschwitz*, 195.

38. Jacques Stroumsa, *Tu choisiras la vie* (Paris: Le Cerf, 1998), 141.

39. Stephan Hermlin, "Auschwitz ist unvergessen," in *Äußerungen, 1944–1982* (Berlin: Aufbau-Verlag, 1983), 85–89.

40. See Andreas Kilian, "Henryk Mandelbaum: Ein einfacher Mensch mit einem schweren Schicksal," Sonderkommando Studien, https://web.archive.org/web/20110831102010 /http://sonderkommando-studien.de/artikel.php?c=biografie%2Fmandelbaum. Henryk Mandelbaum died in 2008.

41. See Clément Chéroux, *Mémoire des camps: Photographies des camps de concentration et d'extermination nazis (1933–1999)* (Paris: Marval, 2001).

42. See Philippe Mesnard, "The Sonderkommando on Screen," in *Testimonies of Resistance*, ed. Chare and Williams, 332–45.

43. Levi, *The Drowned and the Saved*, 53.

44. Primo Levi and Leonardo Debenedetti, *Rapporto sulla organizzazione igienico-sanitaria del campo de concentramiento per Ebrei di Monowitz (Auschwitz–Alta Silesia)*, Opere I (Torino: Einaudi, 1997), 1358; my translation.

45. Levi, *The Drowned and the Saved*, 49.

46. Levi, 52.

47. See *Yisker Bukh Suvalk* [Memorial book of Suvalk], ed. Berl Kagan (New York: Suvalk and Vicinity Relief Society of New York, 1961), available at https://www.jewishgen .org/yizkor/suwalki1/Suwalki1.html.

48. See Nathan Cohen, "Diaries of the *Sonderkommandos*," *Yad Vashem Studies* 20.

49. Shlomoh Riman, "Betar," in *Yisker Bukh Suvalk*. https://www.jewishgen.org /yizkor/suwalki1/suw403.html#Page405.

50. The first time Zalmen Gradowski is mentioned with respect to the Sonderkommando is in Ota Kraus and Erich Kulka, *Auschwitz, Death Factory* (in Hebrew) (Jerusalem, 1961).

51. Shlomo Dragon, interview, in Greif, *We Wept without Tears*, 165 (in the German edition, 105).

52. Ber Mark, *Des Voix dans la nuit: La résistance juive à Auschwitz-Birkenau* (Paris: Plon, 1982), 182.

53. Krystyna Oleksy, "Zalmen Gradowski—Ein Zeuge aus dem Sonderkommando," in *Theresienstädter Studien und Dokumente*, ed. M. Kárný, R. Kemper, and M. Kárná (Prague: Institut Theresienstädter Initiative Academia, Prague, 1995), 131–33.

54. Chare and Williams, *Matters of Testimony*, 74–75.

55. Shlomo Dragon, "Les survivants des Sonderkommandos au procès de Cracovie en 1946," in *Des Voix sous la cendre*, ed. Mesnard, Saletti, and Bensoussan, 177.

56. Chare and Williams, *Matters of Testimony*, 68.

First Manuscript

I wish to thank, first of all, my grandparents (*bobe-zeyde*) who raised me in Yiddish and all my Yiddish teachers over the years, above all Yitshok Niborski of the Paris Yiddish Center, exemplary scholar and exceptional human being. —Rubye Monet

NOTEBOOK

1. "Destruction" is the translation of the Hebrew term *Hurban,* which recalls the first and second Destruction of the Jerusalem Temple. The word has come to have the general meaning of great misfortune, catastrophe, disaster. The phrase "third Hurban" was current for a long time before the use of the term "Shoah."

2. The word he uses, *mabl,* is the word used in the Bible for the Deluge.

3. The Kołbasin camp, where in November 1942 thousands of Jews from the ghettos of the Grodno region were rounded up. They were later deported to Auschwitz or to other death camps.

4. Łosośna, a small train station not far from Grodno, to the southwest, in the direction of Białystok.

5. In January 1943, at the time of the deportation from the Kołbasin camp, the Białystok ghetto still existed. The first acts of liquidation date from February 1943.

6. The Jewish Council (*Judenrat*) and many Białystok Jews had the illusory hope that thanks to their well-organized work, they would manage to avoid the liquidation and remain alive.

7. The author apparently believes that the Warsaw Jews had already been exterminated. He has in mind the unclear information coming from Warsaw about the large deportation to death camps that started on July 22, 1942, and lasted until September 1942. Around January 20, 1943, when the convoy that was transporting Gradowski and his family from the Kołbasin camp passed through Warsaw, roughly 70,000 Jews were still living in a smaller portion of the ghetto. Half, 35,000, were confined to "shops"—workshops where they labored beyond their physical limits while living in adjoining "blocks." The other half lived clandestinely with no work permit, typically hiding out in the abandoned houses of deported Warsaw Jews.

8. *Yekke*—a Yiddish word (mildly derogatory) for German Jews. Here it merely refers to Germany.

9. This wooden cabin constituted the guard post of the SS.

10. The reference is to the SS *Hauptscharführer* Otto Moll, who at that time was in charge of cremating the bodies of those who had been assassinated in the Birkenau gas chambers. He chose candidates for the Sonderkommando from among the prisoners. Those selected did not know where they would be working and the nature of that work.

11. The SS leaders of the camp gave the members of the Sonderkommando better food, clothes, and living conditions compared to what prisoners under other commandos received. This more privileged treatment made it easier for other prisoners to stigmatize those in the Sonderkommando.

THE LETTER

1. The text of the letter was rendered back into Yiddish from the Polish translation by Ber Mark because the photocopy of the original was lost when the texts of Zalmen Gradowski were sent to Israel.

2. According to the numbering of German documents, Crematoria II and III are meant here.

3. In other words, Crematoria IV and V, according to the German numbering.

4. On the grounds of Crematorium V, there were five pits; near Bunker 2, there were burning areas and trenches in which Hungarian Jews were burned in the summer of 1944.

5. The camp of Stutthof (Sztutowo) was opened on September 2, 1939, as a civilian and war prisoners camp. It became a concentration camp starting in March 1942.

Second Manuscript

PREFACE

1. Starting in 1933, "*Greuel-Propaganda*" (i.e., "propaganda disseminating atrocities") was the term used in Nazi propaganda to designate all information about what was really happening in Nazi-controlled territories.

2. A variant spelling of Libe.

3. Yiddish form of Vilnius, the capital of Lithuania, that was first occupied by German troops on June 24, 1941. Immediately a reign of terror was imposed on the 60,000 Jews who lived in the city. In the same month, 500 Jews were assassinated in Ponary, about ten miles from Vilnius. In the meantime, Lithuania was forced into the Reichskommissariat Ostland. Between August 31 and September 1, an additional 8,000 Jews were assassinated or hunted down in the city. In early September, two ghettos were created: 30,000 Jews were held in the first, and in the second were between 9,000 and 11,000. Other massacres took place during October and November (in particular the attack on October 1, 1941, called the Yom Kippur Aktion). By the end of the year, 33,500 Jews had been assassinated. These killings were interrupted in 1943 at the start of summer when Himmler's order arrived calling for the liquidation of the ghetto, which was carried out over the last ten days of September with the deportation of the remaining population to concentration camps and to the death camp at Sobibor.

4. Otwock, a suburb of Warsaw, where in the fall of 1940 the Nazis created a ghetto in the northwest part of the city. The Jewish population was enclosed there and subjected to forced labor, working on the dams of the Vistula. There were about 12,000 Jews in this ghetto, of which 2,000 died of malnutrition and typhus. As part of the liquidation of the ghetto that started on August 19, 1942, roughly 2,000 Jews were assassinated on site, while 7,000 others were deported to the death camp at Treblinka. Cf. *Obozy hitlerowskie na ziemiach polskich, 1939–1945*, Informator encyklopedyczny (Warszawa: Państwowe Wydawnictwo Naukowe, 1979), 377.

A MOONLIT NIGHT

1. To understand fully the mystical resistance that is a part of Jewish culture, this text must be read with attention to the importance accorded by Judaism to the moon, a symbol of renewal. The lunar cycle is a crucial element in Jewish worship. Each month begins with the new moon, and it is the custom to sanctify the moon through the ceremony of *Kiddoush-levana*. This is performed in the first half of the month, when the moon is waxing. Although customs differ, it usually takes place at the end of Shabbat, outside under clear skies when the moon is visible, often in the synagogue courtyard, and if possible with a *minyan*, or at least as a group of three in order to exchange the salutations of *Sholem aleikhem*. It is a joyful ceremony, consisting of Psalms and prayers of thanksgiving.

The renewal of the moon functions as a metaphor of the fate of the Jewish people: just as the moon is reborn after a period of decline and total disappearance, the light of Israel will shine anew in all its brightness. With his invocation to the moon, Gradowski invites it to shroud itself in clouds, to hide its face, recalling thereby the notion of *hester panim*, a symbol of God's silence.

SEPARATION

1. Šiauliai, a city in northern Lithuania (Shavel in Hebrew, Schaulen in German), was invaded on June 26, 1941. A ghetto was instituted in August 1941 and operated until July 1943, when it became a concentration camp. This camp was dismantled on July 21, 1944, and the deportees were transferred to KL Stutthof.

2. Numbers corresponding to the numeric value of the Hebrew letters thus forming the name: ZaLMN—GRADOWSKI.

3. Time indicators concerning this event place it between February and March 1944. Gradowski is probably referring to the reduction of the Sonderkommando that took place on February 24. On that day, members of the Kommando were selected for transfer to the KL Lublin (Majdanek), where they were immediately shot.

4. In the language of the camp, the term probably refers to Jewish Kapos.

5. The author uses the traditional Hebraic term *mekhitse* (border, separation, divider) that represents the separator, divider, or curtain between the sacred and the profane (originally the drapery to separate off the holy of holies in the Temple), between men and women in the synagogue, between the living and the dead.

6. It is only afterward that the men of the Sonderkommando found out the fate of their comrades: "Less than three months later, we learned what had happened to them in Lublin. In April 1944, nineteen Russian prisoners with their German Kapo arrived in Birkenau from Lublin, where they had been working in the Sonderkommando. . . . Even before we had a chance of talking to one of the Russians, we realized what had happened to our teammates; several of the newcomers wore clothing and boots which had belonged to the Kapos and foremen in our group." Filip Müller, *Eyewitness Auschwitz: Three Years in the Gas Chambers*, ed. and trans. Susanne Flatauer (New York: Stein and Day, 1984), 90. This testimony is confirmed by Shlomo Dragon in an interview in Gideon Greif, *"Wir weinten tränenlos…": Augenzeugenberichte der jüdischen "Sonderkommandos" in Auschwitz* [*We Cried without Tears*] (Köln: Böhlau Verlag, 1995), 107.

7. The term *Mishna* refers generally to all aspects of oral law. It was put down in writing and constitutes the foundation of Talmud.

8. A "set table" (*Shulkhan Arukh*) is the title given to the classical codification of Jewish religious law (*Halakhah*), prepared by Joseph Caro of Safed in the sixteenth century.

9. Concerning these cards and file numbers, it's worth noting that in Judaism there exists a prohibition against census taking. It is forbidden to count the children of Israel. In order to carry out a census of the population in the desert after leaving Egypt, every adult was asked to deposit a half-shekel coin, and the coins were counted (Exodus 30:11–12): "The Lord spoke to Moses saying, 'When you take the census of the children of Israel for their number, then every man will give a ransom for himself to the Lord, when you number them, that there may be no plague among them when you number them. This is what

everyone among those who are numbered shall give: half a shekel.'" With this method, the men were not counted head by head, "like sheep," which would have brought about plague and destruction, but instead the coins were counted, and thus no epidemic or death could strike them. Alternatively, each person wrote his name on a paper that was then given to be read by Aaron and Moses, and the slips of paper were counted. In this way, every name was repeated. When David counted his people directly (Samuel II, 24) a plague struck the country, causing the death of seventy thousand people. Still today, in Yiddish, to count those present, a ruse is employed: "Not one, not two, not three, etc." A pious Jew does not count those present to see if there are ten men for a *minyan* (the quorum for prayer), instead reciting a verse containing ten words.

10. The direct testimonies are not in agreement about the composition of the selected group and the motives that led to the reduced size of the Sonderkommando. Filip Müller writes, "Most of them had worked under the direction of Hössler in a Kommando whose mission was to remove traces of bodies near bunkers I and II. Once this work was completed, their presence was useless." Müller, *Eyewitness Auschwitz*, 90. Alter Feinsilber, on the other hand, claims that the decision was a repressive measure in response to an attempted escape by one or more of the Sonderkommando's members: "This group . . . was reduced by half, because two hundred prisoners were sent to Majdanek at the start of 1944 following a failed escape attempt by one of the prisoners in the group. . . . As a punishment, two hundred prisoners were singled out. They were told they would be going as specialists to the Majdanek camp. It turned out that upon arriving at Majdanek these people were shot and then burned." See the deposition of Feinsilber in *Des voix sous la cendre: Manuscrits des Sonderkommandos d'Auschwitz-Birkenau*, ed. Philippe Mesnard, Carlo Saletti, and Georges Bensoussan (Paris: Memorial de la Shoah/Calmann-Levy, 2005), 214–15.

11. A compilation of prayers, the phylacteries placed on the arm and forehead, and the prayer shawl.

12. *Minyan* (number in Hebrew): a prayer assembly of at least ten men, the minimum required to pronounce the communal prayers.

13. "The people of Israel have a magnificent creation that is unique to them, namely the holy and venerable day of Her Majesty Shabbat. In the popular imagination, Sabbath became a living being complete with a body of splendid beauty," explains Hayim Nahman Bialik. Friday evening, each person dons his Sabbath clothes to go meet the Sabbath Queen, and this meeting must take place before sunset. After the lively verses of Psalms 95–99, the *Lekhah dodi* is sung to welcome in the Sabbath Bride: "Come, my beloved, the face of Shabbat appears, let us receive her!"

14. The words are from Jeremiah 30:16, but the order in which Gradowski cites them is taken from the Sabbath song, *Lekhah dodi*, in which are cited the words of Jeremiah: *V'hayu limshisah shosayikh* (Jeremiah 30:16); "they that spoil thee shall be a spoil."

15. *Sholem aleikhem* ("Peace be with you . . ."): the welcoming prayer to the angels, sung at home on Friday evening after the return from the service, to welcome the Sabbath and the two angels accompanying the worshipper who returns home from the house of worship, according to the Talmudic passage. ("Peace be with you, angels of the divine service, angels of God Supreme . . . Enter in peace, angels of peace, angels of God Supreme . . . Bless me with peace, angels of peace . . . Leave in peace, angels of peace . . .").

THE CZECH TRANSPORT

1. In the preface that accompanies the first edition of the text, Haïm Wollnerman recalls having carried out Gradowski's wish: "I want to respect the testament and wish of the author who in each of his prefaces asks the discoverer of his writings to investigate among his relations in America to discover who the author was and who his family was, and to request a photo to be added to the publication of his writings. [...] According to the wish of the author, I wrote to his uncle in America at the address indicated to ask for details and for a photo of him and his family. At that time, in 1946, the postal service in Germany did not function normally, and therefore it took months to receive confirmation that they indeed had a nephew by the name of Zalmen Gradowski, originally from Suwałki. They readily recognized the handwriting of their nephew, and they sent me a photo of Zalmen Gradowski with his wife Sonia-Sarah." Zalmen Gradowski, *In harts fun Gehenem: a dokument fun Oyshvitser zander-komanda, 1944* (Jerusalem: Haïm Wollnerman, 1977), 4.

2. Special work, referring to his work in the Sonderkommando.

3. Purim (meaning "lots") is sometimes called the Festival of Lots. This popular and joyous holiday, celebrated on the fourteenth day of Adar (late February, March) commemorates the saving of the Jews in the Persian Empire from the plot to destroy them. This plan was the work of the evil Haman, a descendant of Amalek, the prime minister of King Ahasuerus (identified as Xerxes I, Xerxes the Great, king of Persia). As told in the *Megillah* (scroll) of Esther, the Jewish people were threatened with extermination in the 127 provinces of the empire on the 13th of Adar, which was chosen at random (by casting lots) as the favorable day for the massacre of the Jews. But they were miraculously saved thanks to the intercession of Queen Esther. A reading of the scroll of Esther is conducted during the evening and morning services. Purim is noted for its joyful, carnivalesque atmosphere.

4. Gradowski is alluding to the assassination of Jews deported from the ghetto of Theresienstadt who arrived in Auschwitz on September 8, 1943. The action, which necessitated a massive deployment of SS, began with the *Lagersperre*, or camp lockdown, ordered on March 8, 1944, in the early evening after the Jews who were to be sent to the gas chambers had been transferred from the sector BIIb of Birkenau to the former quarantine camp BIIa. In the following hours, approximately 4,000 Jews were assassinated in Crematoria II (women) and III (men). Cf. Müller, *Eyewitness Auschwitz*, 129–61. Concerning Gradowski's pages about the assassination of Czech families, see M. Kárný, "Eine neue Quelle zur Geschichte der tragischen Nacht vom 8 März 1944," *Judaica Bohemiae XXV*, nos. 1–2 (Prague, 1989): 53–56.

5. *Tisha be-Av*, the ninth day of the month of Av (July/August), is generally taken as the date for the mournful commemoration of the two Destructions of the Temple (the first carried out in 586 BC by the Babylonians under Nebuchadnezzar; the second in AD 70 by the Romans under Titus). This date is associated with different exiles and dark times in Jewish history including, for example, July 12, 1290, when Edward I signed the edict banishing all Jews from England, and two centuries later the expulsion of Jews from Spain. Gradowski here uses the date to refer not to the destruction itself but to the commemoration: a day of great joy has been turned into a day of deepest mourning. After the war, the destruction of the Jews was called the "third destruction" (*driter Hurban*). It was later

replaced by the term Shoah. *Hurban* is translated in Gradowski's text variously as either "disaster," "destruction," or "ruin."

6. First opened in September 1943, after the arrival of two transports of mostly Czechoslovakian Jews, the "Bauabschnitt BIIb," as it was called in official camp documents, or more commonly the *Familienlager* (family camp), functioned until the final liquidation on July 10–11, 1944. On that date, of the 17,517 Jews deported from Theresienstadt to Auschwitz, there were less than 3,500 survivors, and their number decreased further in the following months. Only 1,167 were still alive when Auschwitz was finally liberated. For a complete review of the history of the family camp, see Miroslav Kárný, "Das Theresienstädter Familienlager (BIIb) in Birkenau," *Hefte von Auschwitz* 20 (Oświęcim, 1997): 133–237.

7. Promoted to the rank of SS *Obersturmführer*, Johann Schwarzhuber (here spelled Schwatzhuber), born in Tutzing in 1904, began service in the concentration camps starting in 1938 at KL Sachsenhausen. He was the commander of the men's camp at Auschwitz II–Birkenau from November 1943 to September 1944, when he was transferred to KL Ravensbrück. He would be taken prisoner and tried in the Ravensbrück garrison trial. He was convicted, sentenced to death, and executed in May 1947. Cf. French L. MacLean, *The Camp Men: The SS Officers Who Ran the Nazi Concentration Camp System* (Atglen, PA: Schiffer Military History, 1999), 219.

8. SS *Oberscharführer* Peter Voss (sometimes spelled Vost or Vast) was in charge of the Birkenau crematorium from 1943 to May 1944; he was subsequently named *Kommandoführer* of Crematorium III. See the testimony by the former member of the Sonderkommando, Stanislaw Jankowski (Alter Feinsilber) in *Inmitten des grauenvollen Verbrechens: Handschriften von Mitgliedern des Sonderkommandos* (Oświęcim: Verlag des Staatlichen Auschwitz-Birkenau Museums, 1996), 45n56.

9. SS *Oberscharführer* Walter Quackernack (here spelled Kwakernak) served at KL Auschwitz in the political department (*Politische Abteilung*) as the head of the civil status registry office, the *Standesamt*. Put on trial after the war by a British tribunal, he was sentenced to death and executed on October 11, 1946.

10. SS *Unterscharführer* Josef Schillinger, after beginning his service at the auxiliary camp of Chełmek, was then put in charge of the cooking facilities at the men's camp at Birkenau. On several occasions he was among the SS personnel assigned to escort columns of Jews selected for the gas chambers. On October 23, 1943, a transport of 1,800 Polish Jews arrived at Auschwitz from Bergen-Belsen. At the entry to the gas chamber of Crematorium II, when the victims, all women, realized they were to be gassed, one of them managed to grab a revolver from one of the SS and shot Schillinger, who died while being transported to the hospital at Katowice, and SS *Unterscharführer* Wilhelm Emmerich, who was only wounded.

11. The reference here is to Crematoria II and III at Birkenau, as numbered in German administrative documents. For a complete reconstruction of the location of the crematoria and gas chambers that functioned at Auschwitz, see Jean-Claude Pressac, *Les crématoires d'Auschwitz: La machinerie du meurtre de masse* (Paris: CNRS Éditions, 1993).

12. On March 1, 1944, a rumor circulated in the family camp that the Jews from the transports of September 1943 (of the 5,000 arrivals, roughly 3,800 were then still alive) would be transferred to work camps at Heydebreck. On the strategies implemented by

the SS to avoid reactions by the Jews, see Miroslav Kárný, "Frage zum 8 März 1944," in *Theresienstädter Studien und Dokumente* (Prague: Institut Theresienstädter Initiative Academia, 1999), 9–42.

13. The reference here is to Crematorium II.

14. "Pouring in the gas." The verb *schitn* (from the German *schütten*) is generally used to speak of pouring powders, such as sand. The reference here is to the moment when the SS poured crystals of Zyklon B through an opening in the roof of the gas chamber, where they would then turn to gas once in contact with the air.

15. The reference here is to Crematorium III. See figure 7.

16. The reference here is to Crematorium II.

17. A play on words—*heylig* in Yiddish means holy, combined with Heil, as in Heil Hitler.

18. The author uses the traditional Hebrew term *tahare-bret* (purification board), a surface on which the ritual purification of the dead is carried out. The use of this term in this context bitterly underscores the profanation of the dead—unpurified and unburied—as cremation is strictly forbidden by Jewish law. These dead are thus excluded from the Jewish community promised in the world hereafter at the time of the Messiah's coming. But one can also hear in the author's words the idea that in this place of horror, with this "work" of destruction that the "devil" requires of them, they themselves take responsibility for, or are at least mindful of, even if only with gestures or prayers, the task of representing the *khevra-kadisha*, the traditional holy assembly whose mission is to assure the accomplishment of the last duties toward the dead—in other words, the funeral service in all its customary ritualistic and mystical aspects. Serving the dead is indeed considered the most altruistic of commandments in the Torah, dictated by love of one's fellow man, a truly disinterested action since it is performed on behalf of one who is forever incapable of reciprocity.

Afterword

I would like to dedicate this afterword to the memory of my parents—Phillip Davidson (né Davidovitz) and Lorraine Davidson (née Shulman)—as well as to Diane Brentari. Without Diane, I would never have been able to complete this project.

I am profoundly grateful to Elizabeth Branch Dyson for her brilliant editorial advice, to Erin DeWitt for her remarkable copyediting, to Rubye Monet for her magnificent translation, and especially to Philippe Mesnard for his extraordinary collaboration on this project and his many acts of friendship.

I am indebted to Maureen Kelly and Kirsten Collins for their meticulous research assistance.

Throughout this time of difficult and painful medical problems, a number of other people have provided exceptional support, encouragement, and inspiration. I must thank Ilsetraut Hadot, Daniele Lorenzini, Maggie Schein, Josef Stern, James Woodruff, and John Zorn, as well as Margaret Mitchell and Richard Rosengarten, Jessie Meltsner and Brian Britt, and Bianca Torricelli and Roberto Righi.

My brothers, Larry Davidson and Chuck Davidson, have been a constant source of kindness and wisdom.

During the past forty years, I have had innumerable conversations about the Shoah with Peter Galison. Our discussions have helped to shape my thought.

—Arnold I. Davidson

1. See, in this book, 5–9; citations hereafter will be parenthetical.

2. A useful edition and translation of Maimonides' *Mishneh Torah* can be found on the website www.sefaria.org.

3. *The Family Haggadah* (Rahway, NJ: Mesorah Publications, 2020), 45.

4. The Lubavitcher Rebbe, Rabbi M. M. Schneerson, *The Divine Prism* (Jerusalem: Heichal Menachem, 2011), 72.

5. Rabbi Joseph B. Soloveitchik, *Halakhic Morality: Essays on Ethics and Masorah* (Jerusalem: Maggid Books, 2017), 17–18.

6. Aharon Ziegler, *Halakhic Positions of Rabbi Joseph B. Soloveitchik*, vol. VII (Brooklyn: KTAV Publishing, 2017), 48.

7. *Megillas Eichah / Lamentations* (Brooklyn: Mesorah Publications, 2017), 68–69.

8. See 198n13. A helpful general article about this ritual is Dovid Zaklikowski, "Kiddush Levana: Sanctification of the Moon," Chabad.org, https://www.chabad.org/library/article_cdo/aid/1904288/jewish/Kiddush-Levana-Sanctification-of-the-Moon.htm.

9. *Sanhedrin* 42a. References to the Talmud will be to the Steinsaltz edition and translation found at www.sefaria.org.

10. *Kiddush Levanah*, in *Siddur for the Sabbath and Festivals with an Interlinear Translation* (Brooklyn: Mesorah, 2018), 664.

11. *Sanhedrin* 42a; *Kiddush Levanah*, 668.

12. *Kiddush Levanah*, 662.

13. *Kiddush Levanah*, 662.

14. *Kiddush Levanah*, 668.

15. *Sanhedrin* 42a. This opinion contrasts with the view that we do not bless the moon, "since this is its nature . . . not an unexpected occurrence that requires these blessings."

16. *Kiddush Levanah*, 665.

17. *Kiddush Levanah*, 667.

18. *Aleinu*, in *Siddur for the Sabbath and Festivals with an Interlinear Translation*, 656.

19. For the use of the idea of spiritual exercises in the context of Auschwitz, see my two essays "Gli esercizi sprituali di Primo Levi," in *La vacanza morale del fascismo: Intorno a Primo Levi*, ed. Arnold I. Davidson (Pisa: ETS, 2008), and "Écrire depuis l'échafaud," in *Traces de vie à Auschwitz: un manuscrit clandestin*, ed. Philippe Mesnard (Lormont, FR: éditions Le Bord de l'eau, 2022).

20. *Megillas Eichah / Lamentations*, 138–41.

21. See Moshe Halbertal, "*Eikhah* and the Stance of Lamentation," in *Lament in Jewish Thought*, ed. Ilit Ferber and Paula Schwebel (Berlin: De Gruyter, 2014).

22. Cited in *Jeremiah* (New York: Mesorah, 2016), xxvi.

23. *Shemoneh Esrei*, in *Siddur for the Sabbath and Festivals with an Interlinear Translation*, 341.

24. *Sanhedrin* 105a.

25. *Pirkei Avot* 5:20.

26. Francine Christophe, *Une petite fille privilégiée* (Paris: Harmattan, 1966), 202.